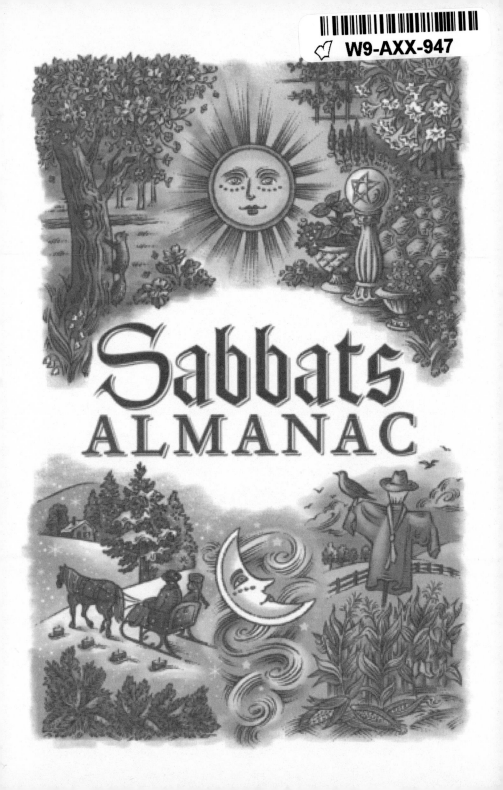

W9-AXX-947

Sabbats
ALMANAC

Llewellyn's Sabbats Almanac:
Samhain 2014 to Mabon 2015

© 2014 Llewellyn Worldwide Ltd.
Llewellyn is a registered trademark of Llewellyn Worldwide Ltd.

Cover art © Carolyn Vibbert/Susan and Co.
Cover design by Ellen Lawson
Editing by Ed Day
Interior Art: © Carolyn Vibbert/Susan and Co., excluding illustrations on pages 39, 74, 76, 110, 113, 148, 185, 220, 222, 255, 257, and 291, which are © Wen Hsu

ISBN: 978-0-7387-2693-9

Llewellyn Worldwide Ltd.
2143 Wooddale Drive
Woodbury, MN 55125-2989

Printed in the United States of America

2014

JANUARY
S	M	T	W	T	F	S
			1	2	3	4
5	6	7	8	9	10	11
12	13	14	15	16	17	18
19	20	21	22	23	24	25
26	27	28	29	30	31	

FEBRUARY
S	M	T	W	T	F	S
						1
2	3	4	5	6	7	8
9	10	11	12	13	14	15
16	17	18	19	20	21	22
23	24	25	26	27	28	

MARCH
S	M	T	W	T	F	S
						1
2	3	4	5	6	7	8
9	10	11	12	13	14	15
16	17	18	19	20	21	22
23	24	25	26	27	28	29
30	31					

APRIL
S	M	T	W	T	F	S
		1	2	3	4	5
6	7	8	9	10	11	12
13	14	15	16	17	18	19
20	21	22	23	24	25	26
27	28	29	30			

MAY
S	M	T	W	T	F	S
				1	2	3
4	5	6	7	8	9	10
11	12	13	14	15	16	17
18	19	20	21	22	23	24
25	26	27	28	29	30	31

JUNE
S	M	T	W	T	F	S
1	2	3	4	5	6	7
8	9	10	11	12	13	14
15	16	17	18	19	20	21
22	23	24	25	26	27	28
29	30					

JULY
S	M	T	W	T	F	S
		1	2	3	4	5
6	7	8	9	10	11	12
13	14	15	16	17	18	19
20	21	22	23	24	25	26
27	28	29	30	31		

AUGUST
S	M	T	W	T	F	S
					1	2
3	4	5	6	7	8	9
10	11	12	13	14	15	16
17	18	19	20	21	22	23
24	25	26	27	28	29	30
31						

SEPTEMBER
S	M	T	W	T	F	S
	1	2	3	4	5	6
7	8	9	10	11	12	13
14	15	16	17	18	19	20
21	22	23	24	25	26	27
28	29	30				

OCTOBER
S	M	T	W	T	F	S
			1	2	3	4
5	6	7	8	9	10	11
12	13	14	15	16	17	18
19	20	21	22	23	24	25
26	27	28	29	30	31	

NOVEMBER
S	M	T	W	T	F	S
						1
2	3	4	5	6	7	8
9	10	11	12	13	14	15
16	17	18	19	20	21	22
23	24	25	26	27	28	29
30						

DECEMBER
S	M	T	W	T	F	S
	1	2	3	4	5	6
7	8	9	10	11	12	13
14	15	16	17	18	19	20
21	22	23	24	25	26	27
28	29	30	31			

2015

JANUARY
S	M	T	W	T	F	S
				1	2	3
4	5	6	7	8	9	10
11	12	13	14	15	16	17
18	19	20	21	22	23	24
25	26	27	28	29	30	31

FEBRUARY
S	M	T	W	T	F	S
1	2	3	4	5	6	7
8	9	10	11	12	13	14
15	16	17	18	19	20	21
22	23	24	25	26	27	28

MARCH
S	M	T	W	T	F	S
1	2	3	4	5	6	7
8	9	10	11	12	13	14
15	16	17	18	19	20	21
22	23	24	25	26	27	28
29	30	31				

APRIL
S	M	T	W	T	F	S
			1	2	3	4
5	6	7	8	9	10	11
12	13	14	15	16	17	18
19	20	21	22	23	24	25
26	27	28	29	30		

MAY
S	M	T	W	T	F	S
					1	2
3	4	5	6	7	8	9
10	11	12	13	14	15	16
17	18	19	20	21	22	23
24	25	26	27	28	29	30
31						

JUNE
S	M	T	W	T	F	S
	1	2	3	4	5	6
7	8	9	10	11	12	13
14	15	16	17	18	19	20
21	22	23	24	25	26	27
28	29	30				

JULY
S	M	T	W	T	F	S
			1	2	3	4
5	6	7	8	9	10	11
12	13	14	15	16	17	18
19	20	21	22	23	24	25
26	27	28	29	30	31	

AUGUST
S	M	T	W	T	F	S
						1
2	3	4	5	6	7	8
9	10	11	12	13	14	15
16	17	18	19	20	21	22
23	24	25	26	27	28	29
30	31					

SEPTEMBER
S	M	T	W	T	F	S
		1	2	3	4	5
6	7	8	9	10	11	12
13	14	15	16	17	18	19
20	21	22	23	24	25	26
27	28	29	30			

OCTOBER
S	M	T	W	T	F	S
				1	2	3
4	5	6	7	8	9	10
11	12	13	14	15	16	17
18	19	20	21	22	23	24
25	26	27	28	29	30	31

NOVEMBER
S	M	T	W	T	F	S
1	2	3	4	5	6	7
8	9	10	11	12	13	14
15	16	17	18	19	20	21
22	23	24	25	26	27	28
29	30					

DECEMBER
S	M	T	W	T	F	S
		1	2	3	4	5
6	7	8	9	10	11	12
13	14	15	16	17	18	19
20	21	22	23	24	25	26
27	28	29	30	31		

Contents

Ostara

Beltane

Litha

Lammas

Contents

Mabon

Introduction

NEARLY EVERYONE HAS A favorite sabbat. There are numerous ways to observe any tradition. This edition of the *Sabbats Almanac* provides a wealth of lore, celebrations, creative projects, and recipes to enhance your holiday.

For this edition, a mix of writers—**Blake Octavian Blair, Dallas Jennifer Cobb, Linda Raedisch, Suzanne Ress, Denise Dumars, Thuri Calafia, Patricia M. Lafayllve,** and **Sybil Fogg**—share their ideas and wisdom. These include a variety of paths such as The Troth and Eclectic as well as the authors' personal approaches to each sabbat. Each chapter closes with an extended ritual, which may be adapted for both solitary practitioners and covens.

In addition to these insights and rituals, specialists in astrology, history, cooking, crafts, and family impart their expertise throughout.

Corrine Kenner gives an overview of planetary influences most relevant for each sabbat season and provides details and a short ritual for selected events, including New and Full Moons, retrograde motion, planetary positions, and more.

Melanie Marquis explores the realm of old-world Pagans, with a focus on customs such as ritual bread baking for Lammas and lesser-known facets of well-known symbols like the pumpkin and the maypole.

Ellen Dugan conjures up a feast for each festival that includes an appetizer, entrée, dessert, and beverage.

Lexa Olick offers instructions on craft projects that can also be incorporated into your practice.

Natalie Zaman focuses on sustainable activities the entire family can share in conjunction with each sabbat.

About the Authors

Blake Octavian Blair is an eclectic Pagan, ordained minister, shamanic practitioner, writer, Usui Reiki Master-Teacher, tarot reader, and musical artist. Blake blends various mystical traditions from both the East and West along with a reverence for the natural world into his own brand of modern Neopaganism and magick. Blake holds a degree in English and Religion from the University of Florida. He is an avid reader, crafter, and practicing vegetarian. Blake lives with his beloved husband, an aquarium full of fish, and an indoor jungle of houseplants. Visit him on the web at www.blakeoctavianblair.com or write him at blake@blakeoctavianblair.com.

Thuri Calafia is the author of *Dedicant: A Witch's Circle of Fire* and *Initiate: A Witch's Circle of Water*. She is an ordained minister and Wiccan high priestess, teacher, and creator of the Circles system and Circles School. She lives in the Pacific Northwest.

Life is what you make it, and **Dallas Jennifer Cobb** has made a magical life in a waterfront village on the shores of great Lake Ontario. Forever scheming novel ways to pay the bills, she practices manifestation magic and wildlands witchcraft. She teaches Pilates, works in a library, is an elected official, and writes to finance long hours spent following her heart's desire—time spent in nature and on the water. She lives with her daughter and three cats. Contact her at jennifer.cobb@live.com.

Ellen Dugan, the "Garden Witch," is an award-winning author and psychic-clairvoyant. A practicing Witch for more than thirty years, she is the author of more than a dozen Llewellyn books: *Garden Witchery*, *Elements of Witchcraft*, *Cottage Witchery*, *Autumn Equinox*, *The Enchanted Cat*, *Herb Magic for Beginners*, *Natural*

Witchery, How to Enchant a Man, Garden Witch's Herbal, Book of Witchery, Practical Protection Magick, Seasons of Witchery, Witches Tarot, and her newest title: *Practical Prosperity Magick.* Ellen wholeheartedly encourages folks to personalize their spellcraft—to go outside and to get their hands dirty to discover the wonder and magick of the natural world. Ellen and her family live in Missouri. For further information, visit her website at www.ellendugan.com. Ellen is also on Facebook, Instagram, Twitter, and Pinterest!

Rev. Denise Dumars M.A., is a founder of the Iseum of Isis Paedusis, chartered by the Fellowship of Isis. She is a widely published author and a college English instructor, whose writing and academic bio can be found at www.DeniseDumars.com. When not teaching college English or writing, she helms Rev. Dee's Apothecary: a New Orleans-Style Botanica, which can be found online at www.Dyana Aset.com. She travels to New Orleans, her favorite city, at least once a year to study magick, and studies in Mexico as well, where she often observes El Dia de los Muertos.

Sybil Fogg has been a practicing witch for over twenty-five years. Her real name is Sybil Wilen, but she chose to use her mother's maiden name in pagan circles to honor her grandparents. She's also a wife, mother, writer, teacher, and belly dancer. Her family shares her passion for magic, dance, and writing. She lives in Saco, Maine, with her husband and children. For more, please visit her website: www.sybilwilen.com.

Corrine Kenner specializes in bringing metaphysical subjects down to earth. She has written sixteen books, including *Astrology for Writers, Tarot for Writers, Tarot and Astrology,* and *The Wizards Tarot.* Some of her work has been translated for a worldwide audience; her books are available in French, Italian, Japanese, Polish, Portuguese, Romanian, and Russian. A former newspaper reporter and magazine editor, Kenner has also edited five anthologies and several astrological publications, including *Llewellyn's Astrological Calendar, Daily Planetary Guide,* and *Sun Sign Book.* Kenner was raised on a farm in North Dakota. She has lived in Brazil and Los Angeles, where she earned a degree in philosophy from California State University, Long Beach. She currently lives in Minneapolis, Minnesota, with her husband, a software developer. They have four daughters.You can find her at www.corrinekenner.com.

Since 1996, **Patricia M. Lafayllve** has lectured and performed rituals throughout the United States. She is a member of Two Ravens Kindred and The Troth, where she has served as Steward, High Steward, Godwoman, Rede member, and Steerswoman. Patricia is the founder of The Troth's Lore Program and served as its Provost. She lives in southeastern Connecticut. Visit her online at walkyrja .wordpress.com.

Melanie Marquis is the author of *The Witch's Bag of Tricks* (Llewellyn Publications, 2011) and a *Witch's World of Magick* (Llewellyn, 2014), the founder of United Witches global coven, and a local coordinator for Denver Pagan Pride. She's written for many Pagan publications including *Circle Magazine*, *Pentacle Magazine*, and *Spellcraft*. She's a regular contributor to Llewellyn's annuals. A freelance writer, folk artist, children's book illustrator, tarot reader, nature-lover, mother, and eclectic witch, she's passionate about finding the mystical in the mundane through personalized magick and practical spirituality. For more, visit www. melaniemarquis.com, www.unitedwitches.org, or www.facebook .com/melaniemarquisauthor.

Lexa Olick is the author of *Witchy Crafts: 60 Enchanted Projects for the Creative Witch* (Llewellyn 2013). She has previously contributed to other Llewellyn almanacs, such as the *Herbal Almanac* (2013) and the *Witches' Companion* (2014). She is a graduate of the University of Buffalo, where she studied art and art history. When she is not writing or crafting, she spends her time traveling, gardening, and adding to her collection of antique glassware. She currently lives in New York with her family and several hyperactive pets.

Linda Raedisch is the author of two books for Llewellyn, *Night of the Witches: Folklore, Traditions and Recipes for Celebrating Walpurgis Night* and *The Old Magic of Christmas: Yuletide Traditions for the Darkest Days of the Year*. An eclectic writer with an art background, Linda is interested in the practical aspects of prehistory, history, and religion. She lives in northern New Jersey.

Suzanne Ress has been practicing Wicca for about twelve years as the leader of a small coven, but she has been aware of having a special connection to nature and animal spirits since she was a young child. She has been writing creatively most of her life—short stories, novels, and nonfiction articles for a variety of publications—and finds it to be an important outlet for her considerable creative powers. Other outlets she regularly makes use of are metalsmithing, mosaic works, painting, and all kinds of dance. She is also a professional aromatic herb grower and beekeeper. Although she is an American of Welsh ancestry by birth, she has lived in northern Italy for nearly twenty years. She recently discovered that the small mountain in the pre-alpine hills she and her family and animals inhabit was once the site of an ancient Insubrian Celtic sacred place. Not surprisingly, the top of the mountain has remained a fulcrum of sacredness throughout the millennia, transforming from Celtic "Dunn" to Roman fortress to its current form—Catholic chapel, and this grounding in blessedness makes Suzanne's everyday life especially magical.

When she's not on the road or chasing free-range hens, **Natalie Zaman** is trying to figure out the universe. She is the co-author of the *Graven Images Oracle* deck (Galde Press), and the YA novels *Sirenz* and *Sirenz Back In Fashion* (Flux) and *Blonde Ops* (St. Martin's Press). Her work has appeared in Llewellyn's *Magical Almanac*, *FATE*, *SageWoman*, and *newWitch* magazines, and she currently writes the recurring feature "Wandering Witch" for *Witches and Pagans* magazine. Find Natalie online at http://nataliezaman.com or at http://broomstix.blogspot.com, a collection of crafts, stories, ritual, and art she curates for Pagan families.

Samhain

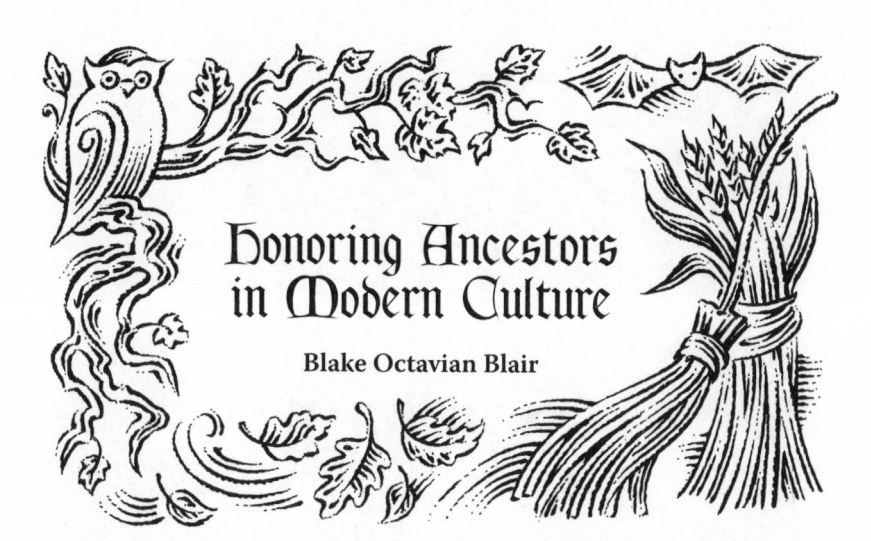

Honoring Ancestors in Modern Culture

Blake Octavian Blair

WHILE MANY OF US honor and work with our ancestors year-round, Samhain is definitely the season of the ancestors. We call upon our ancestors not only to honor them, but also for their guidance, strength, and support. We hope to continue to include them as an active part of our lives. The concept of who our ancestors are and what constitutes an ancestor varies among individuals, traditions, and cultures. For many in modern mainstream Western society, the word "ancestor" conjures up the concept of blood-related relatives who are now deceased. However, that narrow perception is thankfully changing and the concept of who our ancestors are is both shifting and expanding, as is the return of their reverence in modern culture.

The mainstream Western concept of ancestors mainly consisting of blood relations is not the global or historical gold standard definition. Blood relation, while sometimes a contributing factor, is often secondary to other criteria. This is quite often an easy concept for Pagan and magickal folk to understand, as we are frequently part of nontraditional families and communities full of nonblood ties and bonds. If you are initiated into a specific Craft tradition's lineage, everyone initiated into that lineage before you are also your ancestors. Even solitaries are not exempt from this, as all those who helped forge the path(s) before you in the Craft, whether they were solitary or not, are indeed also your ancestors. The very path we walk upon ties us together just as tight as any other connective fiber. (Many modern witches count Scott Cunningham, for example, among their ancestors.) This is and has always been the normal way to conceptualize and define ancestors among many indigenous peoples and cultures.

Former U.S. First Lady Hillary Clinton is often cited for saying that it takes an entire village to raise a child. This implies, of course, that the sphere of influence that contributes directly to who we are goes beyond genetics or the nuclear family. Many of us have had mentors, teachers, and friends who played a more integral role in our life than a blood relative. Some of these relationships are created through more formal means like traditions and lineages. For example, I consider Mikao Usui, who discovered Usui Reiki, to be my ancestor. Reiki practitioners keep track of their exact lineage through which the Reiki healing energy is passed down from Reiki Master to student like a family tree. Every Usui Reiki Master can trace his/her lineage directly back to Mikao Usui. This is the same for other lineage-based traditions, whether they be Reiki, witchcraft, or otherwise. All those in your lineage (and even the broader tradition itself) can be considered ancestors. Although it is a subject of great debate, I also believe that living people in many of the categories explored within this article can be considered an ancestor as well. However, as we often focus on honoring the deceased during the Samhain season, our discussion here will center on our ancestral relations beyond the veil.

Indirect lineages that can't be traced directly still qualify for ancestral consideration. This is true for many shamanic lineages and the lineage of religions—both your own and those of your family members (which may differ widely). If you incorporate Buddhist practices into your path, for example, a host of Buddhist figures who came before you can be considered your ancestors. Or even if you have never practiced Catholicism, but your parents, grandparents, or other loved ones were devout Catholics, it is okay to honor that part of your ancestry. I know more than one open-minded Pagan who has a cross, rosary, or small Star of David on their ancestral altar or somewhere else in their home. They do this because they honor and respect their loving ancestors who found fulfillment from those paths. The energetic bonds and ties formed by lineages and traditions are extremely powerful, and it is not uncommon for an individual to feel closer to their ancestors acquired through those lines than to those formed via means of blood relation.

Ancestral relations can also be formed through informal means and bonds. Beloved community members and neighbors can be considered ancestors worth venerating. Some individuals who grow up in one place for their entire childhood form close bonds to neighbors or other members of that community. Harking back to the "It takes a village" mentality, these people are rightfully classified as ancestors. "Modern tribes" are also another informal bond through which ancestral lines can run under our modern working definitions. Modern tribes often consist of those groups of friends and like minds that often form organically and naturally through life. These types of loved ones are acquired as college classmates or dormmates, co-workers who become more than co-workers, and through deeper friendships formed within larger subgroups and communities. These informal yet tight-knit groups are living entities that grow and change through the natural path of life as people move, have children, change jobs, and pass from this earthly realm. Distance is no obstacle for modern tribes. It should be noted that while I acknowledge that the terms "tribe" and "tribalism" are often used in context with unfavorable connotations and are often used in conjunction with and to bring up concepts, behavior, and practices that can have potential detrimental effects, that is not how I use the terms. I envision and refer to our modern tribes as those tight-knit groups of close friends and loved ones among which we can consciously choose to not practice detrimental behaviors and practices or "us and them" mentalities and instead strive for uplifting, supportive, and beneficial action as a group that is a subset of the greater community at large.

An ancestral lineage or group that can be considered either formal or informal, depending on context, would be those who paved the way and walked the path of your profession before you. Whether you are a schoolteacher, engineer, nurse, massage therapist, stay-at-home spouse or parent, or clergy, there were pioneers who carried the torch that lit the way for you to carry it forward. This certainly makes them worthy of our veneration.

We can also honor people from broader social movements—both those we have participated in or have been affected by—under this definition of modern ancestry. Members of demographic cohorts who have fought and continue to fight for their civil rights can rightfully claim as ancestors members of those movements as well as those who were killed tragically just for being who they are or for standing up for what they believe in. GLBT persons often honor Harvey Milk, Matthew Shepherd, and those involved with the Stonewall Riots. Women's rights leaders who have helped fight sexism and gender inequities such as Jane Addams and Carrie Chapman Catt have rightfully earned their position among the honored dead. African American leaders such as Dr. Martin Luther King Jr. and Rosa Parks are most certainly without question ancestors of the civil rights movement as well.

✤

So now that we have fleshed out a working definition of what may constitute an ancestor, it is time to explore how in our modern life we might go about honoring them. When we look at the cues from nature, it makes perfect sense as to why this is the season we often place a greater emphasis on our ancestors. Samhain brings with it the Earth in the midst of a season of transition. In many areas, the vibrant green and abundant foliage of summer has been left behind, leaves are turning various shades of autumnal jewel tones, the grass is starting to become patchy in color, the air is turning crisper, and the days are noticeably shorter. A process of waning, of transition, is occurring. This certainly brings about a contemplation of the transition that is death and our loved ones who have made that transition. By stopping to reflect upon and attune with nature during this season, it can help us come to a deeper understanding of the transition of death that our loved ones go through as a natural process when we parallel it to the natural cycle that nature experiences. It becomes less mysterious, even if only slightly. We come to at least understand ourselves as being part of the process of nature. A part of the Great Mystery. As simple an act as it sounds, this reflection and realization can take a great deal of time to digest, but also can be profoundly healing and comforting. For with death, most of us believe in rebirth in one form or another, be it an afterlife, reincarnation, or some combination of the two. In the eyes of many spiritual practitioners, some part or form of us carries on. So why not include departed ancestors as part of our lives?

A great way of doing so is to construct an ancestral altar or shrine in your home. I recommend picking a central location that overlooks a hub of activity. Living rooms and dining rooms are great choices. Although many religions and spiritual traditions have prescribed guidelines for the contents and setup of ancestral altars, it can be as simple or elaborate as you'd like—whatever you find pleasing. For me, the more personalized such an altar is the better. The ancestral altar in our home resides atop a short bookcase in our dining room. The bookcase itself contains our cookbooks. I've covered it with an altar cloth I've sewn out of skull fabric. Some of the items included on our altar include a skull with Celtic knotwork depicting spirits traveling through the afterlife, a novena candle to Santa Muerte, an incense burner, a glass for offerings of drink and a plate for offerings of food, and a few photos of some of our departed loved ones. An interesting inclusion is actually an offering to a playful and benevolent spirit that we encountered in our current apartment. Shortly after moving in, as we were painting cement blocks to make bookcases and using tools to hang things and get settled in to our new home, we discovered we had a spirit who liked to play funny business with our tools. Upon further spirit communication, we found he was the handyman type from a bygone era. We left a screwdriver on the ancestral altar for him and haven't experienced any such shenanigans since! It appears acknowledgement was all he desired! So we also use our ancestral altar for purposes of honoring ancestors of property and land.

For those who may already have an ancestral shrine or altar erected, this is a wonderful time to refresh and rejuvenate the sacred space. In addition to the regular cleaning of the altar, perhaps adorn it with a brand-new altar cloth, a fresh new candle, or add photographs or statuary—the ancestors like gifts too! Many people like to use Samhain as an official time to add effects and items honoring ancestors that have passed within the past year (since last Samhain) to the altar. Many people enjoy including inherited possessions from deceased loved ones in their ancestral altars and shrines. Your grandfather's watch, a dear friend's favorite coffee cup, or a mentor's favorite book. You can design a special family ritual or ceremony for the occasion of adding such items.

I feel that if you have an ancestral altar in a common area of the home, it is a good idea to make the erection, maintenance, and care of it a family/household affair. This makes it a space that carries the energies and adoration of the entire household. Each person will be able to form a connection with the ancestors and feel comfortable using the space as theirs.

As mentioned earlier, honoring the ancestors of the land where you live can be a fulfilling and important practice as well. From those who lived before you on the land where your home stands, to the citizens who blazed the way in your city's history before you. For this reason, a favorite practice of my husband and I is to visit local cemeteries. We like to go at least a few times a year, but always make it a point to go around Samhain. We are blessed with some very old cemeteries in our area that date back as far as the late 1700s! We often bring offerings of candy for the graves of children and other offerings that are favorites of various spirits whose remains rest there. During Samhain season, we often arrive to the sight of apples and pennies adorning the top of many of the tombstones. It is a wonderful feeling to know that we are not the only ones honoring the Beloved Dead during their special season.

This Samhain, ask yourself, who are your ancestors? How will you honor them? There are no answers set in stone—the answers are as varied as the people asking these questions. However, as our consciousness shifts, we are joyously adopting a more modern criteria and definition of the ancestors, which in fact isn't modern at all. We are in many ways coming full circle. May you and your ancestors be blessed this Samhain!

Cosmic Sway

Corrine Kenner

THOUSANDS OF YEARS AGO, when astrologers were first developing the principles of their art, they saw the Sun rise and set against the backdrop of a different constellation each month. Eventually, those twelve constellations became the twelve signs of the zodiac, which led to the development of the twelve-month calendar we use to this day.

Even now, the four seasons of the year are based on the Sun's entry into the four cardinal signs—fiery Aries in spring, watery Cancer in summer, airy Libra in fall, and earthy Capricorn in winter. The sabbats celebrate those four quarter holidays, along with the cross-quarter holidays that fall halfway through each season.

Samhain

The sabbat holidays are annual milestones that mark the Earth's journey around the Sun. Samhain commemorates the end of the harvest season and the beginning of a new year. It's celebrated as the Sun moves through watery Scorpio, at the halfway point between the Autumn Equinox and the Winter Solstice.

This year, the holiday is marked by a close conjunction of Venus and the Sun—which will make it one of the sexiest, sultriest, most sensual Samhains in recent memory.

Scorpio is an intense, passionate sign, characterized by its fixation with the dark mysteries of sex and death. (Scorpio, after all, is ruled by Pluto, the god of the Underworld.) Venus is the planet of love, beauty, and attraction. When she passes through watery Scorpio, linked with the Sun, the sign supercharges her natural inclinations. She becomes erotic.

Venus' seductive appeal is further enhanced by the fact that the romantic planet is also in a harmonious trine with Neptune—which emphasizes glamour and illusion—as well as a sextile Pluto, which adds intensity and drive to her sex appeal.

The Sun and Venus aren't alone in watery Scorpio: Saturn, the ringed planet of limitations and restrictions, is also moving through the sign. He's not close enough to Venus to actually form a conjunction, but his presence does lend discipline and structure to Venus's mood—along with a tendency to operate in secret.

Tarot and Astrology

Tarot and astrology are closely linked. Every card in the Major Arcana corresponds to either a planet or a sign.

Picture the planets as ten characters from the Major Arcana, and the signs as the twelve roles they play—along with the costumes they wear. In this case, visualize Venus as her corresponding tarot card, the Empress. The lovely young wife and mother we're used to seeing? This year, she's wearing a little black dress, Scorpio style. That's because Scorpio corresponds to the Death card, which is dark, mysterious, dangerous, and seductive. She might even be wearing a devilish pair of horns and wielding a pitchfork, in homage to Pluto, Scorpio's ruling planet.

If you'd like to visualize the cards as mythic gods and goddesses, picture the Venusian Empress as Aphrodite, the goddess of love, and the Death card as Hades, the lord of the Underworld.

Practical Astrology

To align yourself with the planetary energies at Samhain this year, look for a way to make your celebration as sensual as possible. Dress to impress—or to seduce. Don't go overboard, though. Saturn—the planet of boundaries, limitations, and restrictions—demands a certain level of restraint.

Planetary Positions

On Samhain, the Sun is in Scorpio, the mesmerizing water sign of darkness and mystery. Venus and Saturn are there, too, as we've already discussed. The Sun will move into fiery Sagittarius on November 21.

The Moon is in airy Aquarius, the sign of social groups, humanitarian ideals, and futuristic thinking.

Mercury, the fast-moving planet of thought and communication, is in airy Libra, the sign of social grace and balance. Mercury's passage through Libra favors public speaking, rational thought, and witty conversation. Mercury is the fastest-moving planet, though, and he passes through all twelve signs in eighty-eight days. He'll enter watery Scorpio on November 8, and fiery Sagittarius on November 27.

Venus is in watery Scorpio; she'll move into fiery Sagittarius on November 16, and earthy Capricorn on December 10.

Mars is in Capricorn, the sign of worldly power, where the god of war is exalted. Mars will move into airy Aquarius on December 4.

Jupiter is in Leo. The sign's fiery energy makes the Greater Benefic even more generous and magnanimous than usual.

Saturn, the ringed planet of boundaries and limitations, is in watery Scorpio.

Generational Planets

The three outermost planets are so far from the Sun that they take years to move through each sign of the zodiac.

Uranus will be in fiery Aries, the first sign of the zodiac, until 2018. Uranus is the planet of the unusual and the unexpected—and at the moment, it's moving retrograde, backtracking through the sign. Whenever it passes through fiery Aries, the impulsive planet's focus on freedom and individualism is heightened and focused.

Neptune will be in watery Pisces until 2025. At the moment, it's retrograde, too. Neptune is comfortable here, marking this as a period that can enhance both dreams and illusions. It can also be incredibly imaginative, exceptionally psychic, or incredibly illusionary.

Pluto will be in earthy Capricorn until 2023, where it will fight to uphold tradition, social standards, and conventional responsibility and self-discipline.

Planets in Aspect

In addition to the Sun's conjunction with Venus, there are several other interesting astrological aspects underway.

Aspects describe the planets' geometric relationships with each other as they orbit around the Sun. They're easy to spot when you see the planets plotted on an astrological chart. Commonly used aspects include the conjunction, sextile (60° of separation), square (90°), trine (120°), and opposition (180°).

The effects of planetary aspects are usually fairly generalized, but they can be intense if they happen to mirror key points in your own birth chart.

At the moment, the Sun is in a harmonious sextile with Mars, which supercharges the planet of energy, action, and aggression. You might find you have the energy to kick-start—or finish—a project that calls for focus and determination.

The Sun is in an even more harmonious trine with a Piscean Neptune, the planet of glamour and illusion. The aspect can lead to flights of fancy, escapist fantasies, and vivid dreams.

The Sun is sextile Mars in Capricorn, which energizes the warrior planet even more than usual.

The Sun is also sextile Pluto in Capricorn, which opens a clear channel of communication to the Underworld. It intensifies Plutonian issues of power and transformation, and unavoidable change.

Mercury, the planet of speed and communication, opposes Uranus, the planet of the unusual and the unexpected. An opposition occurs when two planets are on opposite sides of the zodiac. When Mercury, in Libra, taps into Uranus's Aries energy, you can expect the unexpected. You might get surprising news about a brother, sister, cousin, or neighbor.

Mars's fiery energy is dampened somewhat by a sextile with watery Neptune in Pisces. The combination could be steamy.

Expansive Jupiter, in fiery Leo, is squaring off at a 90-degree angle to Saturn, in watery Scorpio. The uncomfortable connection accents accenting the age-old struggle between the forces of growth and the forces of restriction. In more primitive terms, they're playing out the drama between good and evil. Jupiter used to be called the Greater Benefic, while Saturn was the Greater Malefic.

Uranus, in Aries, is square Pluto in Capricorn. The two outer planets take years to orbit around the Sun, which means this is an aspect that defines an entire generation. Collectively, we'll find ourselves struggling with issues of personal freedom and political responsibility.

Phases of the Moon

October 8: A Full Moon in fiery Aries will be completely illuminated by the Sun, which is on the other side of the zodiac, in airy Libra. When the Moon is full in fiery Aries, it takes on many of the qualities we associate with the fiery sign: a commanding sense of leadership, impulsiveness, and a yearning for independence. Emotionally, this is a good time to wipe the slate clean, rid yourself of old baggage, and set a new course for your relationships. Tonight's Full Moon has an added bonus: a total lunar eclipse, visible throughout most of North America, South America, eastern Asia, and Australia. Total lunar eclipses can only occur during a

Full Moon, when the Earth is positioned perfectly between the Sun and the Moon. During the eclipse, look for the Moon to take on a blood-red color, true to her placement in the fiery sign of Aries.

October 23: The lunar eclipse will be followed by a partial solar eclipse during the New Moon, when the Sun and the Moon are conjunct in watery Scorpio.

November 6: A Full Moon in earthy Taurus will be brightly lit by the Sun, 180 degrees away in watery Scorpio. The Moon represents emotional well-being, and it's exalted in earthy Taurus, the sign of comfort and security.

November 22: A New Moon, with the Sun and the Moon conjunct in fiery Sagittarius, could inspire a sense of wanderlust and curiosity. Fiery Sagittarius, after all, is the sign of long-distance travel, higher education, and philosophy. A New Moon occurs when the Moon is directly between the Earth and the Sun.

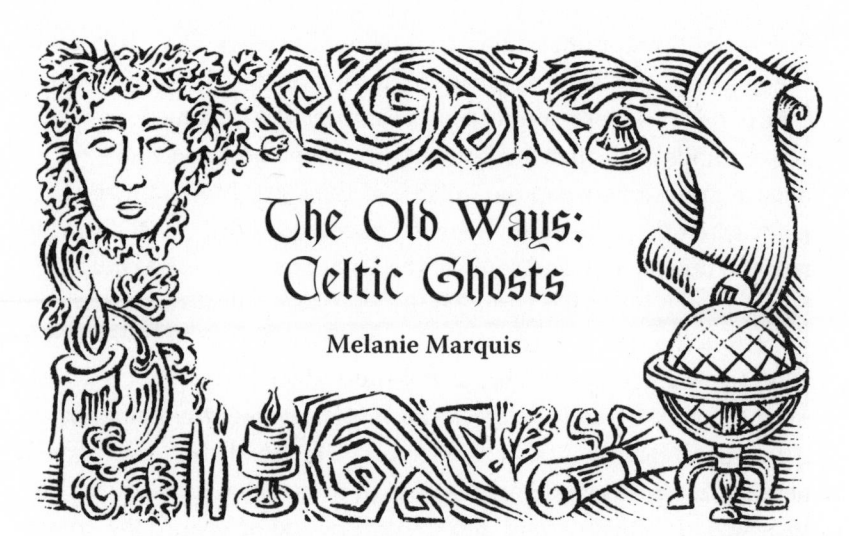

The Old Ways: Celtic Ghosts

Melanie Marquis

ASK A MODERN WITCH what their favorite sabbat celebration is, and there's a good chance the answer will be Samhain. Maybe it's the darker themes and overt mysticism of the day that appeals to us. Maybe it's because Samhain is a time of both quiet introspection and magickal mayhem, which makes for a nice combination. Or maybe it's just the candy. Whatever the reason, Samhain is a major annual celebration for many of today's Witches and other modern Pagans. It makes sense, as much significance was placed on Samhain by the holiday's originators, the Celts. The Celts were an Indo-European people originally from central Europe. They shared a common language and culture, and lived in tribal societies. By the first century BCE, they had spread throughout western Europe, the British Isles, and Galatia, a region in what is now modern Turkey. While the Celtic calendar marked out several major holidays, Samhain was one of utmost importance. To the Celts, Samhain marked a time of endings and beginnings alike. Celebrated annually around November 1, Samhain meant the death of the old year and the start of the new one, the beginning of winter and the initial darkness from whence eventually springs the light. It was the time of harvest, when plants were cut down and stored for winter sustenance.

It was the time of impending cold, when livestock like cattle and sheep had to be sheltered closer to home. Mostly, though, it was a time of death, when roaming spirits captured the beating hearts and active minds of the living. Samhain was a time between times—the middle ground between the finish and the start. It was a magickal night when the souls of the recently deceased could travel onward into the otherworld, and souls of the long-since deceased could return home to visit friends and family who were still alive.

While the belief in ghosts continued year round in Celtic culture, Samhain was the time when these disincarnate souls were most likely to actually interact and mingle among the living. Sacrifices of animals, fruits, and vegetables were made in hopes of appeasing the spirits, and big fires were lit to help guide the ghosts on their way, whether forward into the otherworld or back to the home they enjoyed in life to visit their loved ones.

The Celts believed in the possibility of a bodily life after death. They believed the soul would remain in the body, trapped in the grave or tomb, or would perhaps be given a fresh new material form to carry on with in the land of the dead, the "Otherworld," seen as a subterranean world ruled by a deity with aspects relating to both death and fertility. In the Otherworld, the dead were given fresh corporeal forms to enjoy. Existence in the Otherworld was believed to basically parallel one's life on earth, except that it had the potential to be much better, with greater pleasure, joy, and happiness. The dead could enjoy the same occupations, and expect to have much the same needs and emotions, as they did in life. Evidence of this belief is the widespread use of grave goods in Celtic culture, as well as the practice of feeding the dead. The dead were buried with food, weapons, and sometimes even with slaves, wives, and children (executed especially for the purpose of being there for their loved one despite the body's demise). Food was placed in coffins or around the grave at the time of burial, and at Samhain, a special meal for the dead was served. In Ireland and Brittany, food was placed by the family's hearth for ancestral spirits who came to call. The Celtic

Britons would place a large log in the hearth and then pour libations upon it as an offering to the spirits of the dead.

The hearth was associated with the Otherworld and was seen as a type of portal between worlds. While happy ancestor spirits might stop by the hearth for a pleasant visit, angry spirits seeking revenge could also come to call. The food left by the hearth served a dual purpose: to pay respect to the friendly spirits, and to help placate any dissatisfied, vengeful, or hungry spirits.

To the Celts, existence beyond death could take many different forms. Not every soul journeyed straight to the Otherworld to enjoy an endless afterlife of feasting and pleasures. The Celts held a belief in reincarnation, and they also believed in the idea of earthbound souls attached to particular places like burial mounds, bogs, lakes, or the family hearth. The immortal souls of the dead could appear in a variety forms, from human to furry animal to winged creature, or they could render themselves invisible.

Another possibility for the souls of the departed transformed the spirit into a mystical being. The Irish Celts believed that upon death, certain souls joined the *Daoin Sithe*, a tribe of spirit beings alternately thought of as gods, ghosts, fairies, and nature spirits. The *Daoin Sithe* dwelt in the barrows, burial mounds thought to double as a sort of portal to other realms.

The Scottish Celts in the Highlands believed in a rather unpleasant fate for the souls of the dead people who were deemed evil. It was thought that such souls became demonic spirits of the air, forbidden from entering the Otherworld, and unable to return back to the plane of the living. Known as the *Sluagh*, or the Host, they're believed to fly through the air in large masses. Fortunately, the *Sluagh* aren't necessarily doomed forever: if they find ways to atone for past wrongdoings, they're able to leave the Host and advance onward on their spiritual journeys.

In Ireland, ghosts were divided into two classes: those described as *taibhse*, and those described as *anam*. A *taibhse* was a sort of after-image, the lingering outward appearance of a person or object that can continue on for a time long after the physical form declines. A *taibhse* might look like a dead body or like any inanimate object. A *taibhse* is not a conscious entity, which is to say, if you were to see one, it would not be aware that it was being watched. The *anam*, in contrast, was an actual soul or spirit, a conscious entity that could interact with the world of the living. It was believed that a person could elect to remain an earthbound *anam* if desired, though the reasons for doing so were usually considered illegitimate and unjustified.

Throughout the Celtic lands, and throughout the wider world, local myths and folklore abound with stories of hauntings and spirits that both help and harm from beyond the grave. Would you like to visit with a ghost this Samhain, just as the ancient Celts did? Keep in mind that you're not necessarily looking for some misty white "classic ghost" apparition. To the Celts, a ghost might look like a bird, an animal, a living human, an inanimate object, or a mystical creature such as a fairy. Pay attention to any strange behaviors or characteristics exhibited in birds, insects, other animals, and even in the environment itself. Consider exploring your local graveyard, take a trip to the lake, or perhaps just sit for a spell by the fireplace. Place offerings of food and drink, and invite the wandering spirits of the dead to join you. The dead have visited the living each Samhain for thousands of years, and there's a good chance you might just find yourself in ghostly company.

References:

Imbas.org. "Samhain: Season of Death and Renewal." Alexei Kondratiev. Accessed October 13, 2013. http://www.imbas.org/articles /samhain.html.

Kelley, Ruth Edna. *The Book of Hallowe'en.* Boston: Lothrop, Lee, and Shepard Co., 1919. Accessed October 13, 2013. http://www .sacred-texts.com/pag/boh/index.htm.

Library of Congress Research Centers, the American Folklife Center. "Halloween: The Fantasy and Folklore of All Hallows." Jack

Santino. Accessed October 13, 2013. http://www.loc.gov/folklife/halloween.html.

MacCulloch, J.A. *The Religion of the Ancient Celts*. Edinburgh: T.&T. Clark, 1911. Accessed October 13, 2013. http://www.sacred-texts.com/neu/celt/rac/rac00.htm.

Monaghan, Patricia. *The Encyclopedia of Celtic Mythology and Folklore*. New York: Facts on File, Inc., 2004.

Feasts and Treats

Ellen Dugan

HAPPY NEW YEAR! SAMHAIN is upon us and as Witches we tend to have more events and gatherings now than at any other time of the year. There are Halloween parties for adults and the kids, coven gatherings, and the local Witches Ball. Here are a few good seasonal recipes that are perfect for "making and taking" and they can help to feed a crowd.

Ellen's Mostaccioli

This simple and hearty dish is a Midwestern version of mostaccioli, and it is affordable and goes a long way. It is also great heated up the following day!

Prep time: 20 minutes
Cook time: 8 minutes (pasta), 5–10 minutes (to brown turkey)
Serves: 6–10

1 box of mostaccioli noodles (1 pound), cooked until slightly chewy, as per instructions
1 pound ground turkey
½ cup fresh green pepper, chopped
2 tablespoons dried minced onions

2 cloves garlic, minced

2 teaspoons salt

1 teaspoon pepper

2 8-ounce jars marinara sauce (your choice of flavor, though I use a
    four-cheese variety)

1 tablespoon fresh basil, chopped

1 tablespoon fresh parsley, chopped

1 tablespoon fresh oregano, chopped

1 cup shredded mozzarella cheese

¼ cup shredded Parmesan cheese

In a large pot, cook pasta according to package directions, until pasta is slightly chewy.

Meanwhile, on medium-high heat, brown ground turkey with green pepper, minced onions, garlic, salt, and pepper. Drain the meat.

Add one jar of the marinara sauce to the cooked ground turkey keep warm on low heat.

Once the pasta is cooked, carefully drain the water. Return pasta to the large pot. Then add the ground meat/marinara mixture to the noodles in the large pot, and stir. Add the fresh chopped herbs and, if necessary, more of the marinara sauce. Finally, add the shredded cheeses and stir.

Serve immediately. Refrigerate or freeze any leftovers.

Reuben Dip

This is a different and quick side dish or appetizer to bring to a Samhain gathering or Halloween party. All you have to do is mix it up and zap it in the microwave!

Prep time: 10 minutes

Cook time: 2–4 minutes

Serves: 4–8

4 cups shredded Swiss cheese

1 cup sauerkraut (drained)

1 lb. ham, diced
½ cup low-fat Thousand Island salad dressing
Party rye bread or rye bread crackers

Mix all the ingredients together in a large microwaveable bowl. Microwave in 60-second increments until the cheese is melted, stirring the dip between zaps as you go. Serve warm with rye crackers or party rye bread.

Low-Fat Pumpkin Bread

This is without a doubt the recipe I get the most requests for ... ever! So here you go.

Prep time: 20 minutes
Cook time: 50–60 minutes
Yields: 2 loaves

2 cups sugar
1 can (15 ounces) of solid pack pumpkin
1 cup unsweetened applesauce
½ cup egg substitute (or 2 eggs)
1 teaspoon vanilla extract
3⅓ cups all-purpose flour
2 teaspoons baking soda
1 teaspoon baking powder
½ teaspoon salt
1 teaspoon ground cinnamon
½ teaspoon ground nutmeg
¼ teaspoon ground cloves

In large mixing bowl, combine the sugar, pumpkin, applesauce, egg substitute, and vanilla until ingredients are mixed well.

In a separate bowl, combine the flour, baking soda, baking powder, salt, and spices. Gradually add the dry ingredients to the pumpkin mixture, and mix well by hand.

Pour into two 8 inch x 4 inch loaf pans coated with nonstick cooking spray. (Or pour into 6 mini-loaf pans.)

Bake at 350 degrees F for 50 to 60 minutes or until a toothpick inserted near the center of the loaf comes out clean. Cool for 10 minutes before removing from loaf pans to wire racks.

After it cools, I take one loaf and pop it inside a freezer bag and freeze it. (This baked bread freezes well.)

Options: You may add 1 cup chopped nuts or raisins to this bread. If so, add it after all of the dry ingredients are well incorporated. Then pour the batter into the loaf pans.

Bewitching Dairy-Free Pumpkin Smoothie

This is a healthier and dairy-free version of a Pumpkin Pie Concrete. I experimented with this until I got it perfect.

Prep time: 5 minutes
Serves: 2

1 frozen banana
½ cup pumpkin purée
½ to 1 cup vanilla almond milk
½ cup ice
5 dashes pumpkin pie spice

Pour all ingredients except pumpkin pie spice in to the blender. Attach lid to blender firmly. Blend to desired consistency—start out by adding the smaller amounts of almond milk. After the smoothie is blended, add the dashes of pumpkin pie spice. Blend for a few seconds again and taste to check seasoning level. Also, please note that you can add more pumpkin pie spice/almond milk or ice to your preference.

Crafty Crafts

Lexa Olick

EACH SABBAT-THEMED CRAFT is fairly quick to make. Most of them can be assembled in one sitting, but the drying time can take up to 24 hours or longer. Even if the paint feels dry and the glue seems stable, it's still always important to follow the manufacturer's suggested drying time.

There is no one way to create a project. I've included a few small changes to alter certain projects. Sometimes, a simple change can make a big difference. Of course, these are only suggestions, since there are no limits to creativity!

Samhain is mostly associated with the colors orange, black, gold, purple, brown, and red. It's no coincidence that those are the same colors found in pumpkins, gourds, apples, and fallen leaves. Samhain is about the final harvest and revolves around symbols of death. However, that doesn't mean anything needs to be left outside to rot. All of those items can be gathered together and showcased in a unique Samhain display. They are part of an endless cycle of life, death, and rebirth, so that deserves to be honored.

Items like gourds and apples are easily collected and displayed in baskets, but for variation, we can instead assemble them into glass containers. It adds a bit of class to this mysterious and dark time. An apothecary jar practically rests on top of a pedestal, which further emphasizes the significance of the objects inside. Everything looks more mysterious and magical when it sits behind glass, but such a display also signifies its importance. Samhain is a time to remember ancestors and an apothecary jar can become the forefront of a tabletop display.

Samhain Apothecary Jars

Apothecaries were the precursors of modern pharmacy. They stored precious materials for their remedies in clear, lidded glass jars. These apothecary jars provided very visual and easy-to-access storage, yet there was always something curious about the objects held within. Although the objects were displayed in plain view, their purpose was often unknown. It was a secret only the apothecary knew, so these clear jars still seem a bit sinister today.

Apothecary jars are perfect for stand-alone displays, but they also make wonderful additions to dumb supper tables or altars for Samhain. They can be purchased at any craft or home décor store, but there is something deviously crafty about making your own apothecary jar from scratch.

Supplies
Large mason jar with lid
Spray paint
E6000 adhesive
Drawer handle
4-inch glass taper candleholder
Spanish moss
Small objects and trinkets to fill the jar

Making the Jar: Since you will be spray-painting and gluing, you need to make sure your supplies are free from dust or oils from your fingertips. Wash the mason jar (and its lid and metal screw band), drawer handle, and candleholder carefully with dish soap and water and set them aside until they are completely dry.

Once your objects are clean and dry, place a small amount of E6000 adhesive along the border of the lid and attach it to the metal screw band. Hold it tight for about 1 minute, and then set it aside to fully adhere for 24 hours. Apply E6000 onto the bottom of the drawer handle and place it in the center of the mason jar lid. Just as you did before, hold it tight for 1 minute and then set it aside to fully adhere for 24 hours.

In a well-ventilated area, lay down some newspaper so no unwanted spray paint splatters on anything important. Gather the objects that are to be painted—the lid and the candleholder. Place them on top of the newspaper and spray paint them with the color of your choice. You may need to spray several coats, so make sure to wait until the paint is fully dry before applying another coat. You also have to rotate your objects to make sure you apply an even coat of paint on the bottom and on any hard-to-reach crevices. If your drawer handle has a decorative crystal that you wish to keep intact, cover it with a thick coat of Vaseline before you spray paint it. When you are done painting, wash away the Vaseline and the crystal will be as sparkly as ever!

Once everything is painted and dry, it's then time to piece the apothecary jar together. Place a small amount of E6000 on the top of the candleholder. Attach it to the bottom of the mason jar and hold tightly for 1 minute. Now set it aside for about 24 hours so it can fully adhere.

Filling the Jar: Now that you've created your own one-of-a-kind apothecary jar, it's time to make it even more unique. Apothecary jars look perfect on an altar to honor your ancestors, so the objects you place inside can be photographs, heirlooms, jewelry, or even a private note sealed in an envelope. Personal items make your apothecary jar truly special, but you can also fill it with seasonal items, such as skulls, spiders, or miniature gourds. Whatever you choose, the items are separated between layers of Spanish moss.

Spanish moss is commonly used as filler in floral décor, but it also makes an excellent packaging material. It offers padding to keep your items from sinking into one another, and its dried texture and color makes it a perfect accent for a Samhain display.

Spanish moss is the first thing you add to your apothecary jar. It naturally clings to itself, so gently fluff it out with your fingertips. Place it at the bottom of your jar so it acts like a little "pillow" for your items. Place a couple of items on top of the moss then cover it with another layer of Spanish moss. Repeat until your jar is full. Screw the lid onto the jar and your Samhain apothecary jar is ready to display and admire!

Time to Complete: About 40 minutes to assemble, but may take up to 3 days for the adhesive to cure completely.

Cost: Approximately $15.00, but that price will increase if you chose to fill your jar with store-bought trinkets.

Variation: The apothecary jar doesn't necessarily have to be a tribute to your ancestors. For a more natural display, add snail shells, autumn leaves, apples, or small gourds into your canister. Popular herbs include rosemary, pumpkin seeds, and sage. The apothecary jars are functional as well as decorative. Instead of using them as part of an altar to honor your ancestors or as a general Samhain display, you can also use them as a convenient candy dish for your Samhain celebrations. All you have to do is substitute the trinkets with candy. Since they are still layered between Spanish moss, choose candies that are individually wrapped. That way no one ends up with moss stuck between their teeth!

Sustainable Samhain: Green Resolutions

Natalie Zaman

THIS YEAR, RESOLVE TO go green.

In a world where so much stuff is disposable and constant consumption is the norm, it can take a conscious effort to buy and use only what you need and minimize the waste you generate. Every sabbat is a call to honor God and Goddess and celebrate life at its various stages—but it is also an opportunity to rebalance and reassess: What can I do to make my life simpler? More in tune with nature? Balanced? Adding an environmentally friendly twist to your spiritual practices can ground you, guide you to other green habits, and so give back to the Earth—good karma! What better time to begin than at Samhain, the New Year of the Old Ways.

If your Samhain season is anything like mine, then it will include candy, and lots of it. One of October's great mysteries (for me, at least) is that, Halloween after Halloween, no matter how much candy I give away, I always have leftovers—even after the bowl is restocked with my kids' unwanted loot. I've sent bags of candy to work with my husband, donated sacks to the Vets, nursing homes, and shelters—but the first days of November find many such places inundated with snack sized sweets, and unfortunately, some inevitably ends up in the garbage. The situation presented a challenge:

how to incorporate Halloween candy into a Samhain ritual, one where waste was reduced, if not eliminated.

Inspiration came with a visit by a group of Buddhist monks from the Drepung Gomang Monastery to our state university. In the week that the monks were on campus, they created a Compassion Buddha mandala, a visual prayer for compassion and healing made of colored sand. Translated from Sanskrit, mandala can mean circle, whole world, and cosmogram; whatever the interpretation, all implications point to completeness.

Mandalas can vary in purpose, their positive intentions expressed through color, shape, pattern and number; there is no element that does not hold some kind of import. Perhaps most significantly, the mandala is a reminder of the impermanence of our existence. At the end of the visit, the Compassion Buddha Mandala, so painstakingly planned and carefully crafted, was swept up—as tradition demands—and cast into a body of water as a blessing. Such a sentiment, I thought, is perfect for Samhain as it is a reminder of the only constant in life: Change.

On Samhain and the days that follow, the veil between this world and the next is thin. For many traditions, this is the time of the year to reach out to loved ones who have passed on, and, respectfully, honor the energies that dwell in the shadows. Placed outdoors in a sacred pattern, excess treats collected at Halloween can become an offering to those on the other side. Unwrapped, the candy is biodegradable, and nestled in the soil, will be broken down by insects to become a part of the earth. And while this mandala is not destroyed by human hands and cast into the water, the element of water is used to release its energy.

Make It Your Own!
You will need:
Halloween candy
A small shovel
Water

An outdoor location away from your home or common area if you
share living space. This ritual has the potential to attract wildlife, so for safety and out of courtesy to others, perform it in a
remote area.

Bring your candy to your chosen location. Using the shovel, make a
circular depression in the earth about an inch deep; how large will
depend on how much candy you have to work with.

Unwrap the candy (save the wrappers), and place the pieces in
the depression in a pattern of your choice. If you have lots of candy
and want to create something complex, you may want to draw it
out beforehand, planning what patterns you can make—Halloween
treats come in many sizes, shapes, textures, and colors! Your mandala can also evolve spontaneously. Creating as you go is a potent,
powerful, and fun option, especially if you're working with a group
(or with children!). Do what is most comfortable and practical for
you.

While there are many sacred shapes that can be used for this ritual, consider making a simple spiral. The maypole dance at the opposite point in the wheel of the year spins inward to signify the invocation of life. To honor Samhain, an outward helix acknowledges
the life that will dissipate only to spin inward again and renew.

Before you begin, speak or think this invocation, a call to those
who have passed and are watching:

> *From my heart*
> *To your hearth*
> *In the fading light*
> *I honor and remember you*
> *On this long, sweet night.*

Place a piece of candy at the center of the depression and working clockwise to invoke (transient spirits to your gift, and nature
to break down the sweets), place subsequent pieces around and
around until you reach the outer edge. As you work, invoke the elements you are using to add potency to the spell:

From Fire, sweet
Water frees
Air stirs
And in Earth, complete

Pour water over the mandala once you've finished laying it out. This will help to release the sugars in the candy, which will attract insects such as ants and mites. Cover the mandala with earth; this step will hinder animals from disturbing it before the insects can do their work. Take a moment of silence before leaving the site, and your offering to the workings of Samhaintide and its specters.

And what about those wrappers? There are many things you can make with them (a few clever teens made their prom dresses and accessories out of Starburst wrappers!). Visit Get Green Be Well: (http://getgreenbewell.com/2010/10/25/green-your-halloween-day-25-candy-wrapper-crafts/) and Cut Out And Keep (http://www.cutoutandkeep.net/projects/candy-wrapper-roses) for some easy and fun crafts that will help to lessen the landfill.

Samhain Ritual: Be a Good Ancestor

Blake Octavian Blair

WHILE AT SAMHAIN WE commonly honor our ancestors, doing so also provides a time for contemplation about ourselves. One day, we too will be somebody's ancestor. When they look back at who we were, what about us do we want them to remember? We all have some less-than-admirable traits and qualities; nobody is immune to this fact.

That's why Samhain is a perfect time for banishment, in addition to honoring our ancestors and the dearly departed, so here is a ritual to give a send-off to a part of ourselves that does not serve our highest good! By doing so, we actively take responsibility for ourselves and commit to being the best person, and ancestor, we can be. To accomplish this banishment of these less desirable qualities, ritual participants will write obituaries for those traits and sections of themselves which no longer serve their highest good.

The supplies and procedure for this ritual are relatively simple but often have a very poignant and emotional effect. It can be performed with any number of people from solitary to a large group, however, when done in a small to mid-sized group, it seems to have a way of bringing together the participants in a setting that results in a very comforting and mutually supportive environment.

Writing such an obituary for a potentially painful part of oneself might sound as if it may induce self-anger or self-resentment, however, it surprisingly often results in a stronger sense of self-compassion and empowerment. We realize that often, once we acknowledge less desirable parts of ourselves, they no longer maintain the same ability to control us. Because of the extremely personal nature and poignant results this ritual can produce, it goes without saying that it should be performed in perfect love and perfect trust. What is said in circle—stays in circle.

Before we discuss how the ritual will unfold, let us take a look at the basic supplies that will be needed.

Items Needed

Paper (approx. 1–2 sheets per person)
Pens
Fireproof cauldron or a safe ritual bonfire
Incense or smudge and holder
Lighter
Various offertory herbs (optional)
Light food and drink for cakes and ale
Potluck dish from each participant for after-feast (optional)
Photos of departed loved ones for after-feast (optional)

Before the Ritual

You should try to give an explanation of the ritual to participants in advance—ideally at the time of their invitation. This will give them plenty of time to thoughtfully prepare their obituary. Writing such an obituary is an excellent way to explore detrimental thought patterns, feelings, habits, moods, and other traits as it requires us to acknowledge and confront them head-on. This is why such obituaries can be very difficult to compose. In magick we use the term banishment, which may seem like a strong word, and a strong word it is indeed. However, in context of this ritual, banishment is simply the release from being restrained by these qualities. It is important to remember, we are releasing these traits in an act of compassion. The obituary can be typed or handwritten. On the day of the ritual itself, have pen and paper on hand for any participants who may not have composed their obituary in advance, so that they may do so prior to the start of the ritual proper.

This ritual requires only a very simple ritual space and minimal tools and accoutrements. An altar for the ritual is completely optional, as are quarter candles. If you do choose to use an altar, dress it with candles and a "memento mori" theme with skulls and similar motif. White flowers are a nice altar adornment, as they represent the transformation, cleansing, and new beginnings that can take place from the work of this ritual. Another optional item to have is a bowl or two of offertory herbs available that each person can take a small handful from and drop in the fire with their obituary. A good magickal herb-correspondence book can provide myriad suggestions, but popular herbs for the purpose are tobacco, cedar, and lavender. What is essential is a large fireproof vessel or cauldron (or a safely contained ritual bonfire), and enough space for all participating to gather around the fire or cauldron comfortably in a circle. Cleanse all participants by smudging before processing to the ritual space.

The Ritual

Process to the ritual space and circle around the cauldron/fire clockwise. When the physical circle is formed, cast the energetic ritual circle by your methods of choice. A simplified way of doing this is by circling the space with smudge.

Next, begin the quarter calls:

East: *Spirits of the East! Element of Air, the air that was the breath of our ancestors, the air that is now our breath. Lend us your energy for intellect and for new beginnings. We ask that you join us for our Samhain ritual. Hail and welcome.*

South: *Spirits of the South! Element of Fire, the fires that fueled the love of our ancestors, the fires that now fuel our love for them, for each other, and for future generations. Lend us your energy for love, transformation, and action. We ask that you join us for our Samhain ritual. Hail and welcome.*

West: *Spirits of the West! Element of Water, the water that was fluidity of emotion and life for our ancestors, the water that is now our emotions and lends us life. Lend us your life-giving power and flow of emotion. We ask that you join us for our Samhain ritual. Hail and welcome.*

North: *Spirits of the North! Element of Earth, the very soil of the earth, the very soil our ancestors walked upon, the soil that we now walk upon, that future generations will walk upon. Lends us your stability and your growth. We ask that you join us for our Samhain ritual. Hail and welcome.*

Next, offer a heartfelt invocation inviting the ancestors such as the following:

Our Dear Ancestors! We ask you to join us if you will, as we honor you, honor ourselves, and set forth to be the best ancestors we can be for future generations! Hail and welcome.

Now, one by one, participants take a step forward into the circle, and share a bit about the part of themselves they wrote their obituary for and are banishing. They may share as much or as little as they'd like (not sharing at all is perfectly fine). After sharing, each participant steps forward and offers their obituary to the ritual fire (or lights it and drops it into the cauldron). As the obituary burns, banishes, and transforms that which doesn't serve its author any longer, everyone else in the circle responds, "So mote it be." This procedure continues around the circle until all in attendance have had their turn to share and burn their obituary.

When all obituaries have been ritually burned, cakes and ale can be blessed and sent around the circle. For this ritual, I recommend light fare such as water or sparkling juice and small wrapped choco-lates (who would argue against chocolate?!) because an after-feast often follows.

Dismiss the quarters by reversing the calls given above, ending each with "Hail and farewell!" Then similarly release the ancestors. At this time, you may declare that the circle is open—yet unbroken and recess from the ritual space counterclockwise. (If you have a bonfire, you will want to appoint a firekeeper responsible for con-tinuing to safely monitor the fire.)

After-feast

Holding an after-feast is optional, however, I strongly suggest it. A potluck has become a standard part of a great majority of pagan gatherings anyway and the after-feast helps all to further ground post-ritual. To honor those who came before us, all participants can contribute a potluck dish consisting of a favorite food of a departed loved one. Encourage them to also bring a photo of the departed loved one to place by the dish. During the feast, further stories and memories can be shared.

Samhain blessings to you and your loved ones, past, present, and future, on both sides of the veil!

Notes

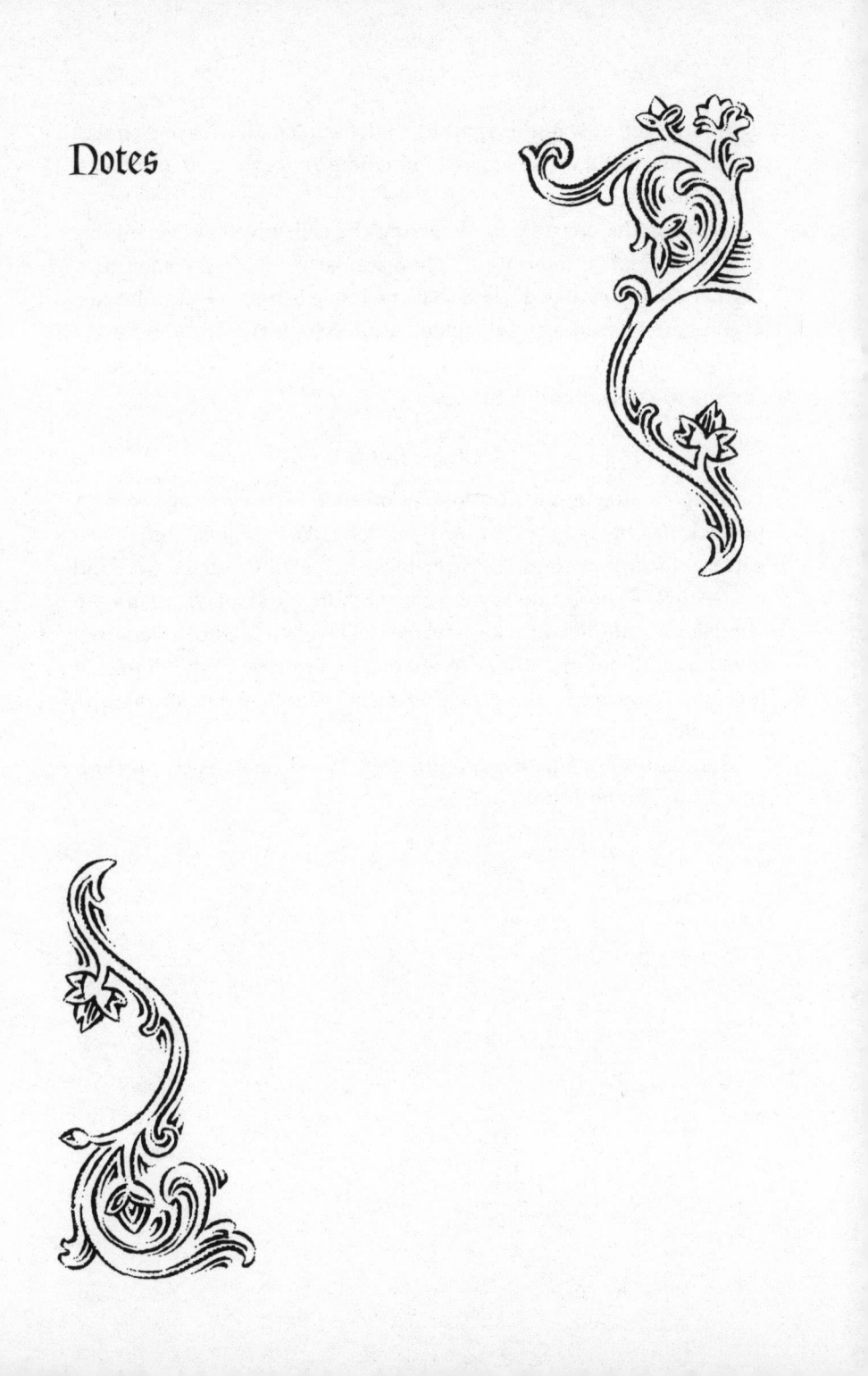

Yule

Winter Solstice: The Lights of Yule

Suzanne Ress

WHEN YULETIDE ROLLS AROUND I always think of my Welsh-American grandmother. I relished visiting her home during the month she had it decorated for Yule. She loved the season and would strew fresh greenery on her mantelpiece and at the center of her dining room table. A large assortment of unusual angel figurines she had collected from her travels was placed on side tables and bookshelves. Doorknobs and archways were decorated with antique bells. And there were candles everywhere: golden beeswax, red, green, silver, white, scented of clove, pine, and bayberry. The atmosphere was exciting.

On December 24, our extended family gathered at her and granddad's house for libations and the exchange of homemade gifts. She played carols on the piano, and we all sang along. Best of all, she lit all of the candles and turned off the electric house lights.

When she died a few days before Winter Solstice, none of us were surprised that she had prearranged her own funeral service in the church she had gone to most of her life, with loads of red candles, holly and fir boughs on the altar, and hauntingly beautiful Bach piano cantatas played a little more slowly than usual.

My widowed granddad soon moved to a retirement home, and, since my husband and I had recently purchased our first house and were expecting our first child, he offered us all of Grandmother's Yule decorations—the bells, the angel collection, and all the candles and their holders—which I happily accepted.

Through many moves, including across the Atlantic Ocean, we've hauled these decorations. By now all the candles are long burnt up, but I still have most of the holders, which I bring out, along with the angels and bells, on December 8, as Italian custom dictates.

The Roman Catholic Church chose this as the date the Virgin Mary was immaculately conceived, and it is a national holiday in Italy. It intrigues me that the Yule season is officially kicked off by celebrating the Virgin, then celebrates the Mother, via birth of the Son god, right after the Solstice, and officially ends with Epiphany, also called *La Befana*, "The Crone," on January 6. Not until January 7 do people take down their holiday decorations and go back to work or school.

Other special dates that fall within the Yuletide period are Saint Nicholas (patron saint of children) December 6, Saint Ambrose (patron saint of learning and of bees) December 7, Saint Lucia (mother of light) December 13, Winter Solstice December 21, Mordnact (mother's night) December 24, Christmas (birth of the Son, or, more anciently, the Sun) December 25, Saint Steven (patron saint of martyrs) or Boxing Day (or Servants' or Animals' Day) December 26, Hanukkah (Festival of Lights) eight days in December; Kwanzaa (Festival of the African People) December 26 to January 1, Saint Sylvester (patron saint of domestic animals) and Berchta (the White Lady) December 31, and Saint Mary (Mother of God) and the Feast of Frey (the horned god) January 1.

Clearly, December is a month for celebrating. I find it interesting that many of the holidays surrounding Winter Solstice, the darkest day of the year, have something to do with light.

Santa Lucia, mother of light and patron saint of eyesight, is celebrated in Denmark, Sweden, Norway, and Finland. On the morning of December 13, one of the girls in the family wears a crown of nine lighted white candles to represent the nine days from Santa Lucia to Yule, and serves breakfast to the other members of the household. Originally this was a Germanic Pagan holiday called Lussi Night. It was thought that the souls of the dead and evil spirits roamed in the darkness for the nine nights between Lussi Night and Yule.

Kwanzaa, celebrated since 1966, has its Kinara candelabra. There are seven candles: three green ones symbolizing the fertile earth of Africa, three red ones symbolizing the blood shed in the African peoples' ongoing struggle for freedom, and one black one in the center of the Kinar, for the skin color of the people. One candle is lit for each of the seven days of Kwanzaa.

One of the major symbols of Hannukah, the Festival of Lights, is a candleholder, the Menorah, with its nine candles, one for each day of the festival, and the central one, used to light the others.

Christians have the Advent wreath, with four red candles and one white candle, to mark each of the four Sundays before Christmas, and Christmas itself.

To me, the Winter Solstice time would simply not be Yule without candles.

Yule was originally a Pagan Germanic festival that lasted for three days—December 22 through December 25—to celebrate the return of the light. This was immediately after the shortest day of the year, when Odin, the god of war and poetry, led a pack of red-eyed hounds, representing the souls of the dead, across the dark night sky in the Wild Hunt. Celebrations included a lot of ale drinking, raucous partying, and animal slaughter. It is thought that the northern European tribes began celebrating Yule only after they had had contact with the ancient Romans and learned of agriculture and Saturnalia.

Saturn, after which Saturnalia was named, represented the harvest and was Lord of Death to the ancient Romans. He was the dark side of the summer sun. Saturn, the planet, is visible to the naked human eye, often especially bright around Winter Solstice. Although people had been watching Saturn since cave dwelling times, it was astrologers in Mesopotamia who called Saturn the black Sun or the Sun of Night. These ancient moon-watchers of the Fertile Crescent studied the movements of the moon in relation to the stars and planets for agricultural use as long as 5,000 years ago.

Daily sunlight is vital for agriculture and the growing season. When humans first began practicing systematic agriculture, the solstices and the equinoxes became very important turning points in the year.

It was believed that appeasing Saturn at the Winter Solstice would allow spring to return. Appeasing Saturn meant offering sacrifices, originally human beings, but later animals, especially pigs and goats. After the sacrificial offering to the god of death, the sun (or son)'s rebirth was celebrated.

Saturnalia was celebrated with animal sacrifice, feasting, banquets, role-reversal between masters and slaves, gambling, singing, drunkenness, and exchanging presents. Typical gifts were candles and figurines made of wax, which symbolized the light necessary for life. In the days after the solstice many candles were lit, representing knowledge and the returning power of sunlight.

The word candle comes from the Latin *candere*, "to shine."

Yule is the perfect time of year to look for the light that shines, not only on a candlewick, but in all living things. Without light there could not be life. Sunlight is, even now, the supreme power and energy that moves the Earth. Think about it—even if you can live inside a windowless apartment, you must eat. Food, in the form of plants (which meat-producing animals must also eat), cannot be produced without sunlight for photosynthesis. Metaphorically, but also literally, light is life.

Every living creature, human and other, has a light inside—her spirit. Light is also thought of as knowledge and creativity. Enlightenment is self-realization. Light dispels darkness, shining like a candle to illuminate the truth.

At Yule, when days are short and cold, I like to celebrate the light within myself—and the lights inside my friends, family, pets, and strangers.

Even casual meetings with strangers offer great opportunities to celebrate inner light and life. While out shopping, or walking crowded city streets, I try to be conscious about making eye contact with oncoming strangers. After all, a person's eyes are the windows of his soul. By holding neutrally friendly eye contact just a little longer than is customary and accompanying it with a heartfelt smile, one can usually elicit a glimmer, or sometimes a beam, of warm light from a stranger. Frequently, his whole face lights up.

In situations in which a few words are exchanged, with post office or store clerks, gas station or parking lot attendants, or someone out walking her dog in the park, a little more time can be spent. I like to visualize a person's inner light coming from his or her sternum, or heart chakra area, and radiating outward. By concentrating on this image, I find that most casually encountered strangers do begin to open up and shine within seconds and, hopefully, the light feeling stays with them for a little while afterward.

While talking with someone I may know, but not so very well, say a neighbor or casual acquaintance, I try to see him as a constantly evolving organism. I visualize him as he might have been ten years earlier, then as a teenager, a child, a newborn baby in his mother's arms. As we make small talk and exchange holiday greetings, I picture him as a decrepit old man, so old that perhaps he's lost his senses and returned to being as helpless as a newborn. What I actually see—the form of his physical body, transforms in my imagination, until eventually it ceases to exist. But what always remains the same, as long as he is alive, is his spirit—his light. I try to concentrate on this light—every one of us has it—and I try to draw it out. As his light brightens and becomes clearer, he begins to shine.

With close friends and family, I know so much more about them that I don't need to rely on visualization. Seeing their inner light is easy! Rather than worry or become bothered by minor problems (or as I like to think of them, "blips" in our relationship), I focus on the reasons that brought us together in the first place—all of the wonderful qualities I know she has and all of the positive feelings we have shared. In short, I focus on feeling the love that unites us.

One of my grandmother's most outstanding qualities was her optimism. She was a lighthearted person who saw the good side in all people and situations. Being light of heart means being able to love easily, laugh easily, forgive easily, accept whatever life offers us with ease and grace, and, probably most important of all, to have the capacity to lighten up the other people around you and accept what they have to offer.

During Yule time I often hear from distant friends or acquaintances who suddenly resurface to wish me peace and joy. Friends and neighbors open their hearths and homes to welcome me and my family in, or they present me with a homemade gift. Personally, I do not feel that this show of open heartedness is false, but that the spirit of the holiday season makes it easier for people to uncover the inner light that is always there.

Let's not forget about our pets and other domestic and wild animals, at Yule time. Every living creature has a light inside! Many people give presents or prepare special meals for their pets; others hang treats with seeds and dried berries for wild birds out doors on tree branches, surely appreciated at this meager season of the year. But make sure to take extra time to really be with the animals around you, to look into their eyes and see their light shining from within. Complement it with your own light; appreciate your cat, or your dog, or the timid fox, or the little black-eyed wild sparrows, or even the big spider in the bathroom, for the unique individuals that they are.

On the days leading up to the Winter Solstice where I live, the sun goes down as early as 4:00 p.m. I kindle a fire in the wood-burning stove and enjoy its warmth and dancing flames. Later, when family and friends gather to eat an evening meal together, I light all of the candles in my grandmother's holders in the dining area and turn off the electric lights to make a peaceful, warm, magical atmosphere where it's easy to let one's inner light shine.

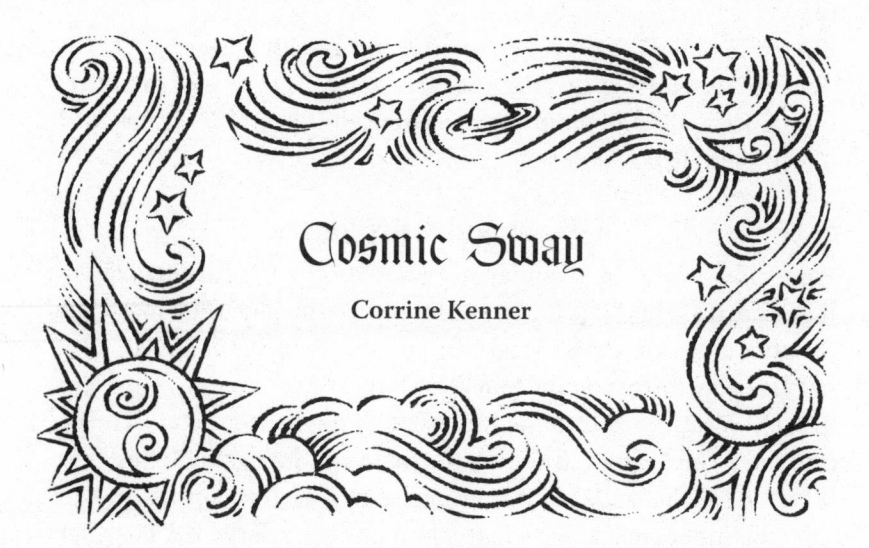

Cosmic Sway

Corrine Kenner

THE EIGHT SABBAT HOLIDAYS commemorate the Sun's rise and fall over the course of a year. On a symbolic level, the Sun's movement through the zodiac parallels the mysteries of existence, just like the Moon's cycle of waxing and waning reflects the cycle of life and death.

Yule is celebrated on the Winter Solstice, which also happens to fall on the longest night of the year. After a long season of darkness, it's time to celebrate the return of the light—the newborn Sun that promises to add light and heat to our days.

It's no coincidence that the Winter Solstice also occurs when the Sun moves into earthy Capricorn. In fact, the Winter Solstice occurs at the moment when the Sun reaches its southernmost position in the sky, directly over the Tropic of earthy Capricorn. This year, however, it's something of a coincidence that the Sun happens to be joining three other planets in the sign: Mercury, Pluto, and Venus.

Whenever there's a stellium—a gathering of three or more planets in the same sign or house—the energy of those planets is focused and intensified. They work in unison. They collaborate. They're part of a team.

In this case, the earthy Capricorn planets are celebrating the things we typically associate with the signs of worldly success:

59

financial riches, material prosperity, and earthly rewards. It's why we exchange gifts at this time of year—tangible tokens of our affection for friends and family, which come with heartfelt wishes for a healthy and happy new year.

Tarot and Astrology

You can picture the five planetary bodies passing through earthy Capricorn as their tarot card counterparts. Imagine the lunar High Priestess, the Mercurial Magician, and the Venusian Empress, all at a Yule party thrown in the Sun god's honor.

The Death card is there, too. While it might seem odd to imagine the Grim Reaper at such a festive event, he's actually the host of the party, because Pluto rules the sign of earthy Capricorn. He's there in his ancient rule as Pluto, lord of the Underworld, guardian of the riches and bounty of the earth beneath our feet.

If you'd like to visualize the cards as mythic gods and goddesses, picture the High Priestess as Diana, the goddess of the Moon, Mercury as Hermes, and Pluto as Hades.

Practical Astrology

This is traditionally a season of gifts—but the astrology of this holiday reinforces the importance of gift-giving, not only among close family and friends, but also in a wider circle. This year, give as many gifts as you can afford to everyone you value, from your mother to your mail carrier.

Planetary Positions

At Yule, the Sun is in earthy Capricorn, the sign of business, career, and social status. The Sun will move into Aquarius on January 20.

The Moon is in fiery Sagittarius, the sign of long-distance travel and philosophical exploration.

Mercury is in earthy Capricorn, which makes the messenger planet assume a practical, methodical approach to its work. Mercury will race into airy Aquarius, the sign of social groups and causes, on January 5.

Venus is also in earthy Capricorn. In this case, the goddess of love tends to value function just as much as form. She'll move into airy Aquarius on January 3, and watery Pisces on January 27.

Mars in airy Aquarius, where the god of war naturally focuses on long-term planning and battle strategy. Mars will move into watery Pisces on January 12.

Jupiter is retrograde in fiery Leo, a sign that prompts the Greater Benefic to become even more generous, compassionate, and optimistic.

Saturn is in watery Scorpio, which tends to make the ringed planet of boundaries and limitations even more reserved than usual. The placement suggests an atmosphere of mystery and secrets— at least until Saturn moves into fiery Sagittarius on December 24. While Saturn will slide back into watery Scorpio this summer, just for a few months, Saturn will eventually establish itself in the sign of the archer, and it will stay there until December 2017.

The generational outer planets remain in the same signs:

Uranus is in fiery Aries.

Neptune is in watery Pisces.

Pluto is in earthy Capricorn.

Planets in Aspect

The moment the Sun enters earthy Capricorn, Mercury and the Sun are in a wide conjunction; the messenger planet is just ten degrees away. That means Mercury is able and willing to relay messages without any hesitation, delay, or confusion.

Mars in airy Libra, however, is squaring off against the Sun, essentially working at cross-purposes by focusing on relationships instead of business.

Mars and Uranus, in Aries, are on opposite sides of the zodiac. Oppositions generally illustrate two sides of the same coin. In this case, Uranus is focused on independence, while Mars is concentrating on intimacy.

Jupiter, in Cancer, and Saturn, in Scorpio, are in a harmonious trine. Their sympathetic relationship suggests they agree on the give and take needed in matters of home and partnership.

Neptune, in Pisces, is in a harmonious sextile with the Sun in Capricorn, which offers clarity and structure to Neptune's intuitive vision of the world.

Phases of the Moon

It's interesting to note that the Moon is full in each sign once a year, six months from the time the Sun is in that sign. That's because the face of a Full Moon is illuminated by the Sun when it's 180 degrees across the zodiac wheel. On December 6, for example, a Full Moon in airy Gemini will be illuminated by the Sun in Sagittarius. The energy of a Gemini Moon makes small talk and conversation easier. There'll be no shortage of curious questions and witty repartee.

December 21: A New Moon in earthy Capricorn will align itself in a conjunction with the Sun, which is also in earthy Capricorn. A New Moon is a great time to start new projects. You can shepherd them toward completion as the Moon waxes toward Full, and tie up any loose ends as the Moon wanes.

January 5: A Full Moon in watery Cancer, across from the Sun in earthy Capricorn, stays focused on matters of hearth and home. Call your mother—or your children. Nurture your pets, plants, and any other people in your life who could use a little love.

January 20: A New Moon in airy Aquarius, where the Sun and Moon are conjunct, makes this a good time to get together with groups of like-minded friends and allies. Share your experiences and your ideas, and make plans for future work together. A New Moon is dark, but a day or two after its birth, you'll see a waxing crescent Moon in the sky. It's easy to determine whether a crescent Moon is waxing or waning. As the Moon waxes toward Full and then wanes, its curves will seem to spell the word "DOG."

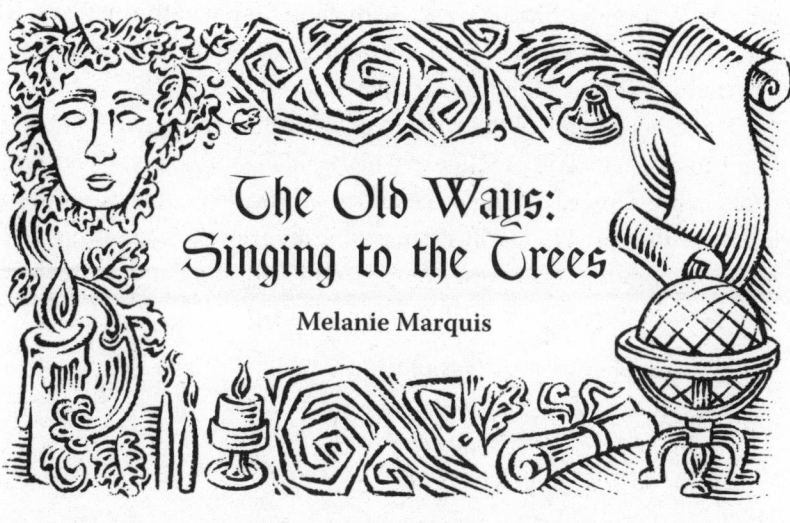

The Old Ways:
Singing to the Trees

Melanie Marquis

DESPITE THE COLD WEATHER, Midwinter is a time of music, merrymaking, and arboreal-centered revelry, when many modern Neopagans and Christians alike join their fellows for feasting, drinking, and singing songs around the holiday tree. These enduring and widespread modern traditions are reminiscent of the once wildly popular, centuries-old practice of wassailing, when residents in west England and other fruit-producing regions would travel from orchard to orchard, singing to the trees and beseeching them for a fine crop in the year to come. Wassails were held around the time following the winter solstice and the start of the new year, most commonly on December 24, January 5 or 6, and January 17, though the specific dates varied from place to place and time to time.

Derived from the old Anglo-Saxon term *wes hal*, meaning "to be whole" or "to be in good health," the wassail's main function was to improve and promote the strength and well-being of the fruit trees, an important source of food, drink, and income. Wassailing ceremonies generally included songs and chants, helped along by lots of cacophonous noise, lots of feasting, and lots of cider-drinking. Raising a ruckus in the orchard served a dual purpose—to awaken the slumbering trees and also to chase off any evil spirits that might otherwise threaten the harvest. By making merry with the trees, it was believed that the health of the orchard could be improved, and a better crop in the coming year thus ensured.

The exact origins of the custom of wassailing the orchards is difficult to discern. The practice is widely believed to have its earliest roots in pre-Christian Anglo-Saxon ritual. However, this is not fact, but speculation. The earliest surviving mention of wassailing the orchards comes from a verse composed in Kent, England, in the late sixteenth century:

Wassail the trees that they may bear
You many a plum and many a pear:
For more or less fruits they will bring,
as you do give them wassailing.

Orchard wassails appear frequently in English literature from 1670 onward, dating the practice to at least as far back as the early Tudor or Medieval period.

However, the essential idea at the heart of the wassail—the belief in the sacredness of trees and the idea of paying tribute to them—is evidenced in England from a much earlier date. We know that the Britons, an early Celtic people who occupied the area prior to the Roman invasion, practiced tree worship. So too did the conquering Romans, who destroyed many of the sacred trees of the Britons, yet nonetheless believed in the divine power of trees and in the efficacy of agricultural-themed rituals. So too did the pre-Christian Anglo-Saxons, Germanic tribes who migrated from the western coast of Europe and occupied the land beginning in the early fifth century. The Scandinavian Norse who entered northern Britain beginning in the late eighth century also believed in the sacredness of trees and paid special tribute to them at Midwinter.

Whatever ancient origins remain reflected in its inner symbolism, the outward form of the wassailing custom as we know it today likely rose in popularity with the spread of apple orchards throughout England. Though apple cultivation began in Britain at the time of the Roman invasion, it declined over time due to various sociopolitical factors. Apple growing experienced its greatest boon in England beginning in 1533, when King Henry VIII authorized a large-scale campaign of apple production throughout the countryside. Apple cultivation expanded widely and quickly gained prominence, especially in Kent and other regions where wassailing traditions soon came to enjoy great popularity. The earliest orchard wassail was 1585 in Kent, fifty years from the start of the king's apple growing program. It seems likely that the tradition as we know it hails from around this same time period, reflecting older traditions, certainly, but taken up in practice in a new form as the need and interest arose. The population of England at that time was largely Christianized, but had still perhaps retained the cultural memories of more ancient pagan ways.

The wassail has all the makings of a pagan agricultural rite, using magickal actions to give nature a mighty boost. As the wassail merrymakers made their way through the orchards, they would often raise their glasses and sing songs to the trees, beseeching the weaker trees to become strong and celebrating the greatness of the biggest, most fruitful trees in the orchard. In many places, the wassailing party not only sings, but also makes a terrible commotion by banging together pots and pans, believing the unpleasant noise will frighten away any malevolent forces. The singing and the noise is used to both banish the bad and welcome the good, an ancient magickal concept we find in many agricultural rituals around the world.

In Devonshire, the wassailing ceremony included song and also gunfire. Accompanied by a large jug of cider, the men would report to the apple orchard, locate the finest tree, and make a singing toast to it, imploring the tree for a fine harvest. One such toasting song ran thus:

> *Here's to thee, old apple-tree,*
> *Whence thou may'st bud, and whence thou may'st blow!*
> *And whence thou may'st bear apples enow!*
> *Hats full! caps full!*
> *Bushel!—bushel-sacks full,*
> *And my pockets full too! Huzza!*

The toast was concluded by firing guns into the upper branches of the tree in order to frighten off any evil influences that might otherwise inhibit the tree's growth, just as pots and pans might be banged together at wassailing ceremonies in other regions.

In Sussex, young boys would go to the orchards singing loudly and blowing a tune on an instrument fashioned from a cow's horn. Beating the poorer trees with sticks and demanding a good harvest as they raised their voices in chorus, the boys shouted their songs and chants so forcefully that the custom became known as apple-howling.

🌿

Traditional wassails are still held annually in many parts of England, and many modern Pagans around the world have incorporated wassailing customs into their midwinter rites, gathering around the trees for singing, drinking, and merrymaking. This season, why not whip up a batch of spiced cider, grab a few friends, head outside, and make some music with the trees old-fashioned style? It's a great way to celebrate and connect with nature while carrying on a time-honored tradition!

References:

Hooke, Della. *Trees in Anglo-Saxon England: Literature, Lore, and Landscape.* Woodbridge: The Boydell Press, 2010.

Hutton, Ronald. *The Rise and Fall of Merry England: The Ritual Year, 1400-1700.* 1994 Reprint. New York: Oxford University Press, 2001.

Miles, Clement A. *Christmas in Ritual and Tradition, Christian and Pagan.* London: T. Fisher Unwin, 1912. Accessed August 25, 2013, http://www.sacred-texts.com/time/crt/index.htm.

Skanland.com. "How we Inherited Christmas from the Viking Yule." Accessed August 25, 2013. http://skandland.com/vikxmas.htm.

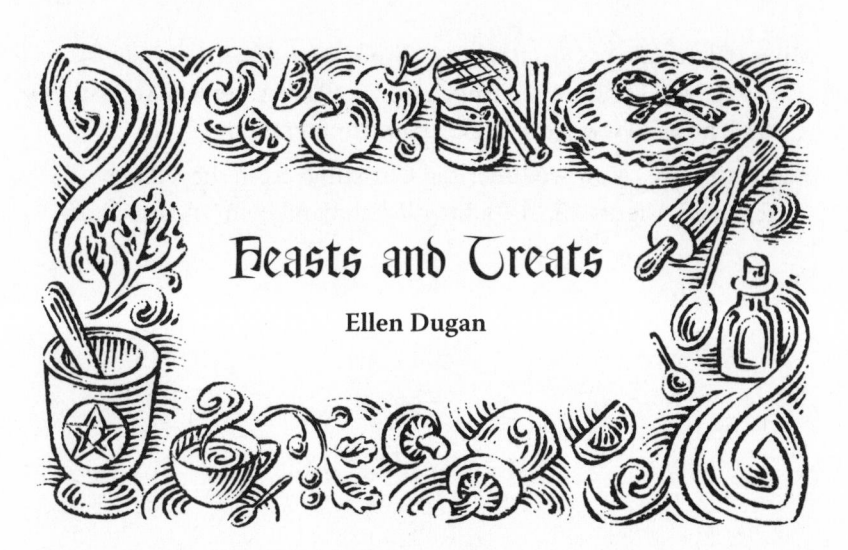

Feasts and Treats

Ellen Dugan

THE WINTER SOLSTICE IS here! In between decorating the home with boughs of holly and trimming the Yule tree, try these savory and hearty dishes. Remember to take a few moments just to savor the magick and joy of the season. Go put a pot of winter stew on, bake some gingerbread, listen to some holiday music, sip some guilt-free hot chocolate, and unwind for a little while! Happy holidays!

Winter Stew

There is something magical about a big pot of stew simmering away on the kitchen stove in the winter. Give this recipe a try.

Prep time: 30 minutes
Cook time: 60 minutes
Serves: 4–6

2 tablespoons olive oil
4 medium stalks of celery, chopped
4 medium parsnips, peeled and chopped
1 medium onion, chopped fine

2 medium red potatoes cut into half-inch pieces (Leave skins on potatoes—just scrub them well.)

2 pounds butternut squash, peeled, seeded, and cut into half-inch pieces

32 ounces (1 package) of ready-to-pour chicken stock or vegetable stock

4 cups of water

½ teaspoon fresh thyme, chopped

1 teaspoon salt

¾ teaspoon black pepper

1 cup light cream

In a large saucepan or Dutch oven, heat oil over medium-high heat until hot. Add chopped celery, parsnips, and onions. Cook until tender—about 10 to 12 minutes—stirring often.

Next, add potatoes, squash, broth, water, and seasonings. Using medium-high heat, heat until boiling, and then reduce the heat to medium-low, simmering an additional 10 to 12 minutes until potatoes and squash are tender.

Finally, stir in the light cream, and heat through for approximately 12 minutes. The stew is now ready to serve. Add sprigs of fresh thyme for garnish. (Note: this stew does freeze well.)

Jennifer M's Stuffed Witchy Mushrooms

This recipe is from my friend Jennifer M. This Italian Witch knows her food! This is an easy recipe! Enjoy!

Prep time: 30 minutes

Cook time: 15 minutes

Serves: 12

¾ pound mild Italian sausage

24 medium- to large-size mushrooms (stuffing mushrooms)

1 pound frozen spinach (thawed and well drained, be sure to squeeze out all of its liquid)

1 tablespoon fresh parsley, chopped

1½ cups of shredded Monterey jack cheese
½ cup of ricotta cheese
¼ cup melted butter or olive oil

Crumble and brown the Italian sausage in a skillet over medium-high heat. This will take approximately 7 minutes. Drain the grease and place cooked sausage in a mixing bowl. Allow the sausage to cool thoroughly.

To prep the mushrooms, twist off the mushroom stems. Jennifer also suggests using a melon baller to scoop out the stem area, which creates more space for the stuffing mixture. Place the prepped mushrooms top-side down and open-side up in a 13 × 9-inch casserole dish.

In a separate bowl, mix the spinach (be sure to take a moment to fluff up the drained spinach for easier mixing), the fresh parsley, and the two cheeses. Stir together well.

Add this mixture to the now-cool cooked sausage and stir well again. Jennifer says it works best to mix this with your (clean) hands.

Stuff the mushrooms with a teaspoon of the stuffing mixture. Make sure the mushrooms are nice and full. After the mushrooms are stuffed, drizzle a bit of the melted butter or olive oil on the tops of the mushrooms.

Bake for 15 minutes in a 375 degree F oven. Serve hot or at room temperature. Refrigerate any leftovers.

Gingerbread

More than any other scent, I associate gingerbread with Yule. Serve this classic gingerbread with a garnish of whipped topping and a dusting of cinnamon.

Prep time: 20 minutes
Cook time: 50 minutes
Serves: 6–8

2⅓ cups all-purpose flour
⅓ cup sugar

1 cup molasses
¾ cup hot water
½ cup vegetable shortening
1 egg
1 teaspoon baking soda
1 teaspoon ground ginger
1 teaspoon ground cinnamon
¾ teaspoon salt

Heat oven to 325 degrees F. Grease and flour a 2-inch deep 9 ×9-inch pan. Beat all ingredients in a large mixer bowl on low speed, scraping the bowl constantly, for 30 seconds. Beat on medium speed for 3 minutes, scraping the bowl occasionally. Pour batter into pan.

Bake until a wooden pick inserted in the center comes out clean. About 50 minutes. Serve warm with whipped cream.

Magickal (No Guilt) Hot Chocolate

I love hot chocolate, but it took me a while to figure out how to enjoy it and not feel guilty afterwards. This is fabulous and tastes wonderful.

Prep time: 5 minutes
Serves: 8–10

1 tablespoon baking cocoa
3 packets of Splenda
1½ cups low-fat milk

Heat milk in microwaveable bowl or large glass liquid measuring cup for 2½ minutes. Remove bowl and whisk in the cocoa and Splenda with a wire whisk until frothy.

Pour into a mug and serve immediately. Garnish with nondairy, fat-free whipped topping or add a peppermint stick for some Yuletide fun.

Crafty Crafts

Lexa Olick

A SNOWY LANDSCAPE IS made up of delicate, one-of-a-kind snowflakes. They are so small, yet they can cover so much. Even people who live in warmer climates recognize snowflakes as a symbol of Yule. They are a model of elegance and are the perfect accent for the winter holidays!

Snowflake Prosperity Pendant

This pendant is formed with lace so it looks like a very dainty snowflake. The tiny snowflake is curled up into a ball so it can cradle the items trapped inside. You wear it around your neck to promote prosperity, but you can also display it in your home. It hangs on a tree and looks just as festive as all the other ornaments. A longer chain is needed for a necklace, but a smaller chain or cord can be used to create an ornament that hangs anywhere. It looks like a snowflake, but it's fragrant with all the aromas of Yule. It's like a tiny diffuser you can take with you wherever you go!

Supplies
3-inch circle of white fabric lace
Craft glue

E6000 adhesive
Water
1 acorn
Sewing needle
White thread
Wire cutters
Chain or cord
Small bowl
30-millimeter Christmas ball ornament (the traditional ones with a
    metal cap around the hook)
Broken cinnamon sticks, broken nutmeg, and whole cloves

Instructions: Choose lace with an intricate design and small holes. It acts as a cage to hold your ingredients inside, so the holes should not be big enough that the items fall through. With smaller holes, you ensure that the items stay inside. If for whatever reason you can only find lace with larger holes, then keep that in mind when you collect your cinnamon, nutmeg, and cloves. The cinnamon sticks and nutmeg are broken into pieces, so make sure to pick the larger pieces to fill your pendant.

Water down some craft glue in a small bowl. Start with 1 part water and 2 parts glue. Add more water if necessary. Soak a piece of fabric lace in the thinned glue. Make sure the material is fully saturated. After a couple of minutes, squeeze out the excess glue. Drape the lace around the underside of an acorn. Smooth it down as much as you can. If necessary, use a rubber band to gather the excess lace at the top of the acorn to help keep it in place. Let the lace sit overnight to dry.

An acorn is a symbol of abundance and security. The lace takes its shape and absorbs some of its properties. When someone carries around an acorn, it wards off loneliness and pain and brings about longevity and luck.

When the lace fully hardens, remove it from the acorn. The acorn has played its role for today, so you can use it as part of

another Yuletide display. For example, acorns look nice gathered together in glass dishes or small baskets.

Now that the lace has formed a small bowl, we can fill it with cinnamon, nutmeg, and cloves. These are all spices associated with Yule and their aroma is stronger when they are broken. Cinnamon is generally used for protection and abundance. Nutmeg is associated with luck and healing. Cloves promote protection and love. These warm spices combine to create a talisman of prosperity and fortune.

When your pendant is full, thread a needle with white string. Gather the opening of the pendant with the needle and stitch it together. Remove the metal cap from the Christmas ornament. Trim the bottom wires of the hook with wire cutters if necessary. Fit the excess lace inside the cap. Trim the lace until it fits snugly inside then apply E6000 adhesive on the lace and hold it inside the metal cap for 1 minute. Set it aside to fully dry for 24 hours.

Slip your chain or cord through the loop on the metal cap. You can now wear your pendant around your neck or display on a tree in your home.

Time to Complete: Construction is completed within 20 minutes, but the lace and glue will take at least 8 hours to fully dry (though 24 hours of drying time is recommended).

Cost: About $20.00

Yuletide Ornaments

The Yule ornaments below are generally hung for display, but as long as you don't string them with ribbon, they can also be used as coasters. Pinecones are stiff and prickly, but they leave a beautiful, natural-looking pattern when pressed into dough. Plus, it's always a good idea to keep a couple of pinecones around the home for protection against evil spirits.

Supplies
½ cup cornstarch
1 cup baking soda
½ cup and 2 tablespoons of water
2 teaspoon salt
Pinecone
Drinking straw
Rolling pin
⅛-inch satin ribbon
Scissors
Large bowl
Cinnamon or glitter
Clear acrylic spray

Instructions: Combine cornstarch, baking soda, water, and salt in a large bowl. Make sure all the ingredients are fully mixed together.

Microwave the bowl on high for 6 minutes so the mixture can thicken. Remove the bowl from the microwave and set it aside to cool. It will thicken again during that time.

When the dough is cool enough to touch, knead the dough gently with your hands until it becomes smooth and malleable. You can powder your hands with flour if the mixture is too sticky. Flatten the dough with either a rolling pin or your hands on a flat, hard surface.

Press the pinecone into the dough and gently lift it away. Repeat until the entire surface has been decorated. Lightly sprinkle the top with cinnamon for a natural-looking ornament and a spicy scent. The aroma of cinnamon warms your home during this cold winter month. For a sparkly, more glamorous ornament, sprinkle with glitter. It will shimmer just like newly fallen snow. Carefully blow off any excess. Now, cut the dough into a 3-inch circle. Press the tip of a drinking straw into the top of the ornament to cut out a small hole. Repeat until all the dough is used up. Set the ornaments aside to dry undisturbed overnight. If the ornaments are still damp in the morning, leave them to dry another day.

When the ornaments harden completely, it is then time to properly seal them. Lay newspaper down in a well-ventilated area and apply a coat of clear acrylic spray to the ornaments. Set the ornaments aside to dry for an hour. Lace an 8-inch ribbon through each hole and tie the top into a knot. The ornaments are now ready to hang!

Makes about 8 ornaments.

Time to Complete: About 30 minutes to create, but it can take up to 72 hours to completely dry.

Cost: Approximately $15.00

Note: When you are making these ornaments, the dough may bake onto your bowl. It may feel hard and stuck for good, but remember that it's just cornstarch and baking soda. It will easily dissolve with warm water. Just leave the bowl to soak overnight.

Sustainable Solstice: Get Cracking

Natalie Zaman

IT'S DECEMBER, AND WE are fast approaching the Winter Solstice, the longest night of the year. Less daylight and more darkness is perfect for hibernation and contemplation, but first comes celebration—of the return of the sun, whose power will continue to grow in the coming days. Yule festivities are welcome revels, for even though the light continues to grow in the months that follow, this time seems to be the darkest and coldest; spring, summer, light and warmth feeling impossibly far away.

Although the Winter Solstice occurs at the latter end of December, the reminder that it's on its way starts about three months earlier when piles of catalogs begin to arrive in the mail. One year when the glut seemed excessively large, I decided to conduct an experiment and saved every booklet I received from one company between October and January (can't forget the post holiday sales!). A new catalog was sent to me about once every two weeks. Each had a different cover, but with few exceptions, many of the items inside were the same, their order of appearance rearranged. Eventually, they all ended up in the recycling bin.

At first glance, recycling seems environmentally responsible—until the resources expended to recycle are considered. There are studies that suggest that more fuel is burned and solid waste created in transporting and recycling printed matter to make paper than using the "virgin process"—pulping paper directly from trees. I've since concluded that the best thing I can do is minimize my catalog and print magazine consumption as much as possible, and reuse what I already have as much as I can before sending it into the recycling cycle.

And so, another challenge presented itself: Upcycle the excess—and considering the time of year—into a Yulish activity, something in the spirit of the season. My family's Winter Solstice celebrations encompass the entire month of December: Cakes and hot cider, the roaring Yule log, feasting and revelry, midnight tarot readings, ghost stories, and Charles Dickens... Great George's Ghost! I could give my unwanted catalogs a new life (like the sun!) with a little nineteenth-century sensibility—as Yuletide crackers.

The cracker is a Victorian invention that started out as a piece of candy wrapped in a twist of paper that was lined with a poem. The evolved novelty we know today is far more complex and meaningful.

Have you ever pulled a wishbone? After a feast of fowl, two lucky folks (wishbones are luck charms) take hold of each end of the bird's center breastbone, pull, and... CRACK! The person holding the larger end gets his wish. (And here also is the origin of an unlucky person getting the "short end of the stick.")

A cracker works much the same way; two people take hold of each end of the string that holds the cracker together. They pull—CRACK!—and the person holding the larger end wins the prizes inside: a paper crown, a toy, and a piece of paper with a joke or motto on it. Three gifts, a magical number. Yes, there are Christian connotations, but a close examination of the crackers' contents show that the history behind them is far older.

The image of the crown can easily be seen as a nod to the tale of the Oak King and the Holly King. Each battling the other for power over the course of the year, the Holly King has the greatest strength now, at Midwinter, and so wins the "crown" (until the spring thaw, at least!). More simply, and no less fittingly, a crown can symbolize the god whose season we are in now.

Poem, joke, or motto—all are words. Through words, truces are forged, oaths sworn, stories told, and histories preserved. Written, spoken, or thought, words are the voice of our intentions, magic's most powerful force. An affirmation, spell, or wish for good fortune will keep the "Craft" in a Yule cracker.

And the toy? The traditional Christian story of the Magi is about three wise men (or more succinctly, magicians) who, according to their reading of the stars, sought a king to give him gifts. Even though the Winter Solstice is not an occasion for gift giving, sharing a token of goodwill in the spirit of friendship—a cone of incense, or a crystal or handmade bundle of herbs for self-improvement, joy, or love—is always positive.

Make It Your Own!

You will need:

Glue and scissors

Ribbon and string (or cracker snaps, which can be found at craft shops)

Cardboard tubes (recycled paper towels, toilet paper, etc.)

Catalogs and/or magazines

Cracker contents:

Crowns: Make these from catalog pages advertising seasonal decorations in gold and silver.

Spells, affirmations, and/or blessings: Write these on blank slips of paper or get creative and cut words and letters out to cobble your positive sentiment in the style of a ransom note.

Small gifts: Use incense cones, crystals, tiny bags of herbs and seeds, or appropriately sized objects of significance like keys or coins in place of the "toy."

Make the body of the cracker from the recycled cardboard tubes. The midsection that holds the prizes should be about 4 to 6 inches long. The two end pieces should be equal in size, and smaller, about

2 to 3 inches each. Using two toilet paper rolls: Keep one intact for the midsection and cut the other in half for the ends. For a paper towel roll: Cut the tube in half, set one half aside, then cut the remaining half in half again to make the ends. Line the sections up with the bigger piece in the middle and pass the string or cracker snap through each one.

Carefully wrap the sections in a catalog or magazine page and use some glue to secure the paper to the tube. When the glue is dry, crimp (bunch carefully) the portions between the tube sections and tie them loosely with ribbon. Before you close the cracker, say a blessing over the prizes:

A crown for wealth,
A wish for health.
A gift for giving,
A game for sharing.
For all who play
Bless every day
Of the coming year
With love and good cheer!

Put the prizes in the cracker and tie off the open end.

When you are ready to break the crackers, have each player take hold of an end, and say or sing:

Glad tidings!
Bright blessings!
Good Yule!
Blessed be!

Pull the cracker and share the prizes. The affirmations and spells can be burned with the Yule log to send them as a message or request to the Universe. And for next year, use one of the many available online services to help cut down on the number of catalogs you receive. Less consumption means less energy wasted and a cleaner world.

Bright blessings for a magical Solstice!

Yule Ritual: The Coming of the Light

Suzanne Ress

THE PURPOSE OF THIS ritual is to celebrate the life-giving light that unites us all. It is to be a joyous celebration of togetherness performed on the evening at Winter Solstice. This rather elaborate ritual requires planning and making preparations ahead of time. If desired, invitations may be issued to welcome sympathetic non-Wiccans into your regular circle.

If you live in a place with a very mild winter climate, the ritual and ensuing celebration may be held outdoors. However, keeping in mind that the bodily comfort and warmth of participants is important, in most Northern Hemisphere climes an indoor location is more appropriate. If possible select a large space with many windows and/or skylights.

Items Needed
Five altars (these can be small tables of any sturdy makeshift kind)
Five altar cloths: a yellow, a green, a red, a blue, and a white
Candles: a red one, a green one, a blue one, a yellow one, five white ones, and appropriate safe candleholders
An athame
A pentacle

A chalice

Incense of clove, bay, or pine, in an incense holder

A horned helmet (instructions for making one follow)

Refreshments (suggestions follow)

Many participants, but at least six

All of the altars should be set up ahead of time. One altar shall be placed in the east, one in the west, one in the north, and one in the south side of your selected space. On the eastern altar place the yellow cloth, the yellow candle in its holder, a lighter, and the cured and fermented air element refreshments.

On the southern altar place the red cloth, red candle, a lighter, and the spicy fire element refreshments.

On the western altar goes the blue cloth and candle, a lighter, and the wassail or punch bowl and ale, for the water element.

On the northern altar, which represents the earth element, place the green cloth, the green candle, a lighter, and fruit and nut-based refreshments.

In the center of the room, set up the fifth altar, which will represent the Spirit. It shall be covered with a white cloth and have five white candles placed in its center. On the east side of this altar, place the incense in its holder along with a lighter. On the altar's south side lay down the athame. The chalice shall be placed on the altar's west side. On the northern side, the pentacle and any other objects to be blessed or charged will be laid down.

Once all of the celebrants have assembled, the electric lighting should be dimmed, and people should be instructed to gather in a circle around the central altar, making sure to leave a space of about an arm's length between the altar and themselves. The male person selected to play the part of Odin shall remain out of the circle and out of view. The four persons selected to represent the four elements shall each remain standing near their corresponding altars. The leader shall take her place next to the altar in the center of the circle, specifically on the east side (near the incense).

The **leader** shall call for silence, and begin by lighting each of the five white candles. After a short pause, she shall light the incense, and, looking toward the east, call out:

Element of the East, where are you?

The **person** responsible for the **eastern** Air element altar shall light the yellow candle, and answer:

I am here!

The **leader** says:

Bring us the spirit of Air, without which we perish!

The crowd parts as the Air element candle is carried carefully to the central altar and placed not too close to the edge, near the incense. The air element person now stands with the crowd, which may close the gap.

The **leader** moves deosil around the altar and stops at the southern side. She shall lift the athame with her left hand, indicating the south and call out:

Element of the south, where are you?

The **person** standing at the **southern altar** lights the red candle and responds:

I am here, my lady (or lord)!

The **leader** then says:

Bring us fire, for we need it to survive!

The crowd shall part to allow the fire element to enter, carrying his candle to the central altar and placing it on its south side.

The **leader** lays down the athame, and moves to the western side of the table. She lifts the empty chalice, and cries out:

Element of the west, are you with us?

The **western person** lights the blue candle, and answers:

I am here!

She then carefully carries the candle in one hand and an open bottle of ale in the other, and moves through the parted crowd to the central altar. After placing the candle on the western side of the altar, she pours a small amount of ale into the chalice before retreating into the crowd. The leader shall lift the chalice high and make a blessing of her choice, before taking of a sip of ale. She shall set down the chalice and move to the northern side of the altar.

The **leader** now holds up the pentacle before the crowd, and bids the northern representative:

Oh, element of the north, where are you?

The **final altar person**, who has been left standing in shadowy darkness, lights his green candle and cries in response,

I am here!

The **leader** then says:

Carry to us the earth of which our bodies are made!

The green candle is brought and placed upon the white altar.
Now the central altar is lit up, shining bright with nine candles.
The **leader** shall instruct all of the participants to repeat together nine times over,

We welcome the dark sun!

At this cue, the **male person playing Odin** shall enter the place wearing his horned helmet. In the circular aisle space between the altar and the crowd, Odin can walk fast, dance, or mimic riding a wild horse across the sky, moving around the altar deosil as many times as he sees fit. When he comes to a stop, he shall remove his horns, and, falling to his knees call out:

Welcome the return of the light!

At his words, the electric lighting shall be turned back on. (Disregard this, obviously, if you perform the ritual outdoors.)

The **leader** says:

The light of all life is within us! Let us revel in our joy at the light's return!

All of the celebrants join in, repeating the leader's words:

The light of all life is within us! Let us revel in our joy at the light's return!

The **leader** now proclaims:

Let us celebrate with cakes and ale!

People may now circulate freely from altar to altar, eating and drinking and conversing to their satisfaction.

The revelry may go on for quite a long time, especially if you have invited a large number of celebrants. It is suggested, therefore, that, after the passage of about half an hour, the leader of the group and the four persons representing the four elements should unobtrusively reopen the circle by dismissing each quarter in reverse order they were invoked, letting each element person snuff out his corresponding candle and carry it back to its altar. The four ritual tools shall be put away in their place, and any items that were blessed or empowered on the central altar shall be quietly returned to their owners.

After reopening the circle the party may continue for as long as desired, but please remember never to leave lit candles unwatched!

Suggested Refreshments for Element Altars

Water/blue/west: a bowl of wassail or punch, and ale

Air/yellow/east: cured and fermented foods such as freshly baked bread, cheeses, salami, Virginia ham, prosciutto, spiced beef

Earth/green/north: Fruits and nuts, date bars, fruitcake, oatmeal raisin cookies

Fire/red/south: spicy salsa dip, spicy cheese log, hot pepper chutney

How to Make a Horned Helmet

Cut a cheap plastic head-sized ball in half with scissors. Make two holes where the horns are to be placed. Using epoxy glue and plenty of duct tape, attach two hornlike tree branches (not too heavy!) securely into the holes. Cover the outside of the helmet with several layers of papier maché, further securing the horns to the helmet. When the papier maché is thoroughly dry, paint the helmet red, black, or gold. The horns can be left natural, shellacked, or painted gold or black.

Notes

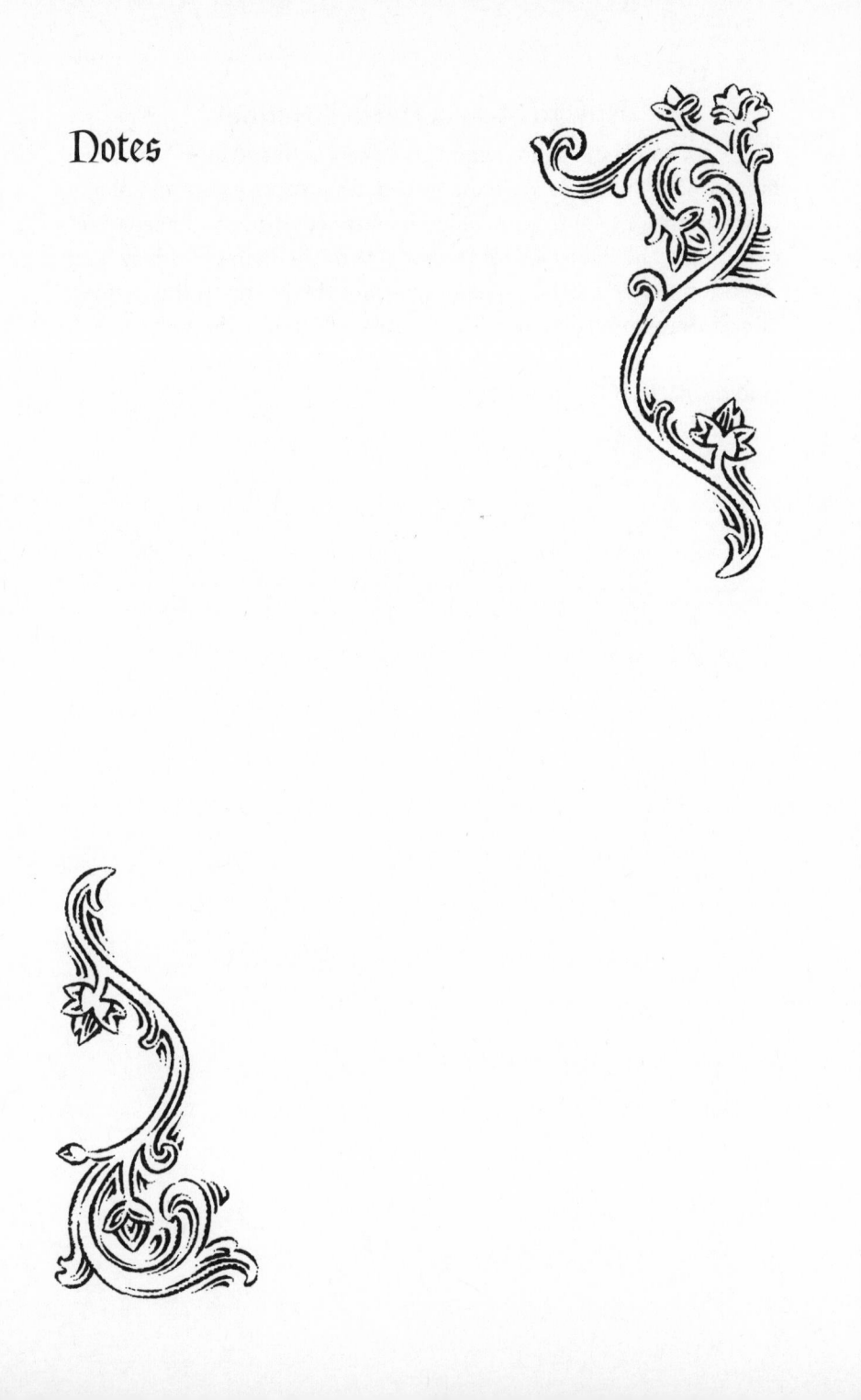

Imbolc

Imbolc: Tending Your Flame

Sybil Fogg

WHEN WINTER FIRST ARRIVES in Maine, it is met with excitement and joy. My children relish the first snow, especially if it grants a day off of school. This snow is formed into snowballs, forts, and snowmen. Snowshoe tracks sprinkle the yard and neighborhood, and snow fairies can be found carved into the powdery white surrounding our home. Alas, after a few weeks, winter becomes rough. The winds whip through with a vengeance. The nights are long; the days are frigid. Eventually we begin to move inside the house, cuddled under blankets, sipping hot cocoa, watching movies, and playing board games. At first we revel in our companionship and learn more about each other. But then we begin to turn inward and study ourselves. We seek to fan a small fire that resides within us. We find a spark that represents Brigid's flame or the fire of Imbolc.

A few years ago, I was talking to my sister about a project I was working on. I'm a writer and dancer and teach both. I often end up juggling freelance articles with looming due dates, creative pieces, and new choreography for upcoming shows. Needless to say, I keep very busy, especially from Valentine's Day through the winter holidays, quieting down for a much-needed rest between Yule and Imbolc.

My sister is a visual artist. In the past, she has worked in many different mediums from paint to wood burning. But she had not been creating in a long while. I asked her about this after realizing I was speaking far too long about my own artistic endeavors. Her reply shocked me. She said she had lost her passion for art. I couldn't imagine losing the desire to create, but she insisted not only was it possible, it had happened to her. I shuddered and gave her a hug, and then went home to my family that day.

I didn't think much about her words right away, but they would creep through my mind at unexpected times. I would be washing dishes or folding laundry, and I would imagine my sister doing these same tasks without wishing that she would be done so that she could get to the computer or dance studio. I would pause mid-fold and stare out the window. Or my feet might tap against a pair of zills or a box of coined hip scarves and the jingle would trigger a reverie of dance and color. Was my sister missing out on something?

Other times, when I was sitting in front of the computer struggling to get something written and the words were refusing to flow, I would wonder if perhaps only having to focus on keeping my home clean, baking cookies for the kids, and working on lesson plans at night would result in a happier me. Maybe she was lucky to have lost her passion. Now she could simply live.

About a year after talking to my sister, I was having dinner out with my husband. We were having a very lively conversation about the different things I was working on and I was trying to persuade him to create a prop for an upcoming performance. This was something he normally did for me as he is a visual artist with a degree in sculpture. I had been working on a specific dance character for a couple of years, the Steampowered Belly Dancer. She required a variety of props to simulate reanimated flesh in an alternate universe where most things were mechanized by steam. My husband had already built her a battery pack full of gears and lights that threaded out and through a corset to hint at the idea that the lights were generating her movements. I wanted to lose the battery pack because it was bulky and wanted lights that wove in and out of my character's flesh and had been talking animatedly about the different ways in which this could be achieved, when he put his hand over mine. My voice trailed off when I looked up at him because I could tell immediately that he had no interest in working on this act anymore. He explained that he had lost his passion for it.

And there was that word again. What was it that caused people, especially those around me, to lose their passion for creating?

As I took stock of our life, I realized that my husband had not created anything of his own in quite a while. We had been busy. He had recently opened a frame shop/gallery, we were looking into buying a house, and our six children were in varying degrees of growing. With so much going on, I had figured he was simply too busy to create any original art. The more I thought about it, though, I realized I was still creating, writing, and dancing. I had worked the entire family into my act without ever thinking about what they wanted to do and wondered if I was draining him.

I thought I would take a step back and not push him to create for me. It seemed if he had space, he would become fascinated with his own work and begin on it again. I decided to use my normal winter break to not ask for anything. It was easy enough to do so. In the 2012–2013 Yule to Imbolc gap, we did not attend one convention. I did not ask him to build any props for any performances, and I took a break from my writing.

The holiday break that year was truly magical. We closed the frame shop for a full week, and I did not do any preparations for my spring semester while the kids were on break. We feasted, we crafted, we played in the snow. The focus was so wonderfully on just the family that when everyone went back to work and school, we all fell into a funk together.

Going back to work was difficult that year. As the days dragged by through January, I felt as though a giant weight was bearing down on me. It was colder than it had been in years, and the snow kept falling. Our daily routines were reestablished. But with the addition of shoveling, driving, and trying to make it around to all of our scheduled activities, I wasn't dancing. It felt too cold to make much of an effort. I wasn't writing because I didn't have any articles due and couldn't seem to bring myself to work on my fiction. Most importantly, I noticed that my husband was not creating.

One day during that dark winter I was sitting in front of the computer just surfing and chastising myself for not writing. My fingers moved over the keyboard they way they did when my thoughts were on fire, but I wasn't thinking. I was reading Facebook updates, looking at Etsy shops, and grumbling to myself about how lazy I had become. I could see my reflection in the computer screen and knew I was growing soft and somewhat flabby—and still wearing my pajamas because I had not had to teach in person that day. I was thinking about story ideas and nixing them one after another. I turned on iTunes, thinking that music would get me up and moving or at the very least thinking about dance combinations, but my mind kept pushing such thoughts away.

I realized I wanted to do nothing more than brew a cup of tea (and that was pushing it), settle on the couch, and watch TV. Every idea I had to create something new, I blasted down. It was then I realized my creative fire had gone out. I had lost my passion!

This realization swept a darkness over me. At first, I moped around the house going through the motions of living. I cooked, cleaned, worked out lesson plans, drove kids around, went on dates with my husband, and spent nights sitting in front of the TV. After surviving the initial shock, I started to welcome the days as being quiet and, to me, seemingly unproductive (though my house had never been cleaner!). As the days moved by and the sun stayed in the sky a little bit longer, I began to grow antsy and bored. It seemed as if the days were beginning to drag on and on. This was much different than the panicky feeling that there was never enough time. I wasn't quite certain what to make of this change, and I certainly wasn't sure what to do with it.

One day after dropping my older kids off at school, I was walking home with my youngest son, Theo. We were moving slowly despite the cold because the sun was bright that day and trying its hardest to bathe everything in light. Theo urged me to take the long way home, so we ducked down a side street and explored the paths behind our house.

Theo was dragging his feet, stopping to investigate bushes and mounds of dirt-caked snow. I wanted very much to see the world through his eyes, but I hadn't been able to shake my sense of gloom. Theo began collecting rocks that appealed to his senses. After filling his pockets to the brim, he began handing me fistfuls to hold. My mind was arguing that this would just bring dirt into my clean house, but I kept my mouth shut, curious to see where this would bring us.

Imbolc was just around the corner, and I had been pushing around ideas of how to celebrate. Normally, we feasted on fresh bread and a large vat of what we called "The Cauldron of Inspiration," a fire-red stew filled with promise to grow our creativity. I was looking forward to Imbolc that year because of the lack of muse in our home. Theo's stones started to give me an idea, but I wanted to see what he had in store for them.

When we could carry no more, we made our way back through our yard and to the house. Once inside, we emptied our pockets onto the table and sorted our rocks by size and shape. Theo insisted that we clean them before advancing. Struck with a sudden inspiration, I bundled him back up and we headed outside to gather snow, as the snowflake is the symbol of Imbolc.

Once back inside we placed the rocks in the bowl of snow and waited for it to melt. Theo sat at the table meditating on the snow while I made us hot chocolate. While the drink simmered, I sat across from my little guy and took up his hands. Together, we watched as the snow turned to water and the dirt from the rocks began to rise to the surface of the pool.

When the smell of chocolate filled the kitchen, I released his hands from mine to dip his fingers into the water and scrub the remaining dirt free from the stones. Leaning forward, I kissed him, noting that children are another symbol of the holiday. I turned off the stove and poured our chocolate into two cups. I was thinking that once the stones were dry, we should paint them in flame colors and draw on symbols that represent early movements of spring when nature begins to poke her head through the cold and grow.

It was then I began to feel something unlock inside my chest and a sense of warmth spread through me. I picked the phone to call my sister and invite her to our Imbolc feast. Our passions weren't gone, they were merely hibernating, growing strong in the dark womb of the Great Mother. I knew my flame of creativity had returned and with it the power to rekindle the fires of those I loved.

Cosmic Sway

Corrine Kenner

IMBOLC CELEBRATES THE COMING of spring, when the Sun is half-way through the sign of airy Aquarius—which is also the halfway point between the Winter Solstice and the Spring Equinox.

On this cross-quarter holiday, the Sun isn't alone in Aquarius. Mercury, the Sun's closest traveling companion, is also in the sign. That's not unusual; Mercury is the nearest planet to the Sun, so it's never more than 28 degrees away in any given astrological chart. As the two move through the sign, both are focused on Aquarian issues, with an eye toward a better, brighter future. That's because airy Aquarius is a fixed air sign, so it's perpetually focused on humanitarian ideals.

Neptune, Venus, and Mars are close behind, passing together through watery Pisces—the sign of mutable water, where energy flows and planets swim through the depths of the unconscious mind. Two of the three planets are perfectly comfortable there. In fact, Neptune, the planet of glamor and illusion, rules the ethereal sign. Venus, the planet of love and romance, is exalted in watery Pisces because it's a sign of emotional connection.

Mars' fiery spirit, however, is dampened by all that water. The god of war is used to staging battles on the dry land of logic and reason. He's not particularly equipped to navigate the swirling waters of mysticism and illusion.

Tarot and Astrology

All of the planets are constantly traveling through all twelve signs of the zodiac. Occasionally, one of those planets will find itself stuck in a sign that seems completely foreign to its own basic nature. A fiery planet like Mars, for example, will feel like a stranger in a strange land when he's submerged in the watery sign of Pisces.

When you find planets in signs that run counter to their nature, you can understand their discomfort by picturing them as their tarot-card counterparts. In this case, Mars corresponds to the Tower card, the natural home to the fiery Aries Emperor. He's an authority figure, the master and commander of all he surveys, and a clear, logical thinker. When Mars is submerged in watery Pisces, however, the techniques he's developed for battles on dry land are no longer effective. He's forced to navigate the watery depths of emotion—not reason—and conduct his battles underwater.

Practical Astrology

As you prepare for the approaching birth of spring, take a look at your own birth chart. Most of us know our own Sun sign, but we don't usually stop to consider the fact that all of the planets and signs follow suit. Each of us is a living, breathing constellation of signs and symbols.

On major holidays—which are, after all, markers of annual calendar events—it's fun to compare and contrast the position of key planets in the sky to their placement on your chart. In this case, find Aquarius on your chart, and look for the 15-degree point. That's the halfway mark between the Winter Solstice and the Spring Equinox, when we celebrate Imbolc. Do you have any planets there? If so, that planetary energy will be triggered when the Sun passes over in real life, and you can expect to see changes and developments in that sphere of influence.

Planetary Positions

The Sun is in airy Aquarius. It will move into Pisces on February 18.

The Moon is in its own sign, Cancer, where it casts a lovely glow on home and family life.

Mercury is retrograde in airy Aquarius, the sign that rules technology. Look for this period to be busier than average when it comes to telephone, email, and web-based communication—and more prone to miscommunication. The fast-moving planet will enter Pisces on March 12, which could lead to some clouded thinking for a few days, as well as a tendency to daydream or wander off on tangents.

Venus is in watery Pisces, where love and romance seem to shimmer in a veil of soft, filtered light. The planet of pleasure and attraction will move into its own sign, the sensual, earthy Taurus, on March 17.

Mars is also in watery Pisces, where the god of war is completely out of his element. He'll be back in command and control when Mars moves into its own fiery sign of Aries on February 20.

Venus will join Mars in Aries on February 20, in a passionate reunion between the goddess of love and the god of war. You'll be able to see the two planets embracing each other in the western sky, just after sunset.

A retrograde Jupiter is still moving backward through fiery Leo. On February 6, it will make its closest approach to Earth, and its face will be fully illuminated by the Sun. You'll be able to see the giant planet with binoculars. You might even be able to spot its four largest moons, as well as some detail in its clouds.

Saturn is in fiery Sagittarius, which tends to lighten its mood. It could even make it possible to break or test the limits of some long-standing boundaries and reservations.

The generational outer planets remain in the same signs:

Uranus in fiery Aries.

Neptune is in watery Pisces.

Pluto is in earthy Capricorn.

Planets in Aspect

The Sun, in Aquarius, is opposite Jupiter in Leo. Oppositions aren't necessarily bad. In this case, the two regal planets have a clear and open line of communication between them, which unleashes a flow of creative energy, confidence, and optimism.

The Sun is also in a harmonious sextile with Uranus in fiery Aries, fueling an atmosphere of excitement.

Venus, in watery Pisces, is squaring off with Saturn in fiery Sagittarius. The ringed planet tends to inhibit Venus' social grace and interaction.

Venus, however, might not notice the full effect of Saturn's limitations. Venus and Neptune are conjunct in Pisces, so Venus is fully immersed in the glamor and illusion of her closest neighbor. When you're under Neptune's spell, it's easy to see the world through rose-colored glasses.

Like Venus, Neptune also happens to be in an uncomfortable square with Saturn—which casts long shadows of imaginary fears and unnecessary guilt.

Mars, in Pisces, and Pluto, in Capricorn, are in a harmonious sextile. The two planets share a deep-seated desire for power and understanding.

One notable aspect actually comes to an end soon. Slow-moving Uranus has been squaring off against even slower Pluto since June 2012. Throughout that time, Uranus—the planet of revolution and rebellion—has been chipping away at institutional and government power and fueling cultural and social revolutions around the world. The last in a long series of exact squares will finally pass away on March 16—but the aftereffects will linger for a few more months.

Phases of the Moon

February 3: A Full Moon in fiery Leo basks in the light of an airy Aquarius Sun. This is a rare opportunity to fuel your self-esteem in a way that would make any fiery Leo happy. Update your hairstyle, wear bright colors, and prepare to be the center of attention.

February 18: The Moon and the Sun move into conjunction in airy Aquarius, leading to a New Moon in the futuristic sign. During a conjunction, we can't actually see the Moon; it's dark, but in a day or two we'll see a silvery crescent in the sky.

March 5: A Full Moon in earthy Virgo reflects the full light of a watery Pisces Sun. Relax. Meditate, stretch, do yoga, and go to bed early.

March 20: A New Moon will be born when the Moon and the Sun form a conjunction in watery Pisces. Some parts of the world will be able to enjoy a total solar eclipse, as well. The path of totality starts in the central Atlantic Ocean; it will move north across Greenland and end in northern Siberia.

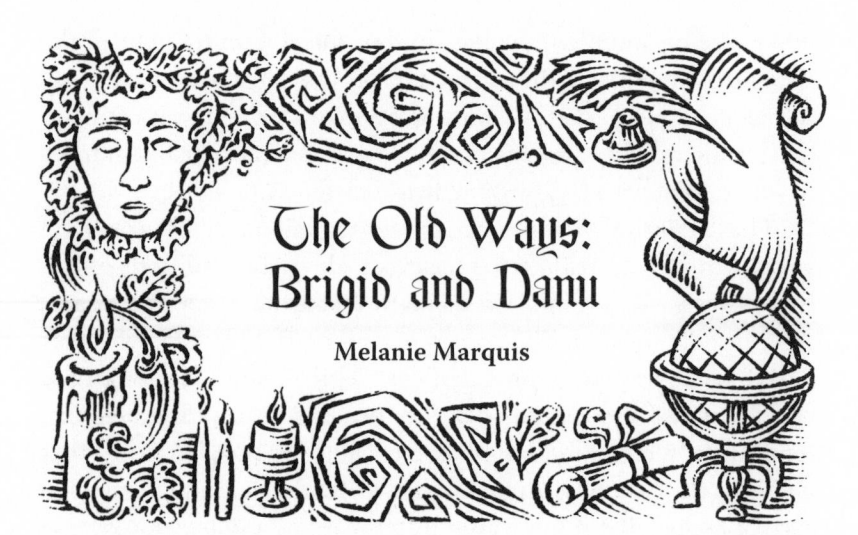

The Old Ways: Brigid and Danu

Melanie Marquis

THE SYMBOLISM AND SIGNIFICANCE of Imbolc can seem a bit confusing and contradictory from a modern perspective. The holiday is focused on the imminent arrival of spring, which isn't due for another six weeks or more, and which is hard to imagine if it's still freezing outside! To the early Celtic people, however, who lived in close relationship to seasonal cycles, Imbolc marked a significant and obvious turning point in the natural year. Occurring roughly at the halfway point between the Winter Solstice and Spring Equinox, Imbolc is a time when the sun's rays are lengthening, gaining strength as winter's freeze begins to melt. It's a time when livestock animals like sheep give birth and produce milk. It's a time of celebration and rejoicing, a time of reassurance in spring's imminent arrival. Winter might still be upon us, but soon the vegetation will emerge renewed.

Imbolc has its origins thousands of years ago in Ireland, and similar variations are celebrated in other Celtic lands. It's unclear when exactly the festival started, but there is some evidence that the date of February 1 was significant to the Celts as far back as 5,000 years ago. There's a certain chamber in the Mound of Hostages at the Hill of Tara in Ireland that was built in alignment with the angle of sunrise on Imbolc morning, so that the streaming light of the rising sun illuminates the chamber. The site dates back all the way to the Neolithic period, an era when humans were first learning to master the crafting and use of metal tools, and also just beginning to experiment with farming and livestock tending.

These cultural changes occurred gradually over thousands of years, and it's impossible to trace exactly how the traditions of Imbolc progressed in result. We do know that around 2,000 years ago, Irish Imbolc was heavily focused on the goddess Brigid, who may have been a version of a much older Celtic goddess, Danu. Brigid was a goddess associated with fire, hearths, inspiration, healing, femininity, fertility, and smithcraft. Danu was an Earth-Mother goddess, the ruler and originator of the Tuathe de Danu, a mystical race of beings that disappeared into the mists and became part of the Earth itself. Danu was heavily associated with both water and fertility; she was a vegetation goddess, and her myths we see reflected in many later Imbolc traditions. In Danu's lore, for instance, there are tales of seeds awakening underneath the goddess's feet as she walked, and there are stories of how her mystical cloak causes flowers to spring forth from the earth wherever the fabric touches. She was seen as the embodiment of fertility, and as a water goddess, Danu helped revitalize the vegetation each spring. Her partner was Lugh, another powerful deity. Danu's father was Dagda, whose duty it was to help awaken the springtime by playing a song on his magickal harp. Dagda also had a large cauldron from which he nourished all the creatures of the earth. In later years, Brigid rose to a greater prominence, but we see in this goddess many characteristics of the earlier goddess Danu and her worship. One Imbolc tradition, for instance, is to leave a garment or other piece of cloth outside on Imbolc Eve, so that the goddess Brigid will come by and bless it, endowing the fabric with magickal power just as Danu's cloak could make the barren earth spring back to life. The sound of Dagda's harp became the music of the Imbolc merrymakers who would play songs and dance late into the night, perhaps in hopes of making such a ruckus that the slumbering spring will open its eyes and take notice. Dagda's cauldron also remained ingrained in Imbolc tradition. Large brewing vessels have been found containing traces of alcoholic beverages, but no storage containers have been unearthed, indicating that the Celts may have enjoyed seasonal, holiday-based drinking.

Slowly, Brigid came to take center stage, and eventually, Brigid morphed into St. Brigid. Brigid's Imbolc celebrations were primarily focused on fire and on the idea of gaining the blessings of the beloved goddess. Large bonfires were lit, perhaps to help thaw the frozen ground and lend the strengthening sunlight a bit of extra power. Offerings such as bread, milk, and butter were placed on windowsills or at hearthsides for Brigid to enjoy as she made her way from home to home on the eve of Imbolc, as encouragements for the goddess to do her thing in awakening the slumbering earth, bestowing blessings on plant, man, and animal alike.

Another curious tradition used to awaken the spring involves, with seeming irony, putting the goddess Brigid to bed. In Ireland and parts of Scotland, a sheaf of corn from the last year's harvest is fashioned to look like a woman, a representative of the goddess Brigid. The sheaf of corn is decorated with flowers and is placed within a wicker cradle where it then receives gifts of shells, blossoms, and other trinkets from local admirers. In some communities, the doll is taken from house to house first before it's laid in its bed. Once the Brigid doll has been put down to rest and the true spirit of the goddess herself has been enticed to enter into the sheaf of corn, this mock-Brigid receives a miniature magick wand, perhaps originally a phallic symbol representing Brigid's relationship with her consort Lugh. In time, the use of Brigid's mini-wand was more of a divinatory nature. When it was time to go to sleep, the woman of the household would smooth the ashes in the hearth, then carefully place Brigid's wand among the ashes. In the morning, the ashes were examined to see if any impressions had been made by Brigid. If the ashes had been disturbed, it was taken as a good sign that Brigid had indeed visited and had indeed blessed the house, its future crops, and its livestock.

Today, many of these old traditions are forgotten, but our modern practices still reflect Imbolc's ancient roots. With candles often substituting for larger fires, we gather and contemplate the growing light of the sun, giving thanks and hoping for our lives to become a little brighter. We place our humble offerings out for the universe to take or to leave, wishing with all our hearts that the higher powers will take notice. We place our faith in the cycles of nature, just as the Celts did thousands of years ago.

References:

Monaghan, Patricia. *The Encyclopedia of Celtic Mythology and Folklore.* New York: Facts on File, Inc., 2004.

National Leprechaun Museum. "Imbolc." Accessed October 13, 2013. http://www.leprechaunmuseum.ie/about-us/irish-folklore -mythology/festivals/imbolc/

Newgrange.com. "Imbolc (Imbolg): Cross-quarter Day." Accessed October 13, 2013. http://www.newgrange.com/imbolc.htm.

Nicholson, Francine. "Imbolc in Yesterday's Ireland and Scotland." Celtic Well. Accessed October 13, 2013. http://www.applewarrior .com/celticwell/ejournal/imbolc/yesterdays.htm.

Vallance, Peter. "Celtic Roots: The Irish Celtic Magical Tradition: The Festival of Imbolc." *Aisling Magazine.* Accessed October 13, 2013. http://www.aislingmagazine.com/aislingmagazine/articles /TAM26/CelticRoots.html.

Feasts and Treats

Ellen Dugan

THE WHEEL OF THE year continues to spin towards the light, yet these are some of the coldest and snowiest days of the year. So curl up in front of a nice warm fire, snuggle up with your favorite warm quilt, and enjoy a few hearty, yet healthier, versions of classic comfort foods this winter.

Magick Meatloaf

Yes, meatloaf. I like something hearty on cold winter nights. This is a healthier version, and it is fabulous. Each slice has 25 grams protein and only 6 grams of fat per serving!

Prep time: 20 minutes
Cook time: 30 minutes
Serves: 4

⅔ cups old-fashioned oats
½ cup fat-free milk
¼ cup egg substitute
1½ tablespoons Worcestershire sauce
½ cup carrots, minced
½ cup green bell pepper, minced

2 tablespoons dried minced onions
1 clove garlic, finely minced
2 tablespoons fresh, flat-leaf parsley, finely chopped
½ teaspoon salt
¼ teaspoon black pepper
1 pound 96 percent lean ground beef
⅓ cup ketchup

Preheat the oven to 350 degrees F. Spray a standard loaf pan with nonstick cooking spray.

In a medium bowl, combine the milk and oats let them sit for 3 minutes until the oats have softened. While this happens, you can chop up the vegetables. Add the egg substitute, Worcestershire sauce, carrots, green bell peppers, dried onions, garlic, parsley, salt, and pepper and mix well. Add the ground beef and mix until well combined. (Use a fork so the mixture stays fluffy.) Transfer into loaf pan and spread out so the loaf is flat on the top. Spread the ketchup over the top evenly. Bake for 30 minutes or until it is no longer pink on the inside. Remove from oven and allow it to rest for 5 to 10 minutes. Cut into 8 slices and serve immediately. Makes 4 servings. Refrigerate any leftovers. Carve into thinner slices for meatloaf sandwiches!

Rustic Parmesan Smashed Potatoes

One of my favorites. Leaving the skin on the red potatoes adds some interest to this dish and makes it more "rustic."

Prep time: 10 minutes
Cook time: 40 minutes
Serves: 4

1½–2 lbs. red potatoes, washed (leave the skins on)
3 tablespoons butter or margarine
¼ cup fat-free sour cream
¼ cup grated Parmesan cheese
Salt and pepper to taste

Wash and scrub the red potatoes well. Chop them up into smaller pieces and cover with water in a pot. On medium-high heat, bring to a boil. Allow potatoes to cook until they are fork tender—about 25 to 35 minutes. Cooking times vary widely, so keep an eye on them.

Drain potatoes. Using a hand masher, smash the potatoes (but not too much—you want them to have texture and to have some small lumps). Now add 3 tablespoons of butter or margarine, stir in sour cream and the freshly grated parmesan cheese.

Stir until butter, sour cream, and cheese are incorporated. Salt and pepper to taste. Serve immediately. Refrigerate any leftovers.

Microwave Oatmeal Muffin for One

This is a fun recipe for when you just need a little something sweetly satisfying on a cold winter's night—or morning for that matter! This is a fun recipe to do with your kids as well.

Prep time: 5 minutes
Cook time: 45 seconds
Serves: 1

In a microwave-safe mug, mix the following ingredients.

¼ cup oats
1 teaspoon brown sugar
1 tablespoon flour (of your choice)
1 egg white
¼ teaspoon vanilla extract
¼ teaspoon baking powder
½ teaspoon cinnamon
1 tablespoon raisins

Stir the ingredients well, then flatten mixture into bottom of the mug and microwave on high for 45 seconds. Allow it to cool for a few minutes. Then pop it out of the mug and enjoy!

White Russian

This is a classic cocktail, and as it is heavy on the cream, it is perfect for Imbolc.

Prep time: 5 minutes

Serves: 1

1½ ounces of vodka

1½ ounces Kahlua

3 ounces heavy cream or milk

In a mixing glass, combine the coffee-flavored liqueur, vodka, and cream or milk. Pour over ice in a highball glass. Happy Imbolc!

Crafty Crafts

Lexa Olick

IMBOLC IS A TIME of cleansing and fire. It's when you should start preparing your home for a visit from Brighid. Magical purification rituals are usually held during this time, but you can also perform a physical cleaning. Brighid is welcomed into your home with such traditional crafts as a Brighid's cross or the Brighid's bed. Crafts to honor her are generally made from cornhusks or woven grain, but as you clear away the clutter in your home, you might discover other recyclable ways to worship her. Something old can be turned into something new, just as the world reawakens into spring at Imbolc.

Imbolc Twig Candleholder

Imbolc is the feast of the goddess Brighid, who is associated with light and the hearth. Candles are burned to purify the home and chase away evil spirits. The warm glow of a flame keeps us safe and evil at bay. The Imbolc twig candleholder looks as if there is a miniature bonfire in your home. It makes every room seem warm and cozy. Plus, it recycles items found around the house! All you need is a glass candleholder and fallen branches from the yard. Imbolc is a time of cleansing, so it's a good idea to begin by physically cleansing your yard. Luckily, some of the items you find can be put to good use. The Imbolc candleholder looks great by itself, but it truly looks ablaze when it's displayed in a group.

Supplies
Votive candle
Clear glass votive candleholder
Dry twigs or tree branches
Garden shears
E6000 adhesive

Instructions: Begin by cleaning the candleholder as thoroughly as possible to ensure the adhesive will stick to the glass. Gently wash it with dish soap and water until all dust and fingerprints are removed. Be sure to dry it well with a towel.

With garden shears, cut the twigs down to the height of the votive candleholder. Cut several twigs at a time, but you can always

cut more later if needed. Apply a thin line of adhesive onto one side of the twig and then hold it firmly against the glass candleholder for 1 minute. Repeat until the entire candleholder is covered and let it sit aside to fully adhere for 24 hours. Once the glue sets, you'll then have a beautiful and natural looking candleholder that will add a warm glow to any room. Imbolc celebrates the growth of light and that light will certainly grow with this new candle!

Time to Complete: About 40 minutes to assemble, but another 24 hours to let the glue set.

Cost: About $5.00 since tree branches are easily found outside

Variation: Instead of using dried branches, you can also use cinnamon sticks. It gives your candleholder the added touch of a spicy fragrance. Plus, it represents the element of fire. If you want to embellish your candleholder further, you can consider tying a bow of raffia ribbon around it.

Brighid's Baskets

Raffia is a natural fiber used to weave baskets or wrap gifts. This project is a combination of both! Below is a simple way to create baskets without weaving. They hold small candies inside, which is perfect for an Imbolc celebration. Raffia can be purchased in a variety of colors, but I think it better suits the purposes of this project to purchase raffia in its natural shade.

Supplies
Raffia ribbon
Craft glue
Balloon
Small individually wrapped candies
Pliers
Wax paper
Pin
Bowl

Instructions: Carefully stretch the opening of the balloon and place small candies inside. Insert as many as you can. I recommend using candies wrapped in gold foil because Brighid is known as the "bright one." It also stands out against the natural texture and color of the raffia. Blow up the balloon to about the size of your fist and tie the end into a tight knot.

Play around with the raffia to make it more pliable. Twist it around your hands and just generally rub it softy with your palms. This will make the raffia more flexible so it will easily cover the balloon.

It is better to work on a hard surface because this project is wet and messy. Cover your work area with newspaper. Thin the glue with water inside your bowl. Start with 2 parts glue and 1 part water. If the mixture is too thick, slowly add more water. You can also thicken the mixture by adding more glue. Dunk the raffia into the bowl and soak it completely in the watered-down glue. Squeeze the excess glue out before you start wrapping.

Begin wrapping the raffia vertically around the balloon. Then change directions and wrap the raffia horizontally around the balloon. Now continue to wrap it every which way. You don't need to cover the entire balloon in raffia because we still want the candies to peek out between the cracks. Cover enough so that the balloon is enclosed, but leave enough cracks in between so that we can see and hear the candies rattling inside.

Cut the raffia and secure it with a generous amount of glue. Brush the remaining watered-down glue all over the raffia-covered balloon to ensure the raffia will set. Place it aside to dry overnight on a sheet of wax paper. If the raffia is still damp by the next morning, set it aside to dry another night. The raffia should be hard and firm before you continue.

Once the raffia is completely dry, pop the balloon with a pin. Carefully peel and remove the remnants of the rubber balloon with pliers. Now the candies are free to shake and rattle inside the Bridghid's basket.

Time to Complete: A little over 20 minutes to make, but up to 2 days to fully dry.
Cost: About $5.00

Note: These are described as baskets and are designed to be used as treat bags or party favors, but that doesn't mean they can't be decorative as well. They make wonderful centerpieces and look very lovely nestled in bunches inside a large basket. They can decorate your home until it's time to welcome your guests with delicious Imbolc treats.

Sustainable Imbolc: In the Box

Natalie Zaman

BY THE TIME FEBRUARY rolls around, I'm finished with winter. The long nights, the bitter cold…the snow. And so I look forward to Imbolc and the evidence that yes, there are brighter days ahead. Life peeks out of death as February rolls into March; a crocus here, a tightly wrapped bud there. Imbolc marks these first signs of life that have lain dormant since the beginning of the God season. Working in the garden has given me a front row seat to observe the subtle changes that take place as the months roll by: The stirring at Imbolc sprouts at the Spring Equinox, then swells at Lammas, and finally, is harvested at the Autumnal Equinox.

Several years of trial and error have made me a more efficient gardener, but a homestead and a quieter life where I live completely in tune with the seasons is still a dream. Due to space constraints, my herbs remain in their pots. Every year I grow a single tomato and devote a small patch to my favorite yellow squash—and the work begins now.

Inevitably, February finds me itching to begin, as if my growing something will somehow speed up the clock and hasten the arrival of spring and its warmer days. My countertops and windowsills become crowded with egg containers filled with seedlings. Each year, they seem to get off to a good start, but I always lose some plants. I'm covered by volume, and usually manage to have enough to fill up my pots and patches. Still, the first weeks after transplant are always iffy, and I wonder, *will my babies be hardy enough to survive?*

Then on one lucky birthday, I was presented with a "Graveyard Gothic Garden"—an octagonal plastic hothouse complete with potting soil and seeds for plants such as black dragon coleus, moonflower, and aloe. This mini-terrarium was very like those plastic boxes you find in the supermarket, the kind that hold small, soft fruits like strawberries and blueberries. My moonflowers did so well that I thought I would try the same method with my vegetable seedlings. Imbolc, "in the belly," would be, for one year at least, Imbolc "in the box" and hopefully my garden would get a better head start.

The boxes made perfect planters: The ventilation holes in the bottom provided drainage, the transparent plastic let in light, the sealable lid kept seeds warm. Planting seedlings at this time of year sets the stirring of Imbolc in motion. Using recycled containers brings the spiritual and the practical together, working with the seasons and respect for the Earth.

Make It Your Own!

You will need:

Plastic lidded fruit and vegetable boxes

Potting soil

Seeds

A representation of a goddess or god associated with planting or fertility and with whom you have an affinity. Each year my planting efforts begin with a plea to the gardening gods (I'll take all the divine intervention I can get!). You can also use a stone or crystal. Moss agate with its green inclusions connect it directly to plant life, while quartz crystal will focus energy and amplify the nurturing nature of this work. There are stones that are associated with specific plants. Use your favorite reference to see which will work best for what you are trying to grow.

A copper penny minted in the current year (Copper is a conductor of heat and energy—exactly what plants need. Using a coin stamped with the year you are planting acknowledges the power of the present.)

Plant your seeds according to the directions on the package. As you prepare the beds, place the seeds and cover them with soil, as you place your stone or god/goddess symbol and the penny, as you water them and place your terrarium in a sunny spot, remember the promise of Imbolc. Speak or think this meditation as you work:

> *With water and earth,*
> *With warmth and light,*
> *By copper and stone,*
> *Are seed and spell sown.*
> *Grow!*
> *Grow!*
> *Grow!*

Studies have shown that plants respond to love and care like all living beings. Watch your seedlings grow and transplant them when they need a larger container or can be moved outdoors. Once you have transplanted your seedlings, clean out your recycled terrariums and use them for storage when it comes time to harvest.

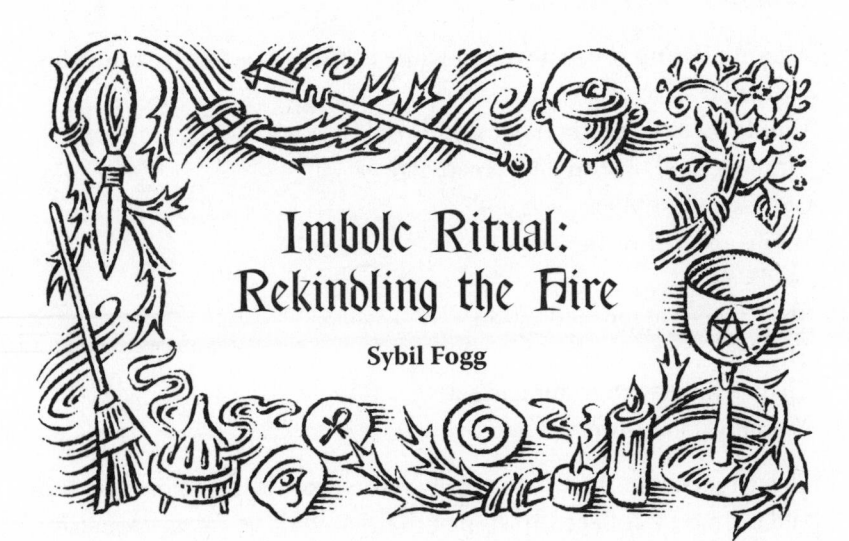

Imbolc Ritual:
Rekindling the Fire

Sybil Fogg

TO ME, THE SABBATS are a time for little magical workings, but I do try to do a ritual to celebrate the turning of the wheel at each holiday and honor my family's place in the natural and spiritual world. Ever since my trying year of keeping the creative fire alive, I have used the following ritual to mark the strength of my passion. This ritual is an excellent way to rekindle the spark of creativity and celebrate the elements of Imbolc.

Items Needed

Rocks gathered from a nature walk
Red, yellow, and orange paint
Paint brushes
Black Sharpie pen
A bowl of snow
As many white and yellow candles and holders as possible
One white spell candle
One yellow candle for the god
One light blue candle for the goddess
Quarter candles
Ritual wine or juice

A food offering (I usually use a white cookie or pastry treat for this
  ritual)
Vanilla oil to strengthen our mind set
Cinnamon oil to stimulate creativity
Clove oil to unblock
White and yellow flowers
Seeds
Myrrh incense for meditation
Athame
Chalice filled with water and salt
As many hand towels as needed

This ritual begins before the New Moon nearest the actual holiday.
Make time to collect the stones that you will be using. A nature
walk in which to make note of the coming spring is the perfect way
to complete this step. I generally take the entire family on a hike
through the woods. This way, we can pause to take in where we see
Mother Earth waking up as green pushes through the snow and animals begin stretches. This also works well as a solitary exercise. A
deep meditation as one weaves their way through the natural world
will awaken the senses. Don't forget to collect the rocks needed for
the ritual as you journey.

The six of us root out stones from underneath the snow and
branches. There is no particular type of stone we are looking for.
Take whatever feels right. The same goes for the amount. Close
your eyes and open your heart. You will know what you need.

The night of the New Moon, gather your paints, paint brushes,
Sharpie, candles, a bowl, and stones. Once outside, scoop snow into
the bowl. If you have an outdoor altar, place your items there to be
charged with the New Moon's energy. If not, use a makeshift altar.
This can be as simple as laying your items beneath your favorite
tree. Apartment dwellers may lay their items (other than the snow)
in a window. Gather snow the first morning after the New Moon.

Once charged by the moon, bring your items inside. The snow will keep in your freezer until needed. Everything else can be placed on the altar.

Make sure to schedule time to bake your treat for the offering. Although, we are busy in this day and age and it can be tempting to purchase an offering, only do so if it is impossible to make it yourself. The magic we infuse in our cooking is potent and sending out this energy creates a connection with our realm and the spiritual that no purchased good can replicate.

The Imbolc Altar
Cover the altar with a white cloth.
Anoint the white spell candle with the oils and place in the center of the altar.
Place the blue candle to the left of the spell candle and the yellow candle to the right.
Put the bowl of snow in front of the candle and pour out the bag of stones.
Lay out the Sharpie, paints, and brushes.
Set out the cakes and wine.
Sprinkle the flowers and seeds around the altar.

After the altar is ready, set the rest of the candles around the room and place the quarter candles in their spots. Light the incense and call the quarters, starting with the east. In our home, our children call the quarters, but this can easily be managed as a solitary ritual.

Quarter Calls
East: Face the east and light the eastern candle.
Hail, the guardians of the East! Spirits of the air! Sprites and sylphs, we welcome you tonight into our circle. Bless us with your flash of creativity and wisdom! Come! We bid you welcome!

South: Face the south and light the southern candle.

Hail, the guardians of the South! Spirits of the Fire! Drakes and salamanders, we welcome you tonight into our circle. Bless us with your fiery passion and action! We bid you welcome!

West: Face the west and light the western candle.

Hail, the guardians of the West! Spirits of the Water! Nymphs and mermaids, we welcome you tonight into our circle. Bless us with your courage and daring! We bid you welcome!

North: Face the north and light the northern candle.

Hail, the guardians of the North! Spirits of the Earth! Gnomes and dryads, we welcome you tonight into our circle. Bless us with your grounding and permanence.

Cast the Circle

In our household, we cast our circle by walking around our working space three times. One member holds the athame in their left hand, blade pointing down. Following, someone holds incense, blowing gently to send smoke in all corners. Another holds a chalice filled with water and salt and sprinkles this in the circle.

Once the final person has made the third round, we lay our tools on the altar and join hands for a moment to fuel the strength of the circle.

Invoking the Goddess and God

Light the blue candle and say:

Our lady of the moon, Maiden Goddess of renewal and making way for the new, we welcome you to our circle on this sacred Imbolc.

Light the yellow candle and say:

Our lord of the sun, Youthful God of the flame and letting go of burdens, we welcome you to our circle on this sacred Imbolc.

Take a moment to meditate on the spark that lies within us all. Think about any projects you have been working on that have lost their appeal over the past year. Try to imagine the process you had gone through to create it and the progress you had made so far. Why did you lose interest? Don't worry if you cannot pinpoint a reason. Just spend some time considering it.

If you do not have any projects currently in the works, meditate on why you are not creating. Imagine that deep inside of you a fire burns. Perhaps it is dampened. Maybe it needs to be rekindled. Imagine this fire sparking and the flame growing.

Sit in front of the altar and light the white spell candle. As you do so, keep in mind this spark. Imagine it igniting within you.

Meditate on the candle for a moment and then take up the stones and pass them around so that everyone has at least a handful.

Place the stones in the bowl of snow. Use your hands to work off as much dirt as possible. The snow will be cold so dry your hands on the towels as needed. As the snow melts, talk to each other about where you get your inspiration. If you are practicing this solitary, meditate on idea growth.

When the snow has melted, gather the stones into the towels and dry them off. They are now infused with Imbolc's magic of inspiration.

This is where the ritual gets fun. Paint the stones in fiery shades to represent the spark within all of us. As the paint dries, use the Sharpie to add symbols that resonate meaning for you. Continue to work as the candle burns down and until the snow has fully melted.

Thank the Goddess and God for their inspiration with an offering of the wine and food.

Hold the wine above the blue candle and say:

Lady of the moon, we thank you for your blessings. Return now to your magical realm. Merry meet and merry part until we merry meet again.

Place the wine glass behind the blue candle.
Hold the treat above the yellow candle and say:

Lord of the Sun, we thank you for your blessings. Return now to your magical realm. Merry meet and merry part until we merry meet again.

Place the dish behind the yellow candle.

Close the quarters starting in the North and moving widdershins.

Blow out the northern candle and say:

Spirits of the North, we thank you for your blessings. Return now to your magical realm. Merry meet and merry part until we merry meet again.

Turn to the western candle and blow it out:

Spirits of the West, we thank you for your blessings. Return now to your magical realm. Merry meet and merry part until we merry meet again.

Turn to the southern candle and blow it out:

Spirits of the South, we thank you for your blessings. Return now to your magical realm. Merry meet and merry part until we merry meet again.

Turn to the eastern candle and blow it out:

Spirits of the East, we thank you for your blessings. Return now to your magical realm. Merry meet and merry part until we merry meet again.

Open the circle by walking around the sacred space three times, widdershins. Let the candles burn throughout the evening to represent the growing fire within us all. Happy Imbolc!

Notes

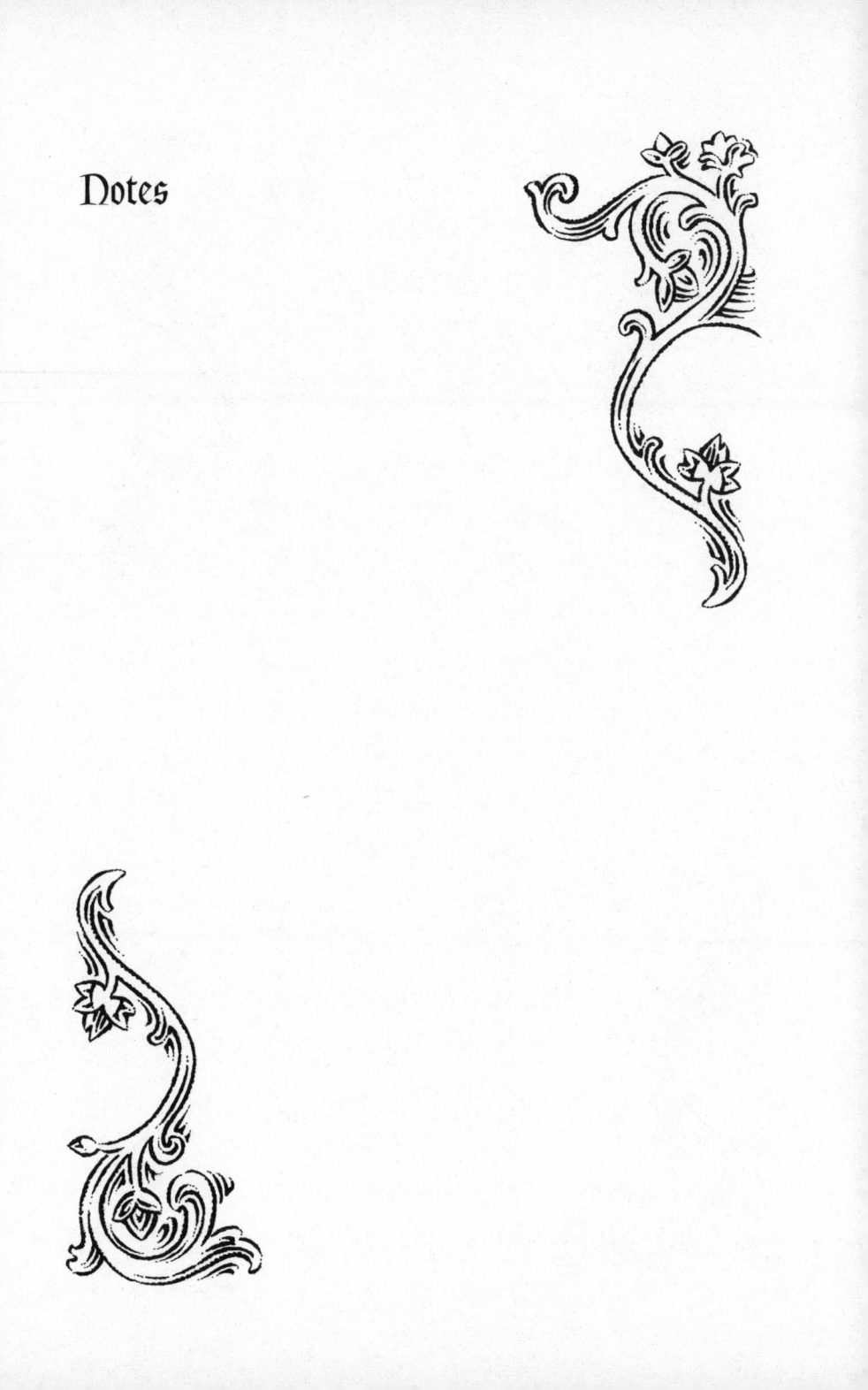

Notes

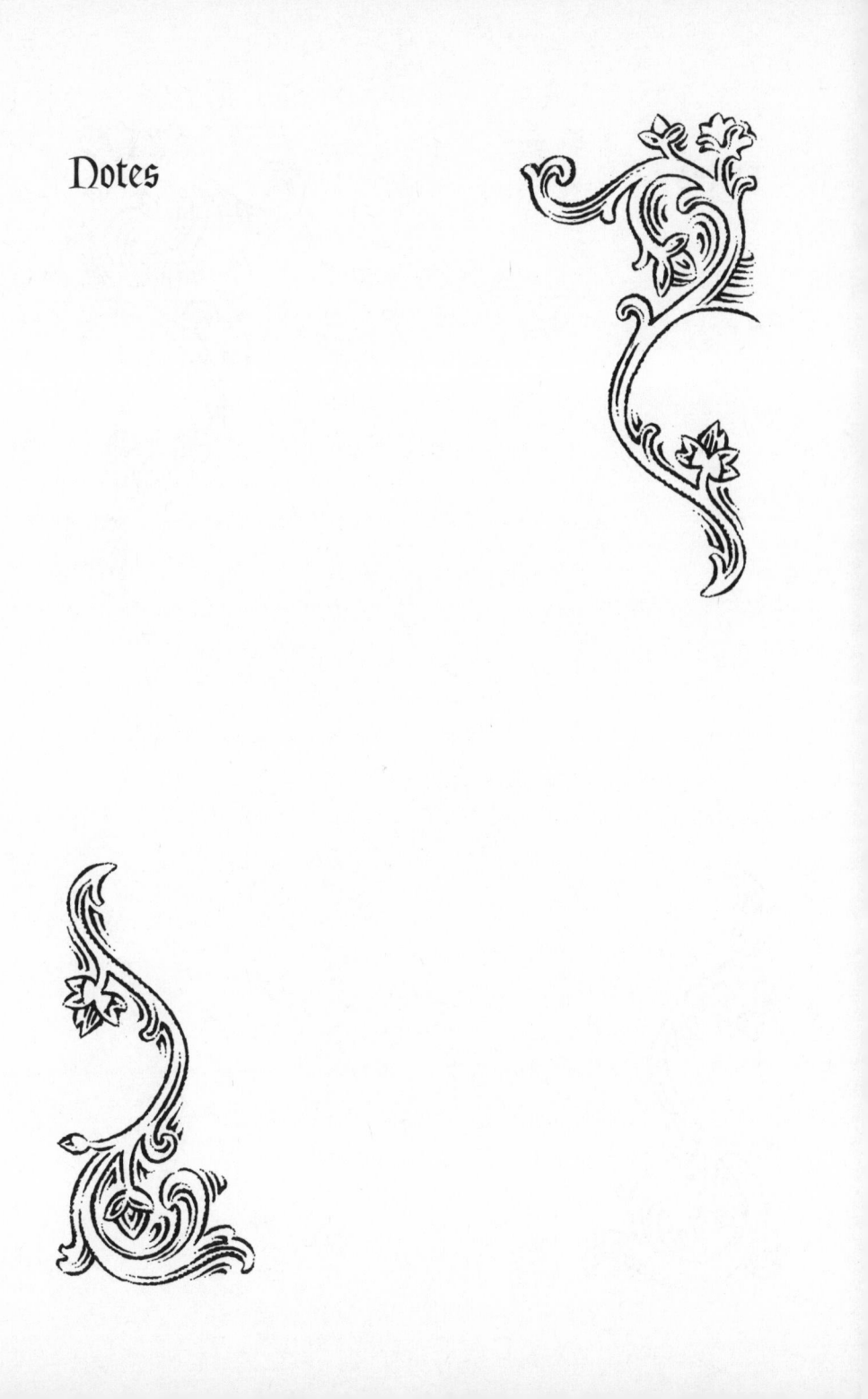

Ostara

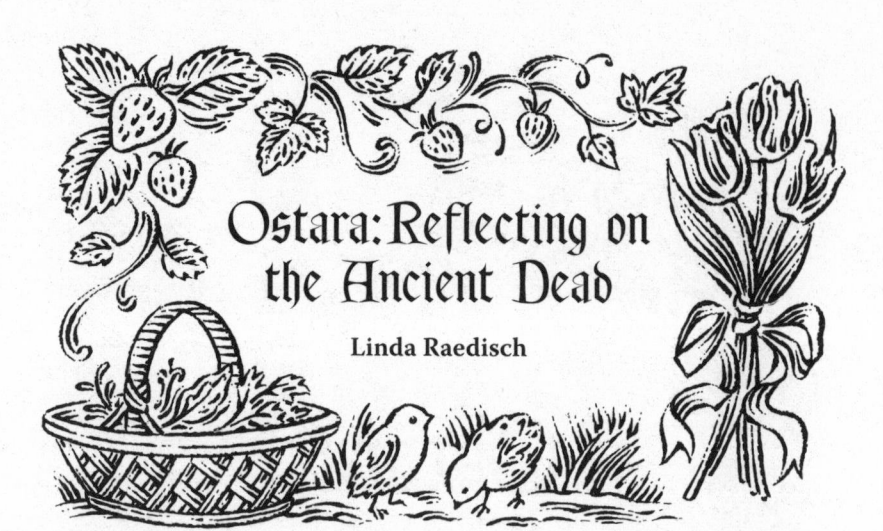

Ostara: Reflecting on the Ancient Dead

Linda Raedisch

As I compose the opening of this essay, I am watched by the shadowed, almond-shaped eyes of a Canaanite individual who lived sometime in the second millennium BCE. Those eyes regard me from the lid of a terra cotta sarcophagus on whose surface the lips, nose, and crossed hands of the deceased have also been molded. Thanks to the miracle of photography, and the convenience of museum postcards, I am able to enjoy this long-gone human's neutral gaze whenever I sit at my kitchen table. My plexiglass napkin holder doubles as a picture frame, and for the past few weeks it has held this image of "Sarcophagus Lid, 'Naturalistic Style,' Ceramic, Northern Cemetery, Beth Shean, Israel, circa 1175 BCE."

Why, you may ask, should I wish to look on the representation of a dead person's face every time I sit down to eat or write? Let us first ask a more basic question: where do we go when we die? Materially speaking, the answer is nowhere; that is, we continue to occupy the same space we always have, just in different forms. Gravity is a powerful force, so where *would* we go? Whether we happen to be reborn in human shape among our furred or feathered friends or settle down to haunt the streams, trees, and soil of our beloved Earth, we are here to stay. Personally, I like the idea of living in a world populated by the ghosts of our ancient aunts and grandmothers. I don't mean to offend the male element out there, either living or dead, but since the dawn of agriculture, the spirits who begin to stir themselves at the Spring Equinox have been mostly female. These girls have a lot to offer—fertility, abundance, prosperity—but they can also be highly dangerous, at least in the Indo-European sphere.

At Samhain, many Wiccans tend to focus on the more recently dead—those they knew personally, as well as those whose names and faces have been made known to them through pictures, documents, and oral histories. Ostara is a good time to remember the more ancient dead—the ones of whom we have no photographs, no written records, nor even any names. Looking into a mirror can help us summon the faces of our distant ancestors up from the depths of the spirit world, but we can also look for them in the faces of those around us. The further we trace our families backward, the more closely the branches of everyone's family trees become intertwined. Imagine you could trace your family back to the Bronze Age, or maybe even further, to the Neolithic, when Near Eastern farmers began to mingle with Europe's indigenous hunter-gatherers. Because the number of your direct ancestors grows exponentially with each genealogical step back, by the time you reach the sixth millennium, the number of your ancestors belonging to that generation far exceeds the world's total population at that time. And that's just you; what about everybody else's ancestors? There simply aren't enough ancestors to go around. The explanation, of course, is that you are descended from people who were already quite closely related to one another, many of them doing double, triple, or even quadruple duty in your family tree, and that you share those distant forebears with everyone else from your hemisphere. If you're of European extraction, you share significant portions of your DNA with everyone else from Europe as well as North Africa, the Middle East, Central Asia, India, and beyond. As the Lakota say, *Mitakuye Oyasin*, "We are all related."

Our ancestors also shared their spiritual beliefs. Along with the technologies involved in tilling the soil, milking the cows, and shearing the sheep, those early farmers brought with them carefully prescribed rituals for petitioning the spirits, who were the source of the ripe seed heads and newborn livestock. Most importantly, it was in the power of those spirits to bestow upon the village newborn humans who would grow up to work the fields, tend the animals, and keep the whole fragile enterprise going. Communion with these spirits who were none other than the dead, was at the heart of the ancient agricultural religion. Because those dead haven't gone anywhere in the millennia since, and because we still rely on water, earth, and the fruits of the Earth for our survival, we, too, would do well to stop and commune with them from time to time. In honoring the dead, we honor ourselves, for, on a molecular level, we *are* the dead.

Samhain is the Witches' New Year, but the Spring Equinox is Nature's New Year. The Earth is coming alive again. This turning point is marked for us First World Moderns by the sprouting of daffodils, a change of wardrobe, and a brighter evening commute, but until quite recently it was a make-or-break kind of season. Labors performed in the spring determined a village's chances of survival the following winter. This was the time to get the spirits of the dead behind one's endeavors or at the very least not to offend the ghosts who haunted the land, for it was they who held the keys to the larders of the Underworld.

Who exactly are these ghosts and what do they have to do with Ostara? We've all heard, ad nauseum, how eggs, specifically Easter eggs, are symbols of fertility, resurrection, and rebirth, but they have also been viewed as convenient receptacles for the soul. Several Russian fairy tales feature a powerful wizard (who has unfortunately come down to us as "evil") who has popped his mortal soul into an egg for safekeeping. An egg could also be a prison for an unwilling spirit: many a Russian fairy tale princess can only be rescued from the clutches of the witch or wizard and restored to the arms of her prince by the breaking of an egg. These themes are quite possibly relics of the shamanism that prevailed in northern climes and eventually blended with the new set of beliefs arriving with the agriculturists from the south.

If things got tough, the hunter-gatherer could get up and head for greener pastures, as it were, while the farmer was shackled to both the land and the dead who lay within it. Because of this period of transition from a highly portable lifestyle to a fixed abode, we have inherited tales of swan maidens and selkies, not quite-human-women who are forced into the mortal realm when their fur robes or feathered cloaks are stolen. What an exciting time it was! If not all things, then at least *more* things were possible in those days than in our own more rational era. Just as huntsman and stay-at-home farmer were crossing over into one another's worlds, the boundaries between human and animal, life and death were more easily overstepped. In those days, a man might marry one of those swan maidens, liminal creatures who would nevertheless keep house, bear children, and even come to love their human husbands. But the swan wife never really belonged to her husband or to the village. As soon as she found the key to the chest wherein lay hidden her magic gown of white feathers, she flew off again to rejoin her sisters, forsaking the tilled fields to resume a life on the wing. She simply could not help herself. But like the selkie, or seal woman, she would always be torn between her mortal family and her wild one, just as many an indigenous, perhaps captive, woman must have been torn between her husband's hearth and the freedom of the forest beyond it.

Yes, I'm sure there's a swan mother somewhere in my family tree, and if there's one in mine, then there must be one in yours too. But wait. We have not yet spoken of the shorn-off branches of the ancestral tree—the ones that blossomed so promisingly but never bore fruit. I am speaking of all those ancient aunties who were born, who aspired to marry and make families of their own, but who died before they got the chance. They are just as important as the grandmothers, and we forget them at our peril. Periodic rituals performed in their honor were an indispensable part of the farmer's year, as important as breaking the ground and sowing the seed.

These girlish spirits go by many names—e.g., *veela*, *rusalka*, *ragana*—and they are as tempestuous as the teenagers they once were. Because all of these girls had succumbed to death while in the full blossom of youth, their unspent fertility was still there for the taking—if you knew how to approach them. One thing they all had in common was their long, unbound hair, the combing of which helped to dispense that untapped fertility. They haunted the wild places just outside the village such as birch groves, streams, or hills. In Russia, living girls repaired to the woods in springtime to dance, sing, make circlets of budding birch and willow, and even swing from the branches, impersonating the playful *rusalki* themselves in order to draw them out. Offerings of linen thread and textiles might be made to the trees where these spirits lived. The Greek *neráïdes* were accomplished spinners and weavers while the rusalki were hopeless at these crafts, stealing white shifts from the clotheslines so they would not have to go naked. A rusalka might even kill for a rag or a torn sleeve, so better to offer them willingly. Roses, parsley, mint, dittany, and hops were pleasing to many of these spirits, while garlic and wormwood kept them at bay.

In old Latvia and Lithuania, a flock of crows might be raganas, who, like witches, gathered periodically on the crests of mountains. Their chieftainess or "Lady Ragana" could appear as almost any animal she liked, but at the Spring Equinox she haunted the waterways as a lovely, long-haired girl. It was this ragana who controlled both the blossoming of the trees and the waxing of the moon. And then there were the tutelary but celibate valkyries in whose honor bonfires were lit in the springtime. In northern Germany, these fires have survived into the twenty-first century as "Easter fires." In the Middle Ages, the birdlike valkyries became "white ladies" who appeared at roadsides, beside streams, or in ruined buildings. When travelers encountered them, the ladies were usually in the process of combing their hair or counting seeds spread out on a white cloth. Often, the white lady offered a boon to the observer, but she might also lure children away with her, into the stream or hillside from which she had emerged. The southern Slavic veelas were active at night, dancing rings around the hapless traveler and eventually dancing him to death. Like the valkyries, however, the veelas might be kindly disposed toward brave warriors, even renouncing veela-dom in order to marry one and bear him children.

Our Canaanite friend from Beth Shean may have known some version of the demonic *lilitu* or *ardat-lili* who preyed upon other women's babies because she had none of her own. You may be more familiar with the ardat-lili as the apocryphal Lilith, Adam's vengeful, childless ex-wife from that murky time before Adam met Eve. Mesopotamian clay plaques show us what the lilitu looked like: a naked, winged young woman with an owl's talons for feet.

❧

When you pay your respects to the Ostara moon this year, spare a thought also to this ragana who has caused it to grow so round and full. Offer a prayer or scrap of cloth to the rusalki, light a fire for the valkyries, and tread carefully over the veelas' dancing grounds. Keep in mind always those women from whom you derived your life directly and those who granted it in a more roundabout way. Soon, dear reader, our own ashes, bones, and essence will be swirling around the planet. Whether we have been mothers, daughters, grandmothers, aunts, fathers, sons, or uncles, we're all going to be around for a long, long time.

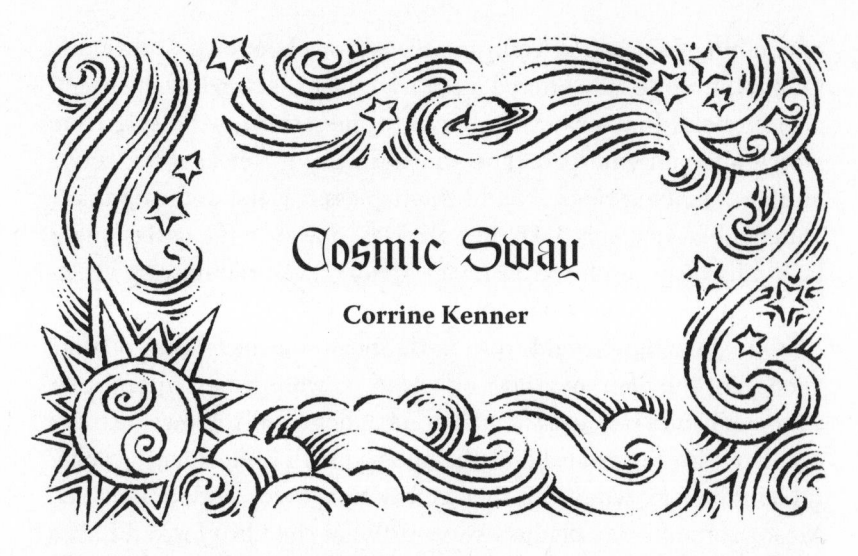

Cosmic Sway

Corrine Kenner

OSTARA MARKS THE FIRST day of spring—and the long-awaited end of winter. For the next few months, the days will grow longer and warmer—but today, on the vernal equinox, there are just as many hours of daylight as night.

It's a time for fresh starts and new beginnings: when the Sun moves into fiery Aries at 6:45 p.m. Eastern time, the astrological year begins. In the process, the Sun will join three planets that are already in the sign.

The Sun meets the Moon first, in a conjunction that accentuates the fiery theme of this year's Aries celebration. The Sun symbolizes the head, and the Moon symbolizes the heart. Whenever the Sun and the Moon are conjoined in a chart, stacked together against the backdrop of the zodiac, they share a single focus and purpose. After all, they have the same world view.

The Sun also joins Uranus, the unpredictable planet of rebellion and revolution, and Mars, the planet of energy and assertion.

Tarot and Astrology

The start of an astrological year is always a grand adventure, and this year, the four planets in fiery Aries are about to embark on a quest for adventure and discovery. They share the same fiery energy. The regal Sun is exalted in fiery Aries, the sign of leadership. The Moon reflects his light. Mars is the god of war that rules the sign, and Uranus can be a rebel fighter for any insurrection or cause that catches his fancy.

Find your tarot deck, and pull the four cards that correspond to the four planets in fiery Aries: the Sun card for the Sun, the High Priestess for the Moon, the Fool for Uranus, and the Emperor for Mars.

The planets always take on the characteristics of a sign when they travel through the zodiac. In this case, you can picture them in a red uniforms—because red is fiery Aries' signature color—and helmets, because Aries rules the head.

If you'd like to add mythology to your visualization, you can also imagine the Sun as Apollo, the High Priestess as Diana, the goddess of the Moon, the Fool as Uranus, the god of the sky, and Mars as Ares, the god of war. In this case, Mars is the group's leader, because he rules the fiery sign of Aries.

Practical Astrology

To align yourself with the planetary energies of Ostara, plot out an adventurous course of intellectual discovery for yourself. What have you always wanted to learn, to do, or to master? Does it seem ridiculous? Uranus, the planet of unexpected developments, wouldn't think so. Will you have to fight to cast off old limits and establish yourself in the field? Mars, the warrior god, will be at your side. Can you resolve any disparity between your head and your heart? Now's the time, when the Sun and the Moon are joined in fiery Aries. This is the time for executive decisions. You can be as bold and daring as any other planet in the action sign.

Planetary Positions

The Sun is in fiery Aries, the first sign of the zodiac, symbolizing new beginnings, new adventures, and new opportunities. The Sun will enter a more grounded phase when it moves into Taurus on April 20.

The Moon is also in fiery Aries, which makes everyone, on some level, yearn for individual freedom and self-expression.

Mercury is in watery Pisces—a difficult placement, because all of that mutable, flowing water tends to wash away the precision that Mercury craves in thought and communication. It's temporary, though: the fast-moving messenger planet moves into clear-headed Aries on March 30, and earthy Taurus on April 14.

Venus in earthy Taurus, the sign that it rules, which puts the planet of love and attraction in her most affectionate mood. Venus will enter clever, quick-witted Gemini on April 11.

Mars is in fiery Aries, which is the warrior planet's own sign, too. Mars has free rein to pursue its own agenda here: enthusiasm and energy run unabated. Mars' energy might not slow down, but it will definitely be more grounded when the planet moves into earthy Taurus on March 31.

Jupiter is still moving backward through Leo. In the fiery sign of creativity and self-expression, the giant planet is free to offer good fortune and goodwill toward anyone who enters his sphere of influence.

Saturn is retrograde in fiery Sagittarius, the sign of adventure and exploration. Saturn's sense of discipline is a useful ally if you're trying to master a new skill—especially if you're working on your own.

The generational outer planets remain in the same signs:

Uranus is in fiery Aries.

Neptune is in watery Pisces.

Pluto is in earthy Capricorn.

Planets in Aspect

At the moment the Sun enters Aries, the Moon and Saturn are in a harmonious trine, highlighting the best of both worlds. The businesslike Aries Moon is closely aligned with the Sun, while Saturn in fiery Sagittarius is in a position to capitalize on any opportunities that come along.

Saturn, however, is also in an uncomfortable square with Neptune in Pisces, which could lead to moments of doubt and unreasonable fear.

Don't worry. Look instead to Mercury and Neptune, which are conjoined in Pisces. That's a combination that lends itself to flights of fancy and active imagination.

Take a deep breath, and you might even find that luck is on your side. Jupiter, in fiery Leo, is in a harmonious trine with Uranus in fiery Aries. Be open to unusual or unorthodox possibilities for advancement and success.

Phases of the Moon

April 4: A Full Moon in airy Libra, with the Sun in fiery Aries, emphasizes the need for grace and equanimity in relationships. The Moon's quiet energy could give you the strength you need to keep your impulsivity in check, even if your first instinct is to lash out at people who offend you.

Tonight's Full Moon is accompanied by a total lunar eclipse. The Earth will be positioned between the Sun and the Moon, and the Moon will pass through Earth's shadow, or umbra. The eclipse will be visible throughout most of North America, South America, eastern Asia, and Australia. Eclipses always bring news of growth and change. Lunar eclipses herald personal developments, while solar eclipses signify public events.

April 18: A New Moon, along with the Sun in fiery Aries, heralds a new cycle of individuality and personal growth. Set your sights on a new adventure or two: make definite plans, complete with a series of step-by-step goals and objectives that will help you measure your progress.

May 3: Still waters run deep during a Full Moon in watery Scorpio, with the Sun across the zodiac in earthy Taurus.

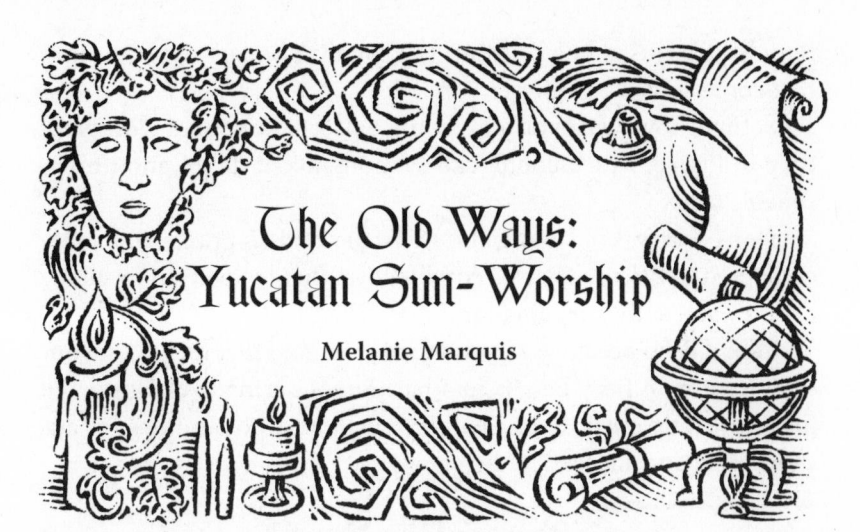

The Old Ways:
Yucatan Sun-Worship

Melanie Marquis

THE SPRING EQUINOX IS a time of magick and festivity in many cultures. It represents an annual tipping point, after which the days finally grow longer than the nights. Around the world, the sun takes center stage at many Spring Equinox celebrations. Solar deities are honored, and ceremonies and rituals are often performed outdoors in the sunshine and open air. In Mexico, "The Land of Eternal Sunshine," the Spring Equinox has been celebrated for thousands of years.

Today, hundreds of thousands of people flock to Mexico's most celebrated sacred sites to witness the rising of the Spring Equinox sun and to absorb the powerful solar rays. It's traditional for the celebrants to dress in white garments, with perhaps a red ribbon, scarf, or sash. The white clothing is believed to better absorb the sunshine, which is thought to be infused at the time of the equinox with especially potent magickal properties able to heal and energize the human body. The red accessories represent energy. Many participants bring quartz crystals to hold skyward, capturing the special power of the equinox sunlight. At the Pyramid of the Sun in Teotihuacan, people climb to the top of the structure in large numbers, holding their hands up to the sky in order to absorb the powerful magick of the sun. At the Temple of Kukulkan, crowds gather to witness the play of light and shadow on the enormous structure as the equinox sun progresses on its daily course. At architectural wonders and everyday community gathering places alike, the Spring Equinox brings celebration, prayer, ritual, dance, and music as people get together to enjoy the magickal sunlight. In many aspects, these modern festivals are very different from the much older Spring Equinox rites held by the ancient Mayans and Aztecs who inhabited the land prior to the Spanish conquest. If we look to the heart of these ceremonies, however, comparing the old ways to the surviving modern traditions, we find at the core a common and enduring feeling of gratitude and awe towards the sun's magnificent power, a feeling Pagans all around the world can understand and share.

The ancient Mayans and Aztecs understood the importance of the sun in relation to their own survival. Their agricultural societies depended on the accurate timing of farming practices, and the Spring Equinox was utilized as a point of reference to indicate the appropriate time to plant the new season's crops. In fact, the equinox was so important that it even figured into the architecture. The Temple of Kukulkan in Chichen Itza, for instance, is oriented so that the sunlight on the Vernal Equinox illuminates the triangular tiles of the pyramid in such a way that the play of light and shadows create the illusion of a large, undulating snake slithering down from the top of the pyramid toward the ground. The base of the pyramid features carvings of giant snake heads, and when the sunlight travels down to the bottom of the structure, the body of the great "snake" is joined with one of the heads, completing the illusion. It's believed that at the point when the snake is whole, the Earth becomes fertilized. The "snake" is a representation of Kukulkan, also known as Gukumatz, or the "War Serpent." Kukulkan was symbolized by a feathered serpent, much like the Aztecs' Quetalcoatl. Today, thousands of visitors come to the pyramid to witness the spectacular sight and to pay tribute to the glorious sun, just as they did in the time of the ancient Mayans. Dances are performed, rituals are enacted, and prayers are made to the four directions and to the elemental forces, continuing a tradition that dates back more than 2,500 years.

Not all ancient Mesoamerican Spring Equinox traditions have been continued, and with good reason. Like many other early polytheistic cultures, the ancient Mayans and Aztecs engaged in both human and animal sacrifice, ritual practices with which our modern sensibilities assuredly do not agree. Warriors in Mayan society were closely tied to the sun god, with survival and victory dependent on the heavenly body and on the deity therein represented. Sacrifices were made to the sun god throughout the year, with prominent ceremonies held at the start of December and also in March, to coincide with the Spring Equinox.

At an armory called the House of Eagles, a ceremony called the *Nauhollin* or "Four Motions"—a reference to the sun's trembling rays—was held. Human victims, usually war captives, were sacrificed within this House of Eagles, offered up as gifts to the sun god of the warriors. The victims were decorated with eagle feathers and white plumes, and they were given a staff to present to the sun god upon their deaths. It was expected that the victims would beg the deity to grant favors to the sun's living sons still on earth.

Larger Mesoamerican ceremonies dedicated to the sun involved nearly everyone in the community. At the Tlacaxipehualiztli, the Aztec's Spring Equinox festival, the solar deity Xipe Totec, a god of vegetation, was honored with extravagant (and rather gruesome) ceremony. One person was chosen to represent Xipe Totec. They were given special clothes to wear and were expected to impersonate the god for a full forty days preceding the festival. At the main event, the mock Xipe Totec, along with countless others, each representing a "rival" deity, were sacrificed and often skinned in a ritual enactment of Xipe Totec's death and rebirth. Xipe Totec was called "The Flayed One," as he was depicted as having an exterior layer of skin that could be shed and sacrificed to the benefit of the earth's fertility. Associated with seeds, his flayed aspect is a representation of a germinating seed that loses its outer "skin" just before it bursts into growth. It was said that Xipe Totec flayed himself and shed his own skin in order to feed humanity. Through the sacrificial slaying of victims, and through the subsequent wearing of the skins by priests who then became as the god himself, it was hoped that Xipe Totec's favor would be won. Offerings of corn were also provided in hopes that the sun would share its blessings and its power with the people.

Ancient Mesoamerican rituals definitely included some violent and grisly aspects, just as we find examples of human sacrifice in early European and early African polytheistic cultures, as well. It's fortunate that humanity has outgrown such practices, and that our traditions have been adapted accordingly, preserving the aspects where we honor nature, but moving forward from having to act cruelly in order to do so. Our magick now reflects a more positive outlook, a trust in nature's ability to provide for her people regardless of the rituals we perform or don't perform. People still gather throughout Mexico on the Spring Equinox to watch the sunrise, hold their arms to the sky, say their prayers, and welcome in the awesome solar power. People still dance and enjoy group rituals. People still get together to offer to the sun their thanks, and to receive the sun's blessings in return. Though our methods of doing so have evolved, beneath the surface of both ancient Mesoamerican Spring Equinox rites and our own modern practices lies an understanding and respect for humanity's utter dependence on that ball of fiery, glowing gases we call the sun. Taking time out at the Spring Equinox to honor natural cycles, express gratitude through simple offerings, and absorb some of those powerful springtime solar rays can lead to a lot of magickal fun, and you'll be carrying on a tradition that has transformed yet endured through thousands of years of endless change.

References:

Ancient-Mythology.com. "Kulkukan." Accessed October 13, 2013. http://www.ancient-mythology.com/mayan/kukulkan.php.

Baird, David, and Shane Christensen, Christine Delsol, and Joy Hepp. *Frommer's Mexico.* Hoboken, NJ: John Wiley and Sons, 2011.

de Landa, Diego. *Yucatan Before and After the Conquest.* Translated by William Gates. Baltimore: The Maya Society, 1937. Accessed October 13, 2013. http://www.sacred-texts.com/nam/maya /ybac/ybac00.htm.

Spence, Lewis. *The Civilization of Ancient Mexico.* 1912. Reprint. New York: Cambridge University Press, 2011.

Students of the World. "Spring Equinox in Teotihuacan." Accessed October 13, 2013. http://www.studentsoftheworld.org /signature-projects/spring-equinox-in-teotihuacan.

Feasts and Treats

Ellen Dugan

AH, SPRING HAS ARRIVED! The grass is greening up, the snow is melting away, and the flowers are pushing their way up and out! The egg is a traditional symbol for many religions of spring, rebirth, and new life. Ostara dishes classically feature eggs and green vegetables, just as you would expect. Try these springy recipes out for yourself, but expect that you will want to make them all year long.

Spinach and Feta Quiche

Quiche is a favorite of mine. This protein-packed dish is tasty, and by adding the egg substitute, you can cut back on the cholesterol.

Prep time: 20 minutes
Cook time: 45–50 minutes
Serves: 6

1 pre-made pie crust
½ cup low fat feta cheese
1 10-ounce package frozen spinach, thawed and squeezed
1 teaspoon dried minced onions
2 eggs
½ cup egg substitute (such as "Egg Beaters")

1 cup low-fat milk
Pinch nutmeg
Salt and pepper to taste

Preheat oven to 350 degrees F. Roll pie dough out into pie plate and crimp the edges. Sprinkle feta cheese over the pie crust.

To make the filling, stir the (thawed and squeezed of all liquid) spinach together with the minced dried onions with a fork. Add the spinach mixture to the prepared pie plate.

Whisk together the eggs, egg substitute, milk, and nutmeg in a medium bowl. Season with salt and pepper, if desired. Pour egg mixture over the filling in the crust. Set quiche on a baking sheet and bake for 45 to 50 minutes or until the top is golden brown and the center is set. Refrigerate leftovers.

Note: Adding ½ cup egg substitute to this quiche is the equivalent of 2 extra eggs. I prefer using an egg substitute like Egg Beaters to make this quiche fluffier and thicker without adding more cholesterol. Also, always sprinkle any cheese added to a quiche over the crust, not the top of the pie. This will keep the crust from getting soggy and the cheese from burning on the top.

Variations: Use finely chopped cooked broccoli and shredded cheddar cheese for a different but equally yummy version.

Asparagus Casserole

My mother-in-law serves this dish every spring. This is a wonderful casserole, and the sliced hard-boiled eggs on top are appropriate for most any Ostara celebration.

Prep time: 30 minutes
Cook time: 30–35 minutes
Serves: 6–8

¾ cup Ritz cracker crumbs
2 cans cut asparagus, drained
3 hard-boiled eggs, sliced
2 tablespoons margarine

2 cups milk
A few drops of Tabasco sauce
2½ tablespoons flour
¼ lb. Velveeta cheese
½ teaspoon salt
Dash of pepper

Spray a two-quart casserole dish with nonstick spray. Put crackers in a large ziplock bag and crush them with a rolling pin. Sprinkle in a few of the cracker crumbs in the bottom of the dish. Add a layer of asparagus, then a layer of hard-boiled eggs, then asparagus again, and finally the remaining egg slices.

In a saucepan over medium heat, melt the margarine or butter and add the flour, stirring until smooth. Gradually add the milk. Bring to a boil and cook for 1 minute. Add the Tabasco, cheese, salt, and pepper and stir until the cheese is melted and the sauce is smooth. Pour the sauce evenly over the asparagus and eggs in the casserole dish. Top with remaining cracker crumbs. Bake at 350 degrees F for 30 to 35 minutes.

Ellen's Low-Fat Applesauce Carrot Cake

This is a lighter and delicious version of carrot cake—it does not even need frosting! It's also great to cut up into squares and pack into school lunches.

Prep time: 20 minutes
Cook time: 25–30 minutes
Serves: 8–10

1 cup all-purpose flour
1 cup whole-wheat flour
½ teaspoon baking soda
1 teaspoon baking powder
¼ teaspoon salt
½ teaspoon cinnamon
¼ teaspoon nutmeg

1 cup sugar
¼ cup egg substitute (or 1 egg)
2 tablespoons vegetable oil
1 cup unsweetened applesauce
1 tablespoon orange juice
1 tablespoon vanilla
1 large carrot, grated
¼ cup shredded coconut (optional)

Mix dry ingredients with sugar. Mix liquid ingredients, including the applesauce. Combine the wet and dry ingredients. Fold in grated carrot and coconut. Bake in a 9 × 9 or 7 × 11-inch pan, coated with nonstick cooking spray at 350 degrees F for 25 to 30 minutes. Cut into squares.

The Ostara Bunny Mimosa

A springtime classic with a twist. This pretty drink has a touch of Grand Marnier for a wicked kick!
   Prep time: 3 minutes
   Serves: 1–4

A bottle of good quality champagne or Prosecco
1 quart of orange juice
Grand Marnier orange liqueur

Pre-chill all ingredients. Fill each wineglass or champagne flute half full with ice and pour orange juice about halfway up. Slowly pour in the champagne or Prosecco. Pour a splash of Grand Marnier Liqueur on top. Garnish with a slice of strawberry and serve these mimosas for breakfast or brunch. Happy spring!

Crafty Crafts

Lexa Olick

OSTARA IS A TIME of growth and new life. The world reawakens around us just as we ourselves may reawaken into a new life. The weather begins to warm around us, filling us with a need for accomplishment and reflection. A popular symbol of Ostara has always been the egg. It reflects the potential that each of us have. An egg hatches and symbolizes that something new is about to happen and that our goals are about to become reality.

Egg Bouquets

Egg bouquets are a beautiful floral arrangement in the shape of Ostara. During this festival, eggs are usually decorated as symbols of fertility. To ensure a rich harvest, eggs are gathered together in baskets and bowls because they are a symbol of life. Not only do they represent rebirth, but also our future plans. Spring is the beginning of a new life and we now embark on that journey.

The egg is a universal symbol of life, creation, and resurrection, but so is the blossoming of a flower. The two can easily be combined for a beautiful display of life and rebirth. These striking, egg-shaped bouquets will add a burst of color to your home.

Supplies
4⅞-inch tall Styrofoam egg
Assorted silk flowers
8-inch grapevine wreath
Aerosol glitter spray

Before You Begin: Larger Styrofoam eggs are a seasonal product that will start to show up in craft stores in late February, but the smaller Styrofoam eggs are easy to find all year round. For that reason, I recommend using a 4⅞-inch tall Styrofoam egg. As you add your silk flowers, the egg will grow anyway. You should end up with nearly an 8-inch tall egg to display in your home. If you still wish to choose a larger egg shape, add the flowers first and then find a larger grapevine wreath to fit at the end.

Choosing Your Flowers: Select your silk flowers wisely. Some flowers associated with Ostara are violets, crocus, dogwood, forsythia, hyacinth, lilac, and olive blossoms. Pastels are considered very spring colors, but colors specifically linked to Ostara are yellow, purple, and green. Purple is a color of faith and trust. Violets are a purple flower linked to tranquility and peace. They offer protection from evil and bring about good luck. Lilacs as well are purple in color and are associated with protection and exorcism. Hyacinths are mainly purple, but you can also find them in mixed colors of yellow, blue, and white. It is a popular spring flower connected to luck, happiness, protection, and peace.

White is a color of purity. Olive blossoms are white and are associated with healing, peace, and protection. The most common color for dogwood flowers are white, but they can also be found in shades of pink and red. Its blossoms are generally used for protection.

Yellow is a sign of wisdom. Forsythias have beautiful yellow petals that can brighten up a room. You are not limited to use a single type of flower, but rather a combination of many. Depending on how you arrange them, your egg bouquets can be striped, dotted, or solid in color.

Making the Egg: Once you have gathered the silk flowers of your choice, it is then time to attach them to your egg. To begin, trim the flower heads off of their stalks, but leave about a 1½-inch length of stem.

Slowly push the stem into the foam egg until it can't go in any further. Continue to push more flowers into the foam until the entire egg is covered. However, you can leave the very bottom of the egg empty so that it sits more steadily on its own. Feel free to alternate flowers for a mixture of color. Set the egg aside once done.

Adding the Nest: Place newspaper down in a well-ventilated area. Lay the grapevine wreath on top of the newspaper and spray with a coat of glitter. Let it dry at least 10 minutes in between coats if you need another layer of glitter. Make sure to turn your wreath around so that you cover it from all angles. Let the wreath sit undisturbed for 20 minutes or until it is fully dry.

When the wreath is ready, place the egg bouquet inside it. If desired, you can weave more silk flowers into the grapevine. The grapevine looks like a nest when your egg bouquet is nestled inside it.

An egg bouquet may look great by itself, but it's even better in a group! For a more impressive display, make several egg bouquets and line them up together.

Time to Complete: About 40 minutes. It doesn't take long to arrange the flowers onto the foam egg, but it may take up to 30 minutes longer for the glitter to dry on the grapevine wreath.

Cost: About $25.00

Variation: Egg bouquets are very elegantly displayed in nests, but there are other ways to arrange a bouquet. Egg bouquets can easily be gathered into a decorative vase instead of relying on a nest. The foam eggs can easily be inserted on top of chopsticks, but I recommend painting those chopsticks first. Lay down sheets of newspaper in a well-ventilated room and spray paint your chopsticks in a color of your choosing. After waiting at least 10 minutes for the

paint to dry, flip the chopsticks over and spray a coat of paint onto the other side. Once they're dry, apply a generous amount of craft glue onto the end of the chopstick and insert it into the bottom of the egg. Continue to insert flowers just as instructed above. This type of egg bouquet looks better in a group of three or more. Once you have created enough stick egg bouquets, place them in a nice decorative vase. To securely hold them inside the vase, fill the surrounding area with either brightly colored jelly beans or marbles. It's good to have variety, so use both egg bouquets in a nest and in a vase to decorate your Ostara display!

Sustainable Spring: A Clean Sweep

Natalie Zaman

THE SILENCE AND STARKNESS of winter is not wholly empty. A time of introspection and incubation, there is a sense of anticipation that intensifies as the days pass, the light grows, and nature unfolds herself. One day, you become certain that something is different. You can hear it; the scritch of tiny feet on frost, the flap of a wing, a twitter and a warble, and then, a full-blown chorus. Nothing announces spring's arrival like bird song. And just like a snap of cold is welcome after a long, languorous summer, so the sun that warms the body and birdly melodies that cheers the soul are welcome changes.

Spring is also a time to throw open the doors and windows, let in fresh air, and begin the season's annual call to clean. And although a good spring clear-out will spruce up your space, you may still feel winter's sleepiness clinging to the energy of your home. This calls for a scouring of an esoteric nature—which can be done with some help from our fine, feathered friends.

Many Native American traditions use smudge fans to cleanse energy, spaces, objects, and even people. Gathering naturally shed feathers is animal friendly and green (they can be released back into the environment when you are finished with them). Use them to create a smudge fan for clearing away unwanted and tired energies.

This work also presents the opportunity to be out and about in the fresh air—a welcome treat after long months indoors.

Make It Your Own!
You will need:

Naturally shed feathers

White ribbon to bind the feathers together; the white color indicates the purity of your intentions and, of course, cleanliness

Before making your smudge fan, clean the feathers you will be using. Remove any debris and dirt, and then wash each in a mixture of salt and water (water with three measures of salt, stirred clockwise for invocation) to purify them of any lingering energies. Blow on the feathers to dry them. This last step will imprint them with your energy.

Hold the feathers in your hand so that all the quill points are even. You can use any number of feathers for your fan, but magical numbers—8 for the sabbats, 4 for the elements, seasons, and directions, 3 for the Goddess, or even 1 if you're working with a particularly large feather—add another layer of significance to your work.

Tie the feathers together at the quills with a generous length of ribbon, then wrap the ribbon around the quills to cover them. Make three knots to bind the fan. As you wrap and knot, speak or think an incantation of intention:

> *A clean sweep I make,*
> *From that which I take.*

Now you are ready to smudge. In addition to the fan, you will need incense or a smudge stick (a bundle of herbs used for clearing energies). Take your environment and needs into consideration when choosing what incense or herbs to burn—dragon's blood dispels negativity, lavender is good for cleansing, patchouli brings peace. Use your favorite reference to determine which you will use.

To smudge, light your incense or herb bundle and keep it in a burner or bowl that will catch the ashes and live embers. Using the fan, gently sweep the smoke over, under, and around the area, object, or person you are cleansing. It is important to visualize the smoke doing its work. Imagine that you are looking at your subject through a murky glass window. As you smudge, see it change: watch any dullness fall away as the smoke touches it; your subject will become clearer and brighter to you. Keep smudging until you feel that all of the cloudy energy is gone.

When you are done with your fan, take the feathers back to where you collected them and release them back into nature. If you gathered the feathers far from your home, don't stress about going back to the exact spot; naturally shed feathers can be released anywhere outdoors. Leave the ribbon on a tree branch (birds use materials like this to build their nests) with these words:

Feathers to sweep,
Ribbon to wind.
Your help my house to keep,
My gift, your nest to bind.
Thank you, friend, and blessed be!

A last word on incantations: Use any pre-written incantations, invocations, spells, and meditations as a beginning. As you become comfortable with ritual, try composing your own. Words are stronger and hold greater meaning when they come directly from the heart of the speaker.

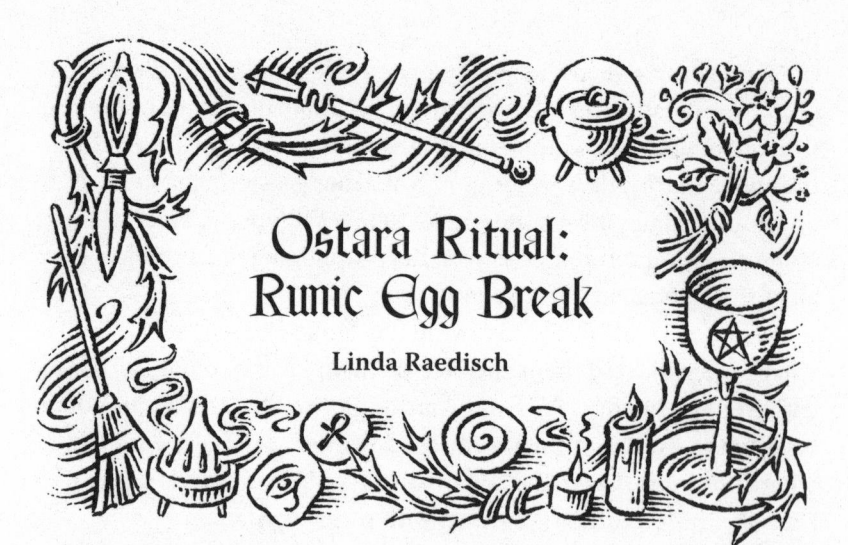

Ostara Ritual: Runic Egg Break

Linda Raedisch

WHILE THIS RITUAL EMPLOYS runes, a very recent development in the scheme of things, it is designed to help the coven or solitary practitioner delve deep into our prehistoric roots. You can substitute other symbols, such as the Greek or Semitic alphabet, as long as you are familiar with the letters' magical attributes. This is a communion not with the recently deceased but with the ancient dead, those whose essence has long ago been swirled into the world around us. It is an acknowledgement of all those who have gone before us, especially those who died young, without having borne any offspring. It was to their ghosts the early farmers appealed in the springtime, urging them to pass over the fields and dispense their unused gifts into the soil and the crops. These teenagers of the spirit world could be a bit tetchy, so they were always approached with caution.

The first part of the ritual takes place indoors, the second outdoors if at all possible. If you have a garden, you will want to ask the spirits to scatter a little magic over your freshly turned vegetable and flower beds. If your coven has its own space in the woods or fields, you will want to ask for blessings upon the wild things that grow there.

The "Maiden" in this ritual is not invoked in the sense of "Maiden, Mother, Crone," for the spirit in question will never step into the roles of mother or crone. She is a girl who has died with her allotted gifts unspent. She is Persephone (called fondly by the Greeks, Kórē, "maiden"), daughter of the vegetal goddess Demeter, drawn before her time into the cold, dark kingdom of the dead but released now to play in the fields and to bask in the glow of the spring moon as she once did. She will always be a girl, but she is also a force of nature. If you are a solitary practitioner, then you will, of course, be playing the role yourself, even if you're no longer girlish! If you are a coven, then you should select either the person who fits the description of teenage girl most closely or who feels strongly drawn to play the role, even if it is a male. It should be someone with a spring in her (or his) step, someone who's ready to have some fun after a long winter shut up in the Underworld. Don't worry; the ritual garments I have suggested can transform almost anyone into a Maiden if the player takes the job seriously enough.

This ritual includes instructions for both solitaries and covens with children on the premises and those without. If you're worried the spirits might be offended when the kids end up with their offerings, remember that children are only recently arrived from the spirit world and are therefore the perfect emissaries.

The Items Needed for Maiden

Here's what you'll need. For the Maiden's ritual garb, a veil such as a large, see-through scarf in any color but black—she's not a widow, after all. Also, black can make the wearer invisible to the spirits and tonight we want to attract their attention. The scarf should have a long fringe to simulate the long, unbound hair of the mermaid, rusalka, veela, nereid, valkyrie, ragana, or other virginal fertility spirit. If you prefer, the enactor may wear a simple mask— nothing scary or garish!—and wear a hat with trailing ribbons that swish when she walks. Of course, if your Maiden happens to be a long-haired, nubile young woman, she may prefer to come as she is. If no one in your coven wants the role or if you, as a solitary, feel uncomfortable performing it, there is a third option: a doll. In fact, in eastern and southeastern Europe, many fertility rituals can and do involve dolls.

The next item on the list is a dozen eggs. On these you will paint or draw your runes. Yes, I know there are more than a dozen runes, but twelve, as you know, is one of our most sacred numbers, and eggs have been coming in batches of twelve for so long that I feel it would be wrong to mess with the tradition. If you find that a dozen eggs are not enough for your purposes, go ahead and up it to two dozen. As for which runes to use, choose those that correspond most closely to the neighborhood where you will be presenting your offerings, that kitchen garden or sacred space in the woods, and what you would like to reap from it.

Ask yourself what spirits you might have encountered and inadvertently offended there. The tree runes are obvious candidates and can be used to represent other species in addition to oak, ash, thorn, birch, yew, and pine. Cen or kenaz (pine) can also carry the meaning of a flame and might represent the fire pit at the heart of your campground or your own hearth at home—there are important spirits dwelling there too! The runes for ice and hail can represent water, that is, any streams, ponds, lakes, or reservoirs nearby. These are favorite haunts of ghostly maidens. The runes for "cattle" and "horse" can stand for any domestic animals on the premises, while uruz, "aurochs," or the Anglo-Saxon ior, "beaver," can stand for the wild fauna who live there. If you are not runecrafty, you can still draw simple pictures of trees, flowers, rivers, birds, etc., but do not spend too much time on the artwork since these eggs will soon be broken. If there are children who need to be entertained the next morning, boil the eggs before marking them. If there are no children, leave them raw.

Items Needed in General

For each participant (minus the Maiden) you will need a slender branch of something that has recently come back to life: birch, pussy willow, forsythia, crabapple, or cherry, depending on what zone you live in.

And now: a word about the moon. Mirrors, still waters, and other reflective surfaces are windows to the world of the dead which overlaps our own. The full moon is the biggest and brightest mirror of all, so if it's at all possible, try to enact this ritual under the full moon closest to the Spring Equinox. (Yes, I know there's a full two weeks between Ostara and the first full moon of spring this year.) If this is not possible, hang a large round mirror in the branches of a tree inside your sacred grove or garden and gather your branches ahead of time so the flowers, leaves, or buds will at least have been washed by the light of the full moon. If they're no longer flowering, that's okay; they'll be "charged up" and therefore useful in the weaving of a magical atmosphere. Of course, it's nice if you can cut your branches the same night that you use them and cover everyone with a confetti-like shower of petals, but it is not obligatory.

The Ritual

For the first part of the ritual you are also going to need kitchen facilities, a clean dish towel that you won't mind never seeing again, scissors, and two large bowls. For the second part you will need one feather large enough that it can be easily found and picked up off the ground as well as white or pale green taper candles, one for each participant including the Maiden. If there's no danger of setting the surrounding vegetation on fire, and if you're sure they'll have burnt down before any children arrive on the scene, you can also offer tea lights, votive candles, and/or stick incense. And if there are children, you'll probably want to throw in some chocolate eggs and other treats among your offerings.

Let's begin! Place the marked eggs in one of the large bowls and cover the bowl with the towel. Remember, these are cooked eggs for the family coven, raw eggs for non-parenting covens. Enter the Maiden, who will remain mute throughout the ritual. She sits herself before the bowl and waits for each coven member to approach her in turn. As they do so, she regards them through mask or veil, then reaches under the towel, draws out an egg, and presents it to the supplicant. (If you are a solitary, then you are, of course, presenting the eggs to yourself.) The supplicant looks to see which symbol she has received, for this should offer some clue as to how she might have trespassed against the spirits in the past year. Did she fill in a chipmunk hole while gardening? Defile a stream or pond? Block the path of a deer, fox, or other landwight when she put up a garden fence? After reflecting thus upon the egg, the supplicant breaks it into the second bowl and discards the shell. Whatever spirit she may have inadvertently imprisoned has now been freed. (If you are working with boiled eggs, each supplicant should place his or hers unbroken into the second bowl and add to them any other offerings they have prepared.)

When everyone has had a turn, the raw eggs, or at least a token amount thereof, must be cooked into an omelet or eggy pancake. It should be large enough to cut into twelve equal portions, or one portion for each participant (minus the Maiden). Place the portions in the first bowl and cut up the dish towel into twelve equal strips. The Maiden will carry the bowl of offerings, the feather, and one of the tapers, which she should light now. Everyone else will carry an unlit taper, a strip of towel, and a branch each. Got everything? Let's go outside!

When everyone has assembled in the sacred space, the Maiden will toss or blow the feather into the air with everyone keeping a close eye on where it lands. There, the first supplicant should stick her branch into the earth, tie the strip of towel around it, and place beside it the slice of omelet (or the hard-boiled egg) as well as any other gifts for the spirits. If there are incense sticks or votive candles, she should light them in the flame of the Maiden's taper. When the supplicant is finished, the Maiden tosses the feather again and the whole process is repeated. If you are a dancing coven, feel free to dance from featherfall to featherfall. You should at least step lively, for you are helping to wake the earth. When all of the offerings have been distributed, all participants should gather before the mirror or facing the moon. The Maiden now lights everyone's tapers from her own. It is time now to form a candlelit procession back to the kitchen to cook up and consume the rest of those eggs. The Maiden may now unveil. She is herself again and free to speak.

Family covens: It's egg hunt time! When the kids wake up, set them loose to find their goodies. Encourage them to smack one another's eggs together to break the shells, then you can teach them how to make egg salad.

Notes

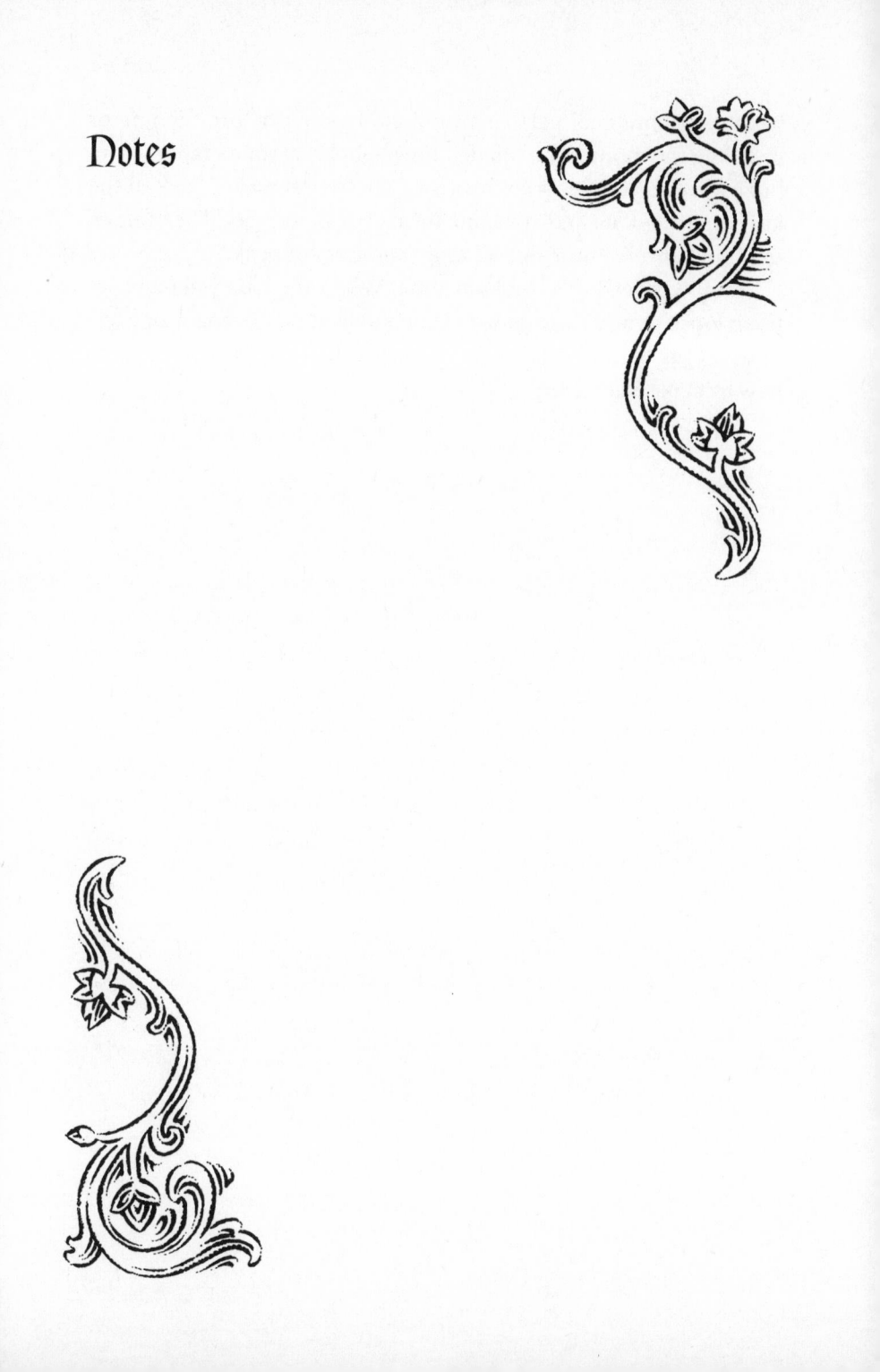

Beltane

May Day

Thuri Calafia

"Over here, Seamus," the raven-haired young woman called out to her companion, her deep blue eyes surveying the multicolored spring flowers in a small clearing in the trees. "There are hundreds of them! And they're beautiful!"

A tall young man with flame-red hair came rushing to Caitlin's side. "Indeed, my darling," he said, his eyes locked on her breasts, "they are beautiful."

Caitlin giggled, blushing slightly. "The flowers, Seamus," she said, sweeping her other hand to show him the scene before them.

"Those are nice, too," he said, slipping an arm around Caitlin's waist. She laughed and stepped away, then took his hand when his brow furrowed and led him into the center of the little grove.

"Come on now," she said, setting down the large baskets she'd been carrying. "We have to collect them, for tomorrow's celebration."

"Aye," he agreed, "for tomorrow. Which means we have all night."

Caitlin laughed as Seamus moved closer. "I suppose you're right," she said, her voice becoming thick with emotion as she touched his arm and raised her eyes to meet his. "And with this many, we won't need to look further. These will fill our baskets with much to spare."

"Let's crush a few, then," Seamus said with sly smile, slipping both arms around Caitlin's waist this time. "I mean, how else would we know if they smell good?" She looked into his clear hazel eyes, which were shining with desire for her, as her own body began to sing with an equal desire.

"True enough, my love," she said as Seamus pulled her closer. "For surely it would be insulting to the gods to bring in the May with imperfect flowers."

"And we must bring in the May, sweet Caitlin," he said, leaning in for a kiss, "in the most perfect way we can."

Bringing in May by gathering flowers, couple by couple, like the one in the story above, was one of the most beloved traditions of Beltane in times past. Although it isn't common anymore, those of us with a little silver in our hair may remember a tradition of giving "May baskets" to our sweethearts, friends, and teachers anonymously when we were kids. Those of us with more curious natures would leave the baskets, and then ring the doorbell and go hide so we could watch the recipient of our carefully gathered flowers smile and pick them up from their front porches.

There is some speculation regarding when Beltane actually occurs, ranging from May Eve, April 30, to the first Full Moon after May 1. In *A Witches' Bible*, Janet and Stewart Farrar state Beltane means "May Day," but Raven Grimassi, in *The Encyclopedia of Wicca and Witchcraft*, says Beltane means "bright fire." The Beltane Fire Society says it may also mean "sacred fire." Indeed, this was when farmers drove their cattle between two fires (called "need fires") to bring luck, fertility, and an abundant milk yield for the year, so holding these fires sacred makes sense. In addition, many of our ancestors would walk between (or jump over) these fires for similar blessings. As the ancient Celts only truly acknowledged summer and winter, Beltane heralded summer and the season of fertility. At this time, the very air is charged with excitement, sexual energy, and passion, which affects animals, crops, and more significantly, us humans.

In those ancient times, while the young people of the villages were away gathering flowers, the more adult members of the family would gather in the freshly plowed fields and bring fertility to the land by making love in sacred orgies. Babies born of these unions were often considered blessed, as they brought the energy of fertility, joy, and summer's blessings to their families with their very conception. The king and queen would secretly steal away to celebrate by making love privately. In those days, the queen represented the land, so the energy raised by the royal lovemaking (and that of their subjects) would bless the land and the people with abundance and fertility. The gods and goddesses of love, lust, and fertility were honored on this holiday, just as they are honored by many Pagans today.

One such goddess is the Greek Goddess Aphrodite. The Farrars, in *The Witches' Goddess*, speak of Aphrodite as being, "in the purest sense," a goddess of love, eroticism, beauty, desire, and passion. Unpredictable, uninhibited, and single-minded, "She was all these things without qualm or apology." This purity they speak of is in the sense of this love goddess being unadulterated, undiluted sexual energy; both desire and fulfillment. Even her name speaks of her power to seduce, as the word *aphrodiasic* comes from the word *aphrodisiakos*, which comes from the Greek "Aphrodite," according to *Funk and Wagnells Standard Dictionary of the English Language*. In *The Grandmother of Time*, Z. Budapest says the word *April* is derived from the Roman word *Aprilus*, which appears to be rooted in the verb *aperire*, which means, "to open." This again speaks to the idea of Beltane occurring in April—the month belonging to Aphrodite. Sadly, this incredibly powerful and alluring, often wise, and benevolent goddess is still often seen as little more than a dumb blonde, even in the Pagan subculture. This is a dishonor to her, as well as a perpetuation of the lie that owning our sexuality somehow diminishes, rather than elevates, our power as people.

Whoever our personal gods of fertility and passion are, they can teach us much about our own sexuality if we take the time to listen. Meditations and other inner work designed to discover ourselves in this way can be extremely rewarding and can help us connect to these archetypal energies both within and without, especially at this special and sacred time of year. For Beltane, like Samhain, is a time when the veils are thin, and the truth of self and spirit is easily accessible if only one opens to the energy.

Beltane Traditions

Probably the most popular and common Beltane tradition is that of dancing the maypole, a beautiful symbolic Great Rite that honors the Sacred Marriage of the Lord and the Lady. Other holiday traditions include, but are not limited to: other types of symbolic Great Rites, walking between two fires or leaping fires for blessings and luck, garden blessings, feasting on symbolically and erotically shaped foods (which may or may not be laced with herbs for love, lust, and romance), drinking May wine, adult-themed parties such as the Haloa, love and lust spells, and of course, the actual Great Rite.

The Maypole – A Symbolic Great Rite

A Great Rite is a sexual act done in sacred space. There are many ways to express this energy that do not involve actual lovemaking, however, such as the tradition of dancing the maypole. In the weeks preceding the holiday, and especially on Beltane itself, the energies of fertility and sexual desire are all around us. This is cause for great joy and celebration, as Pagans everywhere will likely agree that we hold sexuality sacred. When lovers come together in passion, the energy between them builds and builds, and becomes a tangible force that is much greater than the sum of its two (or more!) parts. Sexuality is sacred to Pagans because it honors and celebrates life and love, and in doing so, it serves the life force.

The Great Rite is most commonly symbolized by dancing a maypole, a richly symbolic representation of the Lord and Lady's Great Rite, or Sacred Marriage. The pole itself symbolizes the Lord's phallus, pointing up into the sky, a giant monument to his sexual power and potency. In some traditions, the ribbons twined around it represent the Lady. More often, the Lady's yoni is symbolized by a ring of flowers, which is placed atop the pole.

The ring of flowers is easy to make. Simply purchase a good-sized ring of straw from your local hobby shop (if the straw ring is too small it won't slide down the pole smoothly). Then, you can take flowers of the season, love- and lust-inducing herbs, and poke their stems into the straw base until the top and sides are completely covered. Make sure you don't prepare the ring of flowers too far ahead, or they may begin wilting before the ritual starts. You can combat this a little by holding the ring in a big bowl with a few inches of water—deep enough for the stems to get a "drink"—or by "watering" it occasionally throughout the day. Roses are always a great choice, though they would have to be purchased if not in season. Other good choices are tulips (they are also sacred to Aphrodite), lavender, daisies, hibiscus, violets, columbines, hyacinths, jasmine, orchids (though, like roses, can get pricey rather quickly), and pansies. Herbs for the ring can include patchouli, sweet basil, cinnamon sticks, juniper, lady's mantle, peppermint, rosemary, thyme, willow, yarrow, dill, lemongrass, and any other herbs or flowers you find appealing.

Once your ring of flowers is assembled, have three or four people pull their ribbons out to create a "platform" for the ring to rest on until the dance starts. Then, as the dance progresses and the ribbons are woven round and round, the ring of flowers and herbs slowly lowers itself over the pole, symbolizing the Great Rite of the Lord and Lady, woman-superior style.

A refreshingly different variation on this theme is the male-superior style, which is done at the Spiritual Anarchist's Beltane (SAB), a private festival in the Pacific Northwest. Earlier I spoke of Aphrodite's sexual "purity"—if there was ever a gathering of Pagans who speak to that energy, this would be the place, and the people. Unabashed, uninhibited, openly in favor of the joy and sacredness of both human sexuality and the Sacred Marriage of our Lord and the Lady, these people personify and embody the sexual purity of Aphrodite in a beautiful and vital way.

First, the current May King, whose reign started the previous year, at the appropriate time, takes a team of men off into the woods for special mystery rites, part of which includes the "hunting" of the current year's maypole, which can be either a fallen tree or fresh one. Sometimes this choice is dictated by the current May Queen. From the time it is chosen, the pole is imbued with abundant male energy, and is considered the Lord's phallus, so it is never allowed to touch the ground, or it would lose all that energy. The men then spend a day stripping the bark and carving the end into a wonderfully blatant phallic shape, adding symbols and carved pictures as the spirit moves them.

In the meantime, the women gather around the May Queen, awaiting her orders. At her word, they begin digging a hole for the maypole in a spot that has become tradition for SAB. Now, this isn't just any old hole in the ground. The women make it sacred from the very beginning, as it is consecrated to the Goddess and becomes, for the duration of the festival, the Goddess' yoni. Over the course of the next day (or two), the hole is dug out to the correct depth which is marked by the moment the shortest woman in camp can no longer see out. This takes the effort of every willing woman in camp. The finishing touch is just the right-sized rock for the Goddess' clitoris and dozens and dozens of fresh flowers all around, which emphasize the beauty and mystery of the Goddess and all of nature.

About the time the women are finishing up the Earth yoni, the men come back from their mystery, carrying the giant wooden phallus. The women sing songs of enticement and love to the gods of fertility and passion, and thereby the men who personify him and hold his energy with their intent and their actions. The phallus is then placed lengthwise to the earth yoni, with the "business end" closest to the opening in the ground.

The current May Queen then announces that it's time to choose the new queen. Any woman who feels called may step up and join the others in the circle around the current queen. The current May Queen, through whatever method she feels called to use (usually some system of drawing lots), chooses the next queen. The men step up next, and the new queen chooses her consort (which can be a woman or a man), using whatever method she chooses.

The maypole dance doesn't begin yet, however—the Lord must be made ready. Brilliantly colored ribbons, which were pre-dyed magically by the May Queen, the queens from former years (each one affectionately referred to as a "May Ma"), and other women in the local Pagan community, are rolled out. Each woman in camp chooses one, and attaches it to the far end of the shaft. Once all the ribbons are on, they are secured, and that's when Aphrodite really takes control.

One by one, the women in camp all "dance the pole," which consists of dancing their way, straddling the pole, from the far end down to the beautifully carved head. This they do either simply or quite blatantly, stroking the shaft and carved head erotically, sometimes kissing, licking, or even locking their legs around it and . . . well, let's just say they bless it with their own sacred emanations, enticing and delighting the Lord to his great purpose. Finally, amid much cheering, drumming, and chanting, the Lord and Lady are united as the men, as one, lift, push, and thrust the sacred phallus into the deep earth yoni. Shortly thereafter, the new royal couple withdraws from the revelers to prepare themselves. Once they are invoked with the spiritual energy of the Lord and Lady, the maypole dance begins, and colorful ribbons fly on the breeze as they're woven round and round the pole in a dance as old as time.

A little later in the evening, the bel-fire is lit, also in a traditional place in camp, and the evening continues with much of the same wonderful revelry, drumming, and dancing one finds at most other Pagan sabbat celebrations, with one small exception: everyone is deliciously horny. The new May Queen and her consort sometimes do a symbolic Great Rite with a chalice and blade for the crowd before sneaking off to perform an actual Great Rite (one can imagine the other revelers gathering in the woods in the Old Way), sending bright, sacred, and magical energy to the stars and back, blessing the land, the people, and the holiday in the sublime and sacred tradition of our spiritual ancestors.

Other Symbolic Great Rites

If one doesn't want to do an actual Great Rite or a maypole for her Beltane celebration, there are other symbolic ways to express this energy, such as planting something, burying a crystal that has been charged with magical energies, or joining the chalice and blade as is done in a typical Wiccan ritual. Smaller groups or solitary practitioners can braid magically charged ribbons around an "invisible" maypole by hanging the ribbons from a hook in the ceiling, and then tying off and dividing up the braid later for each participant to use as they will. You can also make a "may gad"—a miniature maypole made by a single practitioner, using a small branch or twig, which is then wrapped with ribbons that carry your wishes. May gads look beautiful lining sidewalk gardens, or stuck in a plant pot on an apartment patio or balcony.

⚜

If one wants to do an actual Great Rite, it's a good idea to set up the space, preferably outdoors, with as many symbols of love, lust, and power as possible (soft, fresh rose petals on the bed are a nice touch), and, if the person or people involved are very good at holding their focus, they can even chant while raising energy in this fashion, which adds to the magic. At the moment of orgasm, the energy can be sent to any purpose, but a good one for this bright and fertile time of year is to bless plants with the energy. One year, my lover and I surrounded the magic circle with all the baby plant starts we'd just made, firing the energy into the little peat pots. We had a great garden that year! If the people involved want the energy to be extra powerful, they can build it over a period of days (I don't recommend more than ten for beginners), by teasing each other sexually every day, bringing each other almost to the point of orgasm, and then backing off and holding the energy until it subsides. This is more difficult than it sounds! Good communication is key—simple code words, such as "My Lord" or "My Lady" can let your partner(s) know to stop or slow their actions when orgasm is imminent. By the time the Great Rite occurs, the stored up energy that's released is like a sparkling rocket!

Revelry

For the party afterward, one can invite people to celebrate in a blatantly sexual fashion, such as in a Haloa celebration like Z. Budapest speaks of in *The Grandmother of Time*. The Haloa was the Greek celebration of women's free speech, and was for women only. As my rituals and parties are open to both women and men, I wanted to include men in the Haloa-type celebration I did one year. At the beginning of the post-ritual party, I laid down the "rules": People were encouraged to flirt blatantly with each other, to say whatever sprang to mind, and to keep in mind that it was all in fun (couples laid their own ground rules for how far the flirting could go). We also had a sexy-joke-telling and bawdy-song-singing competition. For the contest, I first gave each participant a roll of pennies in a paper cup. As each person told their story or sang their song, each member of the audience who laughed had to drop a penny into the performer's cup. For groans or silence, the performer had to give each member of the audience one of their pennies. This helped keep people from telling sophomoric and disgusting jokes just to hear themselves speak. It worked very well; people don't like getting groans, and so the jokes and songs were hilariously funny and sexy. At the end of the evening, the pennies were counted up and prizes were given, but the best prize for all of us was the freedom to be wholly ourselves, even if for only one evening.

Beltane Foods and Drinks

One very traditional and lovely drink for Beltane is May wine. This is commonly made with white wine, lemon slices, and a lovely fragrant herb called sweet woodruff. I have adapted the recipe a bit, so I use champagne and sliced strawberries in mine. In a large punch bowl, I tear some sweet woodruff (a couple of handfuls per bottle is a good measure to go by), then cover this with sliced berries, then more sweet woodruff and another layer of berries. I pour the champagne over all and let it steep for the duration of the ritual. If the sweet woodruff is in bloom, I reserve the pretty white flowers to float on top. By cakes and wine time, the brew should be perfect—delicately flavored, heady, and sweet.

For the cakes, I like to use what I call "hot peach cakes," which are an adaptation of the Fararrs' Aphrodite cakes, found in *The Witches' Goddess*. These are easy to make: you'll need the pastry recipe for a two-crust pie, about a dozen peach halves, a whole, unblanched almond for each one, and some heavy table cream to serve them with (optional). First, roll out the pastry and cut into circles about an inch bigger than the diameter of the peach. Place the peach on top of it and cover with a larger circle of pastry, pinching the edges to seal them. Then, take a knife and cut from the top down on one side almost (but not quite) to the bottom. Dust the very top of the dome with cinnamon, and then push an almond, tip up, into the slit. They will open slightly as they bake. They are delicious served hot, with plenty of cream!

For those who are not inclined to bake, there are many pastries available that can serve just as well, such as cream horns, cannelloni, and of course, the more blatant pastries available for purchase from erotic bakeries. Another option is to buy rolled wafer cookies that come filled with hazelnut or chocolate cream, and then dip one end into melted chocolate a few times. And strawberries, all by themselves, either sliced or whole, can speak to the most erotic shapes if one only takes a moment to look.

Foods for the feast can include stuffed manicotti, stuffed shells, bratwurst, seafood of any kind, and love- and lust-inducing culinary herbs and foods such as sweet basil, cinnamon, avocado, and ginger, to name a few. There is also a lovely damiana liqueur on the market, which is supposed to help induce female lust, though after most Beltane celebrations, the ingestion of damiana liqueur could be like lighting a match to a box of Roman candles!

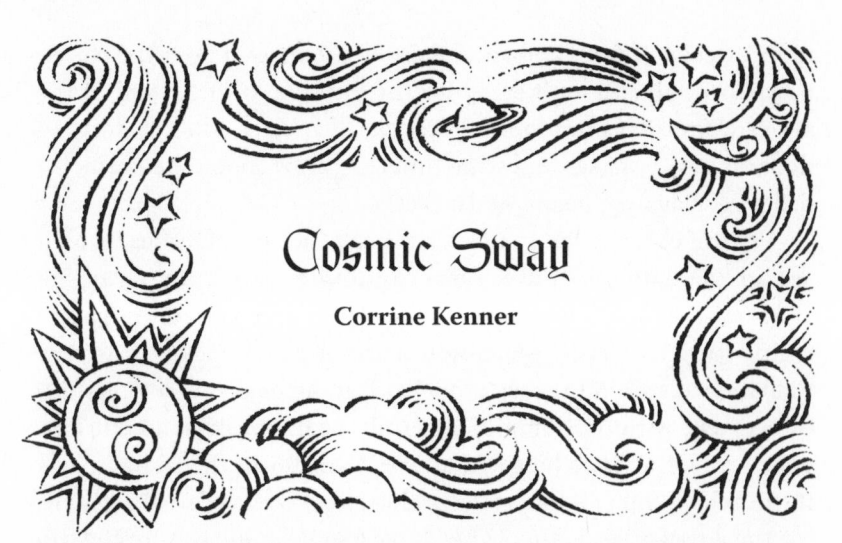

Cosmic Sway

Corrine Kenner

BELTANE, COMMONLY KNOWN AS May Day, marks the halfway point between the Spring Equinox and the Summer Solstice, when the Sun is midway through the sign of earthy Taurus. It also marks the beginning of the planting season.

Farmers want their seed to take root and grow to fruition, so Beltane is a fertility celebration—and this year, primal sexual energy will be easy to find, with Mars, the planet of physical drive and desire, alongside the Sun in earthy, physical, sensual Taurus.

When planets move through earthy Taurus, they assume some of the qualities and characteristics of the sign. They become more physical, like the bull, the sign's signature animal. They also become more sensual, because earthy Taurus is ruled by Venus, the planet of love and attraction.

Intellectual stimulation will play an important role in social interactions, too—and two planets embody the give-and-take of open communication and exchange. On Beltane, Mercury enters airy Gemini, its own sign, where it can make full use of its natural gifts for clever conversation and flirtatious banter. Venus is already there, waiting for him. The goddess of love is especially susceptible to sweet talk when she's immersed in airy Gemini and Mercury whispers in her ear.

Tarot and Astrology

In astrology, the Sun symbolizes the ego and energy of life force. You can see Apollo, the god of the Sun, in most versions of the Sun card—either as a beaming youth or a man in the prime of life. When the Sun is in earthy Taurus, Apollo focuses his energy on all that earthy Taurus represents: physical security, comfort, and stability.

When Mars is in earthy Taurus, too, the Emperor card comes into play. While Mars corresponds to the Tower—one of the few inanimate characters in the cards—the Tower is home to the Aries Emperor.

Mars in Taurus stirs the Emperor's most primal urges. He leaves his Tower and searches for conquests on the battlefield of love, driven by raw physical desire. Picture him chasing young maidens through peaceful meadows and flower gardens, like a bawdy tarot version of King Henry the Eighth.

The Mercury-Venus alliance is also fun to imagine in tarot terms. Mercury corresponds to the Magician card. In airy Gemini, the Magician is at the top of his game, channeling cosmic energy and transforming his thoughts and ideas into physical reality. Venus is the Empress. As long as the Emperor is out of the castle, she'll entertain herself with the Magician's performance.

Practical Astrology

To align yourself with the planetary energies at Beltane, make an extra effort to engage in conversation with the people around you. Ask open-ended questions, and follow up with requests for details and explanations. Like Mercury, be curious. Share your own stories, too, with the kindred spirits who are symbolized by the airy Gemini twins.

Planetary Positions

The Sun is in earthy Taurus. It will move into airy Gemini on May 21.

The Moon is in airy Libra, casting a warm glow over social gatherings and interpersonal relationships.

Mercury is in its own sign. Information flows freely, through clever conversation, witty banter, and stimulating flights of fancy.

Venus is in airy Gemini, too, further enhancing the appeal of love and relationships. She'll enter Cancer on May 7, where domestic partnerships will be a priority. Venus will move into Leo on June 5, and at that point, she'll expect to garner praise for her own beauty and charm.

Mars is in earthy Taurus, where the god of war can either be perceived as stubborn or tenacious. Mars will move into airy Gemini on May 12.

Jupiter is still in Leo. The further each planet is from the Sun, the more time it spends in each sign of the zodiac.

Saturn is retrograde in fiery Sagittarius. On May 23, the ringed planet will make its closest approach to Earth. You'll be able to see its rings and a few of its brightest moons with a medium-sized telescope. Saturn will go retrograde and backtrack into the sign of Scorpio on June 14.

The generational outer planets remain in the same signs:

Uranus is in fiery Aries.

Neptune is in watery Pisces.

Pluto is retrograde in earthy Capricorn.

Planets in Aspect

The Sun in Taurus and Jupiter in Leo are squared off, which suggests that they're working at cross purposes. Both planets favor expansion, but this particular aspect is decidedly uncomfortable, and it bodes poorly for growth management.

Mercury, in Gemini, and Saturn, in Sagittarius, are at opposite sides of the zodiac. The opposition is short-lived because Mercury is such a fast-moving planet, but it could lead to a momentary sense of defensiveness.

Jupiter, in fiery Leo, is still in a harmonious trine with Uranus in fiery Aries—an aspect that opens the door for good fortune and lucky breaks.

Neptune, in Pisces, is sextile the Sun. This is an artist's aspect, both sensitive and creative—and perhaps a little Bohemian.

Phases of the Moon

May 3: Tonight's Full Moon in watery Scorpio is charged by the light of the Sun in earthy Taurus. It's a powerful combination: in this case, the Sun's energy will channel emotional desires into physical energy. Don't be surprised if you find yourself seeking a physical outlet for pent-up emotions. Use that energy to exercise, clean house, or do yard work.

May 18: This morning's New Moon, with both the Moon and the Sun in Taurus, signals an ideal start to the growing season. This is a great time to plant seedlings or prepare a garden—either literally or metaphorically.

June 2: A Full Moon in Sagittarius, with the Sun in Gemini, spurs philosophical discourse and communication. Find a close friend or kindred spirit and talk about life.

June 16: A New Moon, with the Sun and Moon conjunct in Gemini, promises closer connections with friends and neighbors. This can be a practical Moon: use Gemini's energy to run errands, make phone calls, and catch up on family news.

The Old Ways:
Lighting Beal's Fire

Melanie Marquis

BELTANE MARKS THE MIDPOINT between the Spring Equinox and the Summer Solstice. Vegetation is in full bloom, and the sun is continuing to gain strength day by day. It's a time of fertility, a time of growth, a time of purification, and a time to ask for continued blessings. Above all, however, Beltane is a fire festival—in fact, it was one of the most important fire festivals of the Celtic year. It was a celebration of Beal, or Belenos, an early Celtic god of fire and the sun. Beal may have been a derivation of the ancient Babylonian god Baal, dating from the third millenium BCE. His symbols were the bull and oak, and he represented the waxing, brighter half of the year. Beal was born at the Winter Solstice, then died at the Summer Solstice. At Beltane, Beal reached the apex of his cycle, where the myths relate that the young god, at last having reached full maturity, mates with the earth goddess, ultimately making it possible for the crops to grow and the flowers to bloom.

Beltane was celebrated widely throughout the Celtic lands. Preceeding the festival, all the fires in the countryside were extinguished. When the proper time came, fresh fires were lit in homage to the lord of the sun. These "Baal Fires" or "Beal-fires" were what we call "need fires"—kindled from friction rather than from a lighter or a book of matches. The villagers would all light their home fires anew out of flames brought from the Beal-fire, believing that this act would help incur good luck and preserve the family's health throughout the year. In Ireland, the sacred Beltane fire was kindled using a wheel with a spindle placed at the center, the circular wheel seen as a suitable symbol for the sun god. The wheel was rotated sun-wise around the spindle, creating friction and heat and eventually a spark of flame. Once the spark appeared, a highly combustible plant was quickly brought in contact with it, producing a gust of flame from which the rest of the fire was lit. Such Beal-fires were considered sacred, and they were believed to have many magickal properties. It was thought that the fires helped fertilize the land and protect it from evil influences, and that the ashes could be used for powerful magick. Cattle were driven to pass between two fires in order to purify them and protect their health, and often even people who were young enough and brave enough would leap through the Beal-fire flames in the hopes of procuring good health and good luck.

In Scotland, the Beltane fires were built on hilltops. The people would gather there, enjoy a meal, then spend hours singing and dancing around the fire. At last, the Beltane cake—a cake made primarily of flour and egg—was shared. One piece of the Beltane cake was discolored, and whoever received this blackened piece was doomed to be the new star of the show. The unlucky person, called the *cailleach beal-tine*—roughly translated as the "Old Lady of Beltane," was subjected to all sorts of mock cruelty, from being nearly tossed into the fire to being laid on the ground while the revelers pretend like they're getting ready to draw and quarter the helpless victim. After the more terrible mock punishments were over, the *cailleach beal-tine* was pelted with eggs, and for the rest of the night and the next few days, they were talked about as if they were dead. In the Western Perthshire district of Scotland, whoever received the blackened piece of Beltane cake was compelled to leap three times over the fire. The *cailleach beal-tine* ritual was performed as an offering or sacrifice to Beal, and perhaps also offered the Celts a way to relate more deeply to the solar god who was doomed to imminent death at the approaching Summer Solstice.

Fire wasn't the only means the Celts found for honoring Beal. Feasting, drinking, and dancing were also often part of the Beltane festivities. In Ireland, a sacred dance called the *Rinceadh-fada* was performed. The dancers were paired in groups, and each dancer held the corner of a small square of white cloth. The dancers moved gracefully in interweaving patterns and semi-circles as the music, which started slow, increased its pace to a frenzy.

One Scottish ritual practiced by herdsmen in the countryside began with a large, square trench cut into the ground. In the middle of the trench was left a square of turf, upon which a fire was built and a concoction of eggs, butter, oatmeal, and milk was prepared. Everyone participating in the ritual brought a little something to contribute to the mix, "Stone Soup" style. This mixture, called *caudle*, was poured on the ground in addition to libations of beer and whiskey in hopes of pleasing the gods. Of course, the humans saved a good bit to enjoy themselves, too. Each person was also given a special cake made from oatmeal, which featured nine raised, square knobs. The herdsmen would sit near the fire, break off one of the knobs, dedicate it to a deity or other being believed to have the power to protect their livestock, then toss the bit of cake over their shoulder, offering it to the selected entity as a gift in hopes of incurring blessings. The ritual was also used to bribe dangerous animals out of harming the lambs and other livestock, with offerings of oatmeal cake given in the name of the fox along with a plea for mercy.

Even if you don't have the luxury of building an enormous bonfire this Beltane, you can still honor the old ways by using candles as miniature Beal-fires. Instead of cattle, pass your own "livestock" between the flames: charge crystals or other stones to represent assets you have and value, then carefully pass each one between the two candle flames. You might light just one candle, placing it on the ground so you can safely jump over the small-scale fire. Just take care to follow general fire safety guidelines, especially if you have the inclination and opportunity to build larger fires for Beltane fun. This means making sure the fire is contained, that you have an extinguisher nearby, that you don't wear loose clothing that could drag in the flames, and that you allow only responsible, sober adults to get near the fire. If fire isn't your thing, why not honor the spirit of the equinox with some old-fashioned Scottish *caudle*, or perhaps with an Irish sacred dance? There are lots of ways to carry on time-honored Pagan traditions while custom-crafting your own modern Beltane celebration.

References:

Bonwick, James. *Irish Druids and Old Irish Religions*. London: Griffith, Farran, 1894. Accessed October 13, 2013. http://www.sacred-texts.com/pag/idr/idr00.htm.

Frazer, Sir James George. *The Golden Bough*. 1922. Reprint, New York: Bartleby.com, 2000.

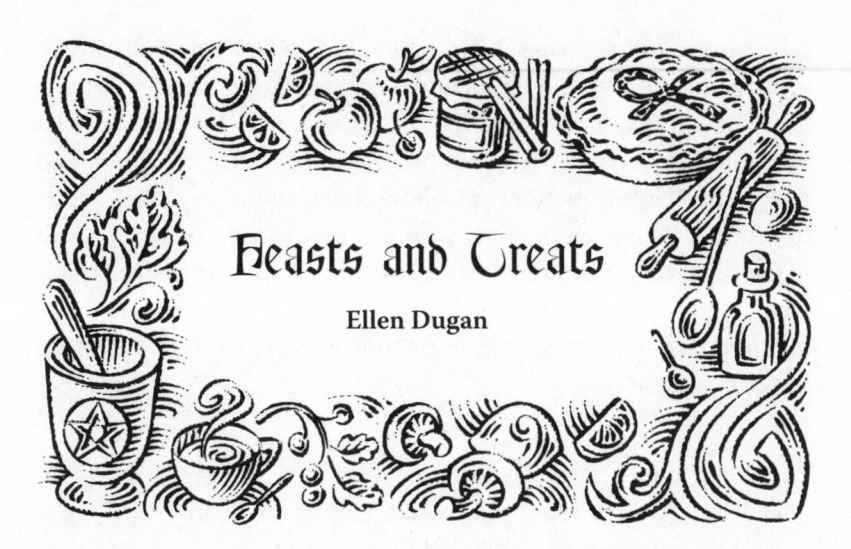

Feasts and Treats

Ellen Dugan

MAY HAS ARRIVED, AND it is time to enjoy the earliest herbs in the garden and to start planting your veggies for the summer harvest. In keeping with a playful Beltane mood, here are some fun and, better yet, interesting and dare we say "surprising" recipes for you to conjure up.

Grilled Mozzarella Sandwiches

We all love mozzarella sticks ... here is a fast and easy way to have the same effect in a fancy little sandwich. Serve with your favorite marinara and dip away!

Prep time: 20 minutes
Cook time: 2 minutes per side of sandwich
Serves: 8–10

4 slices whole-wheat bread
4 slices low-fat mozzarella cheese
1 egg or ¼ cup egg substitute
¼ cup low-fat milk
A couple small sprigs of fresh thyme (strip stems of their leaves)
½ teaspoon salt

Pinch nutmeg
½ cup warm marinara sauce
2 tablespoons olive oil

Place one mozzarella slice on each of the four slices of bread. Put bread together with cheese in the middle. You will have two sandwiches.

In a wide, shallow bowl, whisk the egg/egg substitute, milk, thyme leaves, salt, and nutmeg. Whisk until well blended.

Warm the marinara sauce at 30-second increments in a microwave-safe bowl. Set aside but keep warm.

In a 10- to 12-inch nonstick skillet, heat the olive oil over medium-high heat. Dip the sandwiches into the egg batter, turning to coat, and place them into the pan. Cook until golden brown on the first side, about 2 minutes. Flip over and brown the other side. Transfer the sandwiches to individual plates. Cut in half and serve immediately with warm marinara sauce.

Couscous with Tomato and Cucumber Salad

A lighter type of salad and one of my favorites, this is great all spring and summer! Fresh herbs and tomatoes from your own garden make this dish really pop!

Prep time: 20 minutes
Serves: 4–6

3 cups couscous (cooked)
1 tomato chopped/or 12–20 cherry tomatoes, halved
1 cup fresh cucumber, chopped
2 tablespoons fresh basil
2 tablespoons fresh parsley
¼ cup low-fat Italian salad dressing
½ cup low-fat feta cheese crumbles
Salt and pepper to taste

Cook the couscous according to the package directions. (I use an instant couscous and add a tablespoon of dried, minced onions to the water as it cooks.) When the couscous is finished, fluff with a fork and transfer it into a large mixing bowl. While the couscous cools slightly, prepare the vegetables and herbs.

Add the chopped veggies and herbs to the couscous in the mixing bowl. Add salt and pepper. Pour dressing over the top and mix gently. Lastly, add the feta cheese crumbles and stir again. Taste and add more salt/pepper or salad dressing as desired. Serve immediately or refrigerate. (Be sure to keep leftovers covered and refrigerated.)

Strawberry Pretzel Salad

This is a classic recipe from my mother-in-law's best friend. Wonderful and different!

Prep time: 30 minutes
Chill time: 1 hour
Serves: 8–10

Crust
2 cups crushed pretzels
3 tablespoons sugar
¾ cup margarine, melted

Filling
8 ounces (1 package) cream cheese, softened
1 cup sugar
2 cups non-dairy topping, such as Cool Whip

Topping
1 3-ounce package strawberry jello
1 3-ounce package raspberry jello
3 cups hot water
10 ounces frozen sliced strawberries (allow these to thaw *slightly*)

Mix crushed pretzels with 3 tablespoons of sugar and melted margarine spread in a 13 × 9-inch pan and bake at 375 degrees F for 8 minutes. Cool completely.

Cream the (softened) cream cheese and 1 cup of sugar with a mixer. Fold in the Cool Whip by hand with a spatula and spread it over the cooled pretzel crust.

Mix the 2 packages of jello with 3 cups of hot water in a separate large bowl. Add the semi-frozen strawberries and stir. (The frozen fruit will help the jello to set faster.) Chill the fruit-jello mixture, covered, in the refrigerator until it begins to set—approximately one hour. When the jello has partially set, pour it over the cream cheese layer and smooth. Then return the dish to the refrigerator. Chill overnight. See who can guess what that first layer is actually made of!

May Day Martini

Seriously, there is actually a martini named "May Day!" How much fun is that?

Prep time: 5 minutes
Serves: 2

4 parts vodka
2 parts lemon juice
2 parts cinnamon syrup
4 strawberries sliced

Directions: Fill a shaker with ice cubes. Add all ingredients except strawberries. Shake and strain into a chilled cocktail glass. Garnish with strawberries.

Happy Beltane!

Crafty Crafts

Lexa Olick

DURING BELTANE, IT IS very common to see ribbons and flowers. Both look so gentle and elegant, especially when strewn across a room. This is a time filled with the promise of summer, so flowers are a popular theme. They are a sign of fertility and growth. The blossoming of a flower represents our own goals since it starts as just a small bud that blossoms into endless possibilities.

The arrival of spring celebrates Flora, the Roman goddess of flowers. She is a fertility goddess who protects early blossoms. She is usually depicted as wearing a garland of flowers. This crown of flowers has become a typical tradition of Beltane. They are an essence of spring. Crowns are not only worn, but can also be displayed. They look great simply resting on top of a pillow. However, there are many ways to display a garland of flowers. For example, the delicate blossoms are seemingly weightless when they dangle from the ceiling for an elegant Beltane display.

Beltane Flower Chandeliers

Flower chandeliers are beautiful wreaths that hang suspended from the ceiling. They flow through the air and closely resemble flower crowns and maypoles, which are two popular Beltane traditions.

Made of a combination of silk flowers, wreaths, and ribbon, they look dainty and delicate as they dangle from above. A gentle breeze further emphasizes their elegance. The ribbons dance through the air and the wreath of blossoms is vibrant with color that brightens up any room. Flower chandeliers look graceful and charming as they decorate your home with the Beltane spirit!

Silk flowers may not be natural, but they are stunningly realistic and can last a lifetime. They don't require water, but it is a good idea to keep them well dusted if you display them for a long period of time. A compressed-air duster will keep them looking new and fresh.

Supplies

12-inch green foam wreath

Scissors and wire cutters

3/16-inch satin ribbon for hanging

Variety of ribbon for embellishment (choose an assortment of widths, but I recommend keeping between the widths of ⅛ inch and 1½ inch)

2-inch plastic macramé ring (a key ring will work just as well)

Instructions: A green foam wreath is best because it blends with the green leaves of the silk flowers. However, if for whatever reason you cannot find a green wreath at your local craft store, you can easily adapt a white one. All you need to do is lay down a few sheets of newspaper in a well-ventilated area and cover your wreath, front and back, with a coat of spray paint. The spray paint can either be green or the color that dominates the majority of the petals of your silk flowers. It's important that you choose a color to coordinate with the overall look of the chandelier. Allow the paint to dry completely for several hours before adorning it with flowers.

Take your 3/16-inch satin ribbon and cut it into 4 pieces that measure 40 inches each. Take one strip of ribbon and place the 12-inch wreath at its center. Tie the ribbon in a knot so it is tight against the wreath. This will leave you with two long tail ends. Repeat this step with the remaining 3 strips of ribbon, making sure that there is an equal amount of space between them so that the wreath will stay balanced when it hangs. Altogether, you will have 8 tail ends.

Gather the tail ends together and lift them high into the air so you can see how the wreath will hang. Split the tail ends in half, slip the plastic ring between them, and then knot the ribbon securely together at the top. You can now set the plastic ring down and put your focus on the foam wreath.

Choose colors that best reflect the Beltane celebration, such as green, yellow, purple, and pink. Some flowers associated with Beltane are daffodils, lilacs, daisies, and forsythias. Of course, you can use a variety of different flowers because Beltane is a time when flowers are abundant.

Make sure the flowers you chose are on a sturdy stem. Sometimes the plastic is too thin to sufficiently hook itself into the foam. I recommend you find flowers with wired stems because they are thicker and will not slip away from the foam.

Cut off the flower heads, making sure to leave a 1½ inch of stem. This extra bit of stem will truly anchor the flowers into the foam and bury them deep inside.

Carefully push the stem into the foam until it can't go any further. Continue to push in more flowers until the entire foam wreath is covered. You can alternate flowers for a mixture of color. All you have to do is stagger the flower colors to keep the wreath looking balanced. As you cover the wreath, you'll notice that the ribbon wrapped around it becomes less visible. If there are any gaps between the flowers, you can fill them in with smaller silk blossoms.

The chandelier looks best when there are flowing ribbons that dangle from the wreath. Take a variety of colored ribbons and cut them into lengths that are no shorter than 80 inches. If you find the length is too long, you can always trim them at the end. Gather the ribbon together and find their center. Fold them in half to create a loop and hold it against the knot on the plastic ring. Pull the tail

ends through the loop until it is tight and secure. Then let the loose ribbon dangle from the wreath.

When you hang your flower chandelier from the ceiling, your room will be in bloom with beautiful flowers and graceful ribbons!

Time to Complete: About 1 hour, but if you are arranging your flowers in a specific order, it can take longer.

Cost: About $40.00, but you can lessen the cost if you buy the right flowers. Smaller flowers make a tighter wreath, but they require more blossoms. Large flowers with bigger flower heads and large petals take up more space. If you find silk flowers with fuller petals, the fewer you'll need to complete your wreath.

Sustainable Beltane: A Mummer's Tale

Natalie Zaman

THE WHEEL OF THE year is a mandala, a cosmic diagram of the spiraling dance of the Sun and the Earth, the turn of the seasons, the play of death and life. It is a thing of sacred geometry, each season quartering the circle, every sabbat angled against its neighbors, and joined in the center. Take away its sabbat-spokes, and the wheel becomes the traditional astrological symbol of the Sun. Everything is connected.

Each sabbat has an equal and opposite partner to which it is inevitably connected. They gaze at each other across the expanse of the year, dividing it in half. And while these points in time appear to be paradoxical, they are more like yin and yang—each having a seed of the other inside it.

At first glance, Beltane and Samhain seem to have nothing in common. At Samhain we enter the God season. The world is enveloped in shadow and the spirit of death, that strange energy that whispers of the unknown permeates the very air. Contrariwise, Beltane welcomes in the Goddess season and revels in the power of creation. As May approaches there is no mistaking that life is all around us—and while it is light, this power can be just as unnerving and mysterious as the blackest dark. Who has not been awed by the unstoppable power of the ocean, the relentlessness and ruthlessness of the tiny creatures that break down a corpse, or the power of fire as it consumes all matter and substance into itself?

The perceptions of the life force so honored at these tides are very different, but also similar. On both occasions we are beckoned to put on the guise of God and Goddess. Costumed trick-or-treat, even though more "Halloween" than "Samhain," harkens back to older traditions; the putting on of horns to become the God, the adornments of the Goddess, and death masks. At Beltane, there are mummers.

Most folks know about mummers through the annual parade held in Philadelphia on New Year's Day, but the uniformed teams of marchers with their glittering costumes are quite different from mumming's humble beginnings in the English countryside.

The original mummers were a cast of masked (*mummer* means "disguised") characters who acted out seasonal plays, most of which centered around the common themes of good versus evil and not surprisingly, life and death. These plays were part of Beltane celebrations that also included games and dancing. During the maypole dance, celebrants of Beltane rites become God and Goddess who come together to weave creation—a sacred and powerful means of honoring the life force so prevalent at this time of year. But it can also be fun—and made green with a few stacks of recyclables and a handful of office supplies.

Use newspapers and cardboard to create masks and costumes for your Beltane ritual or the revels that follow—both are equally important in preserving the Old Ways. This activity can be especially engaging when you have a younger group and the process can be turned into a game or contest, another nod to ancient tradition.

Make It Your Own!

You will need:

Clean recyclable materials such as newspapers, magazines, plastic
    bottles and cardboard including boxes, paper roll tubes, etc.
Masking tape

Stapler and staples
Scissors

Divide your revelers into groups (boys against girls, families, whatever works for your gathering). Give each group an equal amount of recyclables, and one each of a roll of tape, stapler, and a pair of scissors.

Present the groups with their challenge: each must construct one costume and/or mask out of the recycled materials. Individuals in each group must work together and use the materials given to create their mumming outfit in the given amount of time. How elaborate you want to be and what those costumes and/or play are will depend on your tradition, the theme of your celebration, and how much time you have to devote to it.

Perhaps each group will have to make masks and perform a traditional play. Anyone not participating in the challenge can cast votes for the best disguises and performances. If you wish to focus on solemnity, each group can make a mask and/or costume to represent God and Goddess who come together at Beltane during your ritual.

All should be honored, but I'm convinced that no matter how serious the holiday or solemn the rite, spirituality is meant to bring comfort and joy. May the Old Ones smile on your Beltane revels!

Beltane Ritual: Erotic Energy

Thuri Calafia

THIS RITUAL IS WRITTEN for a small group, but can be easily adapted for solitary practice, or for larger groups.

Each covener must bring a spool (10 yards) of half-inch ribbon, in the color that best represents the power of their own sexuality as well as the story of how they came to own such power (who or what influenced them, for example). For the party afterward, each covener must also bring a love- or lust-inducing herb as thank you offering for the bel-fire; bawdy songs, tales, and jokes; and something "sexy" for the potluck feast.

The altar is decorated with crafter's lace, candles, and a bouquet of spring flowers in the colors that remind the practitioners of love and lust. Also on the altar are all the regular Witch's tools. If outdoors, a fire is laid ready in the South (the wood is soaked with lighter fluid for a dramatic quick start), and two tables of candles stand opposite for people to walk between, with the bowl of herbs everyone brought all mixed together. If indoors, two tables of candles are set up, framing the South quarter of the circle, and the thank you offerings will be cast into the air outside instead of into a fire.

The circle is then cleansed, purified, charged, and cast in the usual way.

Coveners Call the Quarters

Blessed East, we welcome you
Who bring the winds of change,
Who open up our minds and hearts
And fan the sacred flames.
We seek you and we call you
To our Beltane rites tonight
That all may free their minds in love
And bring their truths to light.
Blessed be.

Blessed South, we welcome you
Who keep the sacred fire,
Who blaze within our minds and hearts
And lead us to desire.
We seek you and we call you
To loan your passion to our will
That all may feel the primal force
These Beltane rites fulfill.
Blessed be.

Blessed West, we welcome you
Whose emotion crests within,
Who frees our loving discourse,
That romance may begin.
We seek you and we call you
To our Beltane rites this eve
That all may find the courage to dare
To flow where passion leads.
Blessed be.

Blessed North, we welcome you
Who manifest desire,
Who teaches us the power held

When Earth banks passion's fire.
We seek you and we call you
To our Beltane rites tonight
That all may manifest their truth
Bringing Mystery to the light.
Blessed be.

HPS Calls the Goddess: *Foam borne Lady who rides the waves of desire, who burns true in women's hearts, who sparks the libido of women and men, we bid you come! Aphrodite, Goddess of allure, desire, and ecstasy, we welcome you this blessed spring evening. Sweet Lady of Love, whose eyes reflect the deep green sea, whose scent is of the ocean, we ask you to be here now! Come join in our celebration of all that is you. Blessed be.*

HP Calls the God: *Mighty, dark and sultry Horned One of the green and wild places, who touches our core in sweet surrender, who drives the aggression in both women and men, we bid you come! Lord Cernunnos, who gives all in the service of the Lady and the life force, who guides us to her, we welcome your presence and your blessing tonight on these rites. Gentle savage, we ask that you be here now! Come join in our celebration of passion and joy! Blessed be.*

HPS Leads the Group in a Guided Meditation: *Everyone, let's breathe together, ground and center . . .*

Tonight, we celebrate Beltane, and we're about to embark upon a journey. . . . Know that what is at the truest, deepest part of you is from the gods, and is therefore sacred. There is nothing to fear here, for it is you whom you are exploring, and only you can see what lies ahead, what lies at the core of your own inner mysteries. You are safe, therefore—safe to explore all that is a part of you, even those things you've never told anyone, even those things you've kept hidden from yourself.

And as you seek this deeper connection, this Mystery, you can see a network of interconnected threads, connecting all . . . to all. And with this visualization, you understand that there is harmony within this individuation, that we resonate with each other, with the world, and most importantly, with all of nature.

Feel the energy on the rise, then, feel the call of all things wild as this season takes hold in your heart, your body, and the deep and vast Mystery far within . . . to your core, illuminating your most sacred, fundamental life force—your passion, your sexuality, your drive, your deepest desires, and know that here, you are safe.

So just take a moment now to explore your truest self . . . it is safe . . . let your mind wander as you feel the circle around you, this bright sphere of light and love protecting you as you explore the depth of your own mysteries . . . and know that when you awaken, you'll be stronger in your convictions.

As you come up from this secret and holy place, hold on to the truths you wish to keep: the truth of yourself, of your ways, your way of loving, knowing that passion and sexuality are good, and healthy, and sacred! Emerge when you are ready, eyes open, spirit awakened, holding fast to the love of the gods you hold dear.

HP Delivers the Ritual's Message: *Here in this place between the worlds, in this sacred time, the air is charged, this circle is charged, and we ourselves, are charged with the intense and erotic energy of Beltane.*

Now, what are we gonna do with that enegy?

In ancient times, our ancestors used this energy in a pointed fertility rite, under the Beltane fires, the fires that beckon to our own inner fires. The spirits of the Lord and the Lady came down into the High King and Queen where they lay together, blessing the land and the people with fertility and abundance.

In other ancient cultures, there was a tradition called the Haloa. This tradition began in ancient Greece, and was the one day every year when women were allowed free speech . . . of course, the talk was blatantly sexual, as women by this time had begun to be robbed of their sexuality. And now, with layer upon layer of cultural baggage upon us, the yoke has fallen upon the shoulders of men as well. But tonight, perhaps we can reconnect a bit with those core beliefs, those inner callings. . . .

Imagine, if you will, a world where the fire in our hearts can blaze freely, where all are valued—woman, man, transgender, gay, straight, bisexual—where all are free to be who we are. Imagine a world where a Haloa would not even be needed, where women and men alike are free to say the things their hearts long to express, where words are neither rewards nor weapons, where censorship of the self is a more serious offense than any acknowledgment of the bright flames of passion within.

Just imagine . . . FREEDOM!

HP lights the need fire.

HPS: *Let this be our challenge then: Now, and for the rest of the evening, try to not just imagine freedom of thought and speech, but to allow that freedom to rule over these rites and the party afterward. The circle will stay up after this ritual, so we'll still be in sacred space as we party, our words and feelings and safe to express. Let's let freedom of speech rule, an orgy of thought, if you will, a dance of life, a Haloa for both women and men, and at the end of the evening, we will part friends, for all that is said here will be held in honor and respect for the courage of those who have spoken.*

HP: *For now, let's share the stories of how we became more sexually free, filling these ribbons with that energy, so we can share the energy with each other when we each take a segment of the ribbon home.*

All share stories as they hold their ribbons, imbuing them with that power. When all are finished, the ribbons are tied together at one end, and looped over a hook in the ceiling (if indoors) or tied to a low tree branch (if outdoors).

HPS: *Since there is no space at this time for a large wooden maypole, let's imagine the God's sacred shaft of light standing here, in this space, a magical maypole. As we twine these ribbons into a braid around it, let's celebrate the life force inherent in our wild side, our spiritual passion, our sexuality, for it is spring, it is Beltane, and it is time to let the veil between the worlds part, that we may touch the power and gifts of the gods yet again. And so we weave . . .*

All chant (from my book, *Dedicant: A Witch's Circle of Fire*):

We weave in love a promise left
In the Lady's keeping
Surround the Lord with passion's gift
Rewards for future reaping.

Power peaks. Energy is fired into the braided ribbons.

Cakes and Wine

HPS blesses the wine: *Wine of May, fragrant and sweet, freshest draught of love, as grail to the lance, let passion's dance fill this bowl from above. May the touch of Aphrodite and Cernunnos flow here, and remind that us we are all as one.*

HP blesses the cakes: *Cakes of May, delicate and rich, symbolic of passion's sweetest gift, may our blessings be sweet, as merry we meet, and the love of the gods merge within.*

Cakes and wine are passed around, and several minutes are allowed for folks to enjoy them.

HPS: *Let's go to our partying then. The circle is permeable, and the gods and guardians are welcome to stay—don't be surprised if they touch you! Because of the nature of this circle, people can enter and leave it at will. But before the first person leaves for the evening, we will stand again in this space to say goodbye.*

Remember that all those you interact with here tonight are aspects of the gods, children of the gods, and their messengers, and are

therefore sacred beings. So mote it be with our words and our games.
Blessed be.

Throughout the evening, coveners go to the need fire and give herbs to it, saying thanks to their ancestors. Some will jump the fire, and some will merely walk between the fire and the table of candles burning opposite. Later, the fire spent, some will take ashes from it, to bless children and pets with a smear of the ashes, as the ancients did.

When the time comes to say goodbye, all return to the circle. Deity and quarters are all thanked in the same spirit in which they were called, and the HP opens the circle. The HPS hands out the segments of braided ribbon from the ritual to each participant.

HPS: *I ask you all to give the same blessing to every one of your sisters and brothers here tonight: (she takes a covener's hand and looks into her eyes) I honor you, my sister. The words you said and the energy we shared here only served to make us closer. May you go forth in the world a freer woman (or man), and be blessed.*

Notes

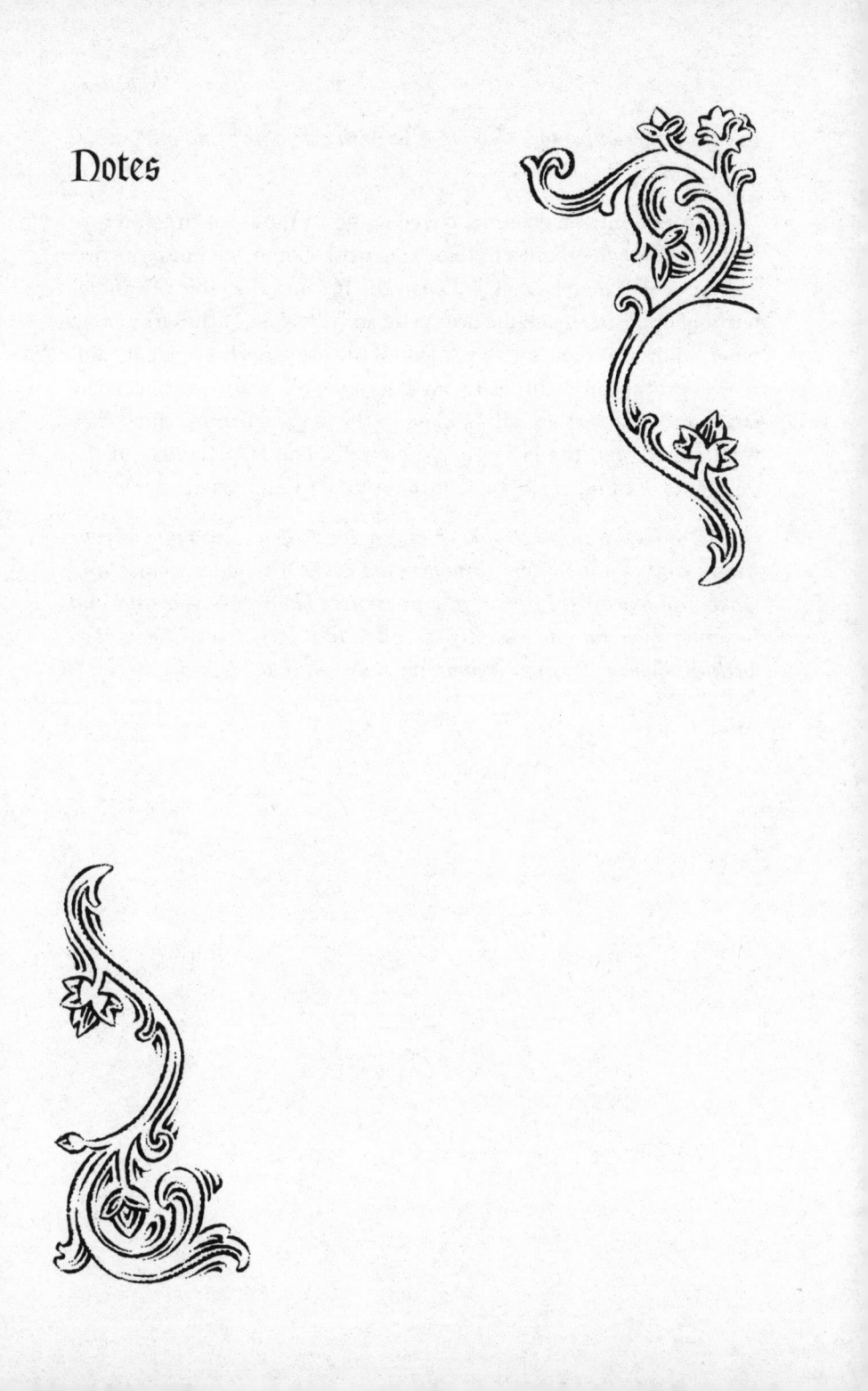

Litha

Litha: Fertile Fires

Dallas Jennifer Cobb

KNOWN COMMONLY AS THE Summer Solstice, Litha occurs between the twentieth and the twenty-third of June, depending on the Earth's rotation around the sun. The sun is at its highest point; this is the longest day of the year. It is partnered with the shortest night.

While our current calendar names Litha as the first day of the summer season, it was historically known as Midsummer, the day halfway between the sabbat festivals of Beltane (May 1) and Lughnassadh or Lammas (August 1). Rather than the "first day of summer," Litha is the middle of the warm season of agricultural growth and harvest.

On the wheel of the year representing the divine relationship between the God and Goddess, Litha is about their intertwined energy. The Earth Goddess, carrying the Sun God's child, is pregnant with potential. She is embraced and honored by the Sun God, who is proud in his masculine glory, excited about becoming a father. She is all goddesses who embody love, sexuality, beauty, and passion. And he is all gods representing strength, power, provision, and virility. She is fecund femininity, and he is virile masculinity. They intertwine, nurturing and protecting their child growing inside.

The swelling energy of the Goddess and the proud energy of the God are bound together today, blessing the sabbat with potent, powerful magic. While this is obviously a good a time for rededication to the God, Goddess, and the Craft, it is also a time for dedication to a mate through handfast or marriage and a time for rededication to all parts of ourselves that combine in divine creativity.

At Litha, we explore the relationship between these paired, so-called opposites that rely so steadfastly upon one another for their survival: God and Goddess, men and women, masculine and feminine, work and leisure, light and dark, waxing and waning, Lugh and Litha. Not only around us in the natural world, but within us energetically, we find the energies of the divine God and Goddess.

Tradition

Traditionally celebrated as the beginning of the harvest season, Litha was often a large, boisterous community festival honoring fertility. Celebrants wore garlands of elder flowers and ribbons representing the fertile Goddess, or crowns representing the triumph of light and the crowning of the Sun God. Clothing was often gauzy, light, and flowing—and white, yellow, or peach colored.

On this day, both the earth and sun are celebrated, as they have collaborated to produce fertile foods, an abundance of fruits and vegetables, and the gorgeous beauty of blossoms and flowers. These early harvested fruits and vegetables are the fruit of the soil and the sun, and the center of this celebration. While the sun's energy seems to dominate everything, especially the night, the earth soaks up that energy, turning it into wondrous creation.

During the day, it was common to journey to the forest to choose and cut branches for magical use: dowsing rods, divining wands, and magical wands. Choice woods include willow (filled with expansive seasonal energy), oak (symbolic of the Oak King), and cherry (the fruitful Goddess). Alive with the waxing energy, these woods were thought to be fluid-filled and more easily tuned in to magical works. Having come through their spring growth cycles, new wood is easily harvested from the ends of branches, and easily trained for magical purposes.

With an abundance of food available at this time of year, the harvesting of the early fruits and vegetables was undertaken in the early part of the day before it became too hot. Strawberries, cherries, and rhubarb; lettuces, cresses, and greens; flowers, blossoms and herbs were all gathered for the evening feast. Many herbs were ritualistically gathered on Litha, dried and preserved for later use in spells and remedies requiring expansive energy.

Returning from the fields and forests with baskets of food along with medicinal and magical harvests, people wore flowers woven into their hair and crowns made of vines.

As the sunlight waned, bonfires and torches were lit, filling the night with warmth and light. Villagers traveled through their villages by torchlight, gathering at the large communal bonfires. Magical, mythologica,l and metaphorical stories were told, akin to Shakespeare's *A Midsummer Night's Dream*—stories of love and loss, of youth and old age, beauty and blight, stories of the God and Goddess, reminders of the potent magic that surrounds us.

As the night wore on, the party grew louder and more boisterous. Music and merriment abound as revelers rejoiced, singing, dancing, and leaping. A symbol of the great and powerful Sun God, great blessing was believed to be in the Litha fire. Jumping over it brought romance and the potential for love to singles, fertility to young couples, and abundance and safety to one's family. Handfasting couples leapt over the Litha fire three times to bless their partnership, bless their resources, and bless their fertility. It was common for couples to snuggle up together near the fire, warmed and lulled by its flames, perhaps envisioning their life together as they watched the glowing embers.

When the fires finally burned out in the wee hours of the morning, it was common to scoop up some ashes to be used in magical charms and spells or to carry some embers home to bless the hearth. The practice of tilling ash into the soil of plants probably found its origins in the Litha practice of carrying ash to the orchards to till in around the base of fruit trees.

Feasting

A table prepared for the Litha feast was dressed with objects and colors traditional to the sabbat: elder, oak, birch, and willow branches decorated the eaves and posts; St. John's wort flowers, sunflowers, or evening primrose blossoms were tied in radiant yellow bouquets; strawberries, new lettuces, and baby greens combined in lively salads; and circular objects that signify the sun were everywhere. An abundance of candles placed on the table illuminate and represent the sun and fire element. Beeswax candles burned with golden luminescence highlighting the seasonal colors on the table: red, gold, yellow, and bright green.

Common to Litha are the herbs so readily available at this time of year: lavender, mint, elder, St. John's wort, hemp, wild roses, thyme, nettle, chamomile, and yarrow. These were used for culinary spicing, made into hot and cold teas, or dried for later use in culinary, medicinal, and cosmetic creations. Oils made from these herbs that carry the expansive magical energy of Litha were commonly used for cooking and salad dressing or rubbed in small amounts on candles to diffuse their scent into the air. In addition to the seasonal herbs, other desirable oils included pine, orange, lemon, and sandalwood, which embody the sun and masculine energies.

Traditional foods for the Litha feast include anything shaped like the sun (oranges, lemons, and grapefruit) and early harvest fruits and vegetables (strawberries, rhubarb, early cherries, summer squash, zucchini blossoms, wild leeks, sorrel, and watercress). Imagine feasting on huge salads made with vibrant greens decorated with the edible petals of calendula and served with round loaves of bread made to resemble the sun and the swelling belly of the Goddess.

Traditionally, ale was made special for the feast—a light golden brew that was effervescent and warming, like the sun, yet yeasty and earthy like the Goddess. Most importantly, the ale was strong and intoxicating like the young Sun God, and satisfied the thirsts worked up from a day of early harvest.

Energy and Meaning

Literally, Litha is the longest day of the year, a day when the sun rises early and sets late, a day that overpowers the night, magnificently. But more than just a sun day, Litha is an earth day, a celebration of how the absorption of the sunlight produces life and life-giving foods. This is a day to celebrate fertile fruits, abundance, radiance, enlightenment, and brightness. This is the pinnacle of our youth, our power, and our harvest. Metaphorically, the Sun God is at the pinnacle of his youthful power. He feels eternal, all-powerful, and ever youthful. He shines his attention on the Earth Goddess, bathing her in radiant love, protection, and provision. And she absorbs his light, feeding the child she shelters within, ensuring the continuance of life.

Litha is both a joyous celebration of the brilliance, radiance, fire, and heat of youthful perfection, but also marks the turning point, the beginning of the decline. With the long day of bright light, we revel in the glory, then light the fires that can burn all night, like the child in the womb growing bright.

While the Sun God stands tall, bright, and powerful in his masculinity, Litha also marks the beginning of his decline, as the wheel turns and he begins the slide toward mid-age, old age, weakness, and death. In a culture obsessed with youth and at a time when we feel ageless and immortal, we too often forget that Litha marks the end of the waxing cycle of expansion and the start of the waning cycle of decline. From here on, old age awaits us. But there is hope here as well.

Deep in the womb of the earth mother grows the next generation, the future and the fruits of our creative endeavor. As the Sun God begins his decline, the Earth Goddess continues to swell, her time of power and the peak of feminine strength still to come.

Today we celebrate the bright sun, the God and masculinity. Tonight we light the sacred Litha fires, which we will leap across, feeling alive. And tomorrow, before we start to slip back toward the darkness, each day moving a little closer to the ultimate darkness of death, we affirm the great light that grows inside each of us. There, we are fully alive.

The Sacred Dance

Litha is one step of the sacred dance of the divine relationship— when the youthful, perfect God begins his decline toward old age, and the Goddess grows the next young God within her, the seeds of their combined dreams. The wheel of the year marks the steps in this sacred dance, the movements of the divine creative relationship that makes eternity possible, makes old age worthwhile, and makes our descent into darkness filled with the fires of hope.

Whether partnered or single, we celebrate the evolving relationship of the sacred pair, God and Goddess, Lugh and Litha, knowing both energies dwell within each of us. Pregnant, creative, and growing, the Goddess is also deeply nourished by the attention of the God. Radiant and youthfully perfect, the Sun God is invigorated by the Goddess's expansion, within her grows his child, and his future. Through the Goddess he finds meaning and maturity, ready to move into his role of protector and provider. Through this sacred dance each learns the strength of their own character, understands the power of their gender identity and how they collaborate in the sacred dance of creation.

As we dance, sing, and tell stories, let's remember the wheel of the year turning. As we light torches and candles, and leap over the Litha fire, let's take the small steps forward in our own glorious dance of life, knowing the God and Goddess energies within us that make us productive, fruitful, and filled with potential. We explore this divine relationship of female and male, Goddess and God, not just today, but going forward, as they dance around the wheel of the year, moving into and out of sacred balance, their feminine and masculine energies twirling, sometimes leading, sometimes following, sometimes in complete balance, but always together.

While we often think of life as a series of polar opposites—positive and negative, white and black, good and bad, female and male, rich and poor—they are in reality a series of pairs in an eternal, divine dance within us. At Litha, with the long day's light, take the time to pause and be illuminated, to see these pairs as interdependent and co-creative, like the sacred Gods and Goddesses, relying upon one another for their very definition and survival.

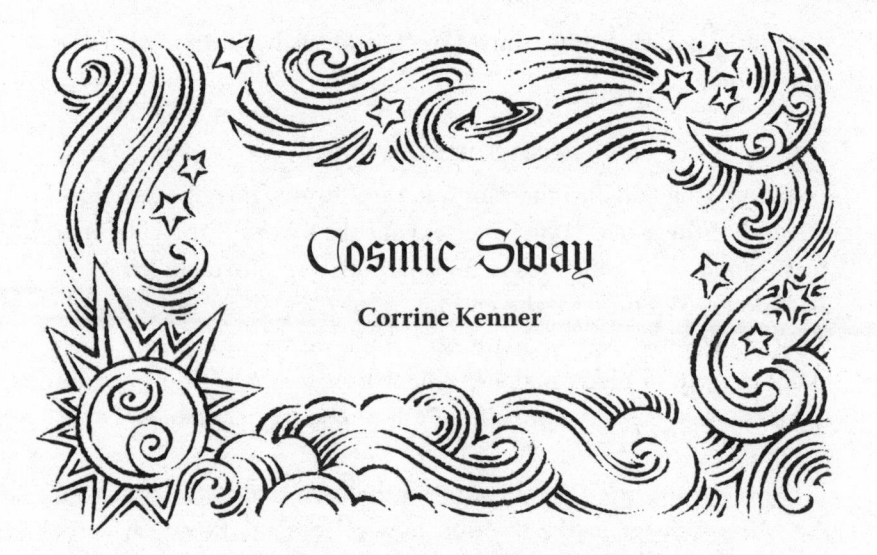

Cosmic Sway

Corrine Kenner

WHETHER YOU THINK OF Midsummer as the first day of summer, the longest day of the year, or the Summer Solstice, it's both an astronomical and an astrological event.

Like most celestial phenomena, the Midsummer holiday can be keyed to a specific moment in time. In this case, that's on June 21, at 12:38 p.m. Eastern time, when the Sun enters watery Cancer.

That's also when the Sun reaches its northernmost position in the sky, directly over the Tropic of watery Cancer. In fact, the word solstice comes from the Latin words for "sun" and "stop." The Sun stops moving north on that day. At that point, the North Pole is tilted toward the Sun, so its rays will shed light on the earth for the longest day of the year.

As it happens, the Sun and the Moon are in an almost perfect sextile at that moment, too. In fact, the two luminaries are almost exactly 60 degrees apart. Sextiles suggest grace and harmony between two planets; they understand and support each other.

Granted, this particular aspect is a little odd, because the fiery Sun is in the watery sign of Cancer, and the watery Moon is in the fiery sign of Leo. It's a perfectly symmetrical balance, though, and the energy between them moves freely and easily, like partners in a cosmic dance.

Tarot and Astrology

To picture the Sun and the Moon in tarot terms, imagine Apollo—the god of the Sun—taking the reins of the Chariot, the card that corresponds to Cancer. It's actually a pretty comfortable fit. After all, Apollo used to drive the chariot of the Sun. What most people don't realize, however, is that most people with a strong Cancerian element in their chart make excellent travelers, adventurers, and fighters—especially if home, family, and country happen to be on the line.

Now picture the High Priestess—the card that corresponds to the Moon—dressed like the lion tamer from the Strength card. That's the card that corresponds to Leo. We don't normally think of the High Priestess as someone who confronts wild animals. She normally seems fairly placid and controlled. In her full capacity as the goddess of the Moon, however, she does rise at night to lead wild animals on a moonlit run through the forest.

In both cases—the Sun as the charioteer, and the Moon as the goddess of the hunt—we see the primal, untamed nature of astrology and tarot.

Practical Astrology

These days, astrology is an indoor sport. Astrologers rely on computer programs, datebooks, and calendars, which make it all too easy to forget that astrology used to be a visual science based on scientific observations of the sky.

To align yourself with the planetary energies of Midsummer, go outside to watch both the sunrise and the sunset today. In the morning, wake up while it's still dark and stand in the shadows as the Sun glides over the eastern horizon. Tonight, stand in the same spot at twilight and watch as the Sun slips away.

In both cases, you'll see the Sun rise and set rise at its northernmost latitude. Look for landmarks that will help you remember its positions; in six months, at the winter solstice, the Sun will rise and set much farther to the south.

Planetary Positions

The Sun is in watery Cancer. It will move into fiery Leo, its own sign, on July 22.

The Moon is in earthy Virgo, where it tends to inspire a desire for physical fitness and mental acuity.

Mercury is in its own sign, airy Gemini. The messenger planet is operating at peak efficiency here, stimulating clear and open communication and clever conversation. Mercury will move into watery Cancer on July 8, and fiery Leo on July 23.

Venus is in Leo, where the planet of love and affection rewards loyal suitors with lavish affection. She'll enter earthy Virgo on July 18. The planet will go retrograde and glide back into the sign of Leo on July 31.

Mars is in airy Gemini, accenting the warrior planet's intellectual ability—but also fueling a tendency toward nervous energy. Mars will move into watery Cancer on June 24.

Jupiter is still in fiery Leo.

Saturn in still in watery Scorpio.

The generational outer planets remain in the same signs:

Uranus is in fiery Aries.

Neptune is retrograde in watery Pisces.

Pluto is retrograde in earthy Capricorn.

Planets in Aspect

At the moment the Sun enters Cancer, it will be in a harmonious sextile with the Moon in Leo. For a moment, the two luminaries have traded places in the natural order of the zodiac, and they're in each other's domains. The switch adds some interest to their cosmic dance.

Even though it's now in Cancer, the Sun is in a close conjunction with Mars, in airy Gemini. The Sun's heat supercharges Mars' masculine energy and physical desire.

Meanwhile, the Moon, in fiery Leo, is in a supportive sextile with Mars—which means Mars is getting a blast of heat and light from both luminaries.

The fiery Leo Moon is also squaring off against Saturn, which is in watery Scorpio.

Even though Mercury in in Gemini, its own sign, the messenger planet is in an uncomfortable square with Neptune in Pisces—which is comfortably established in its own dominion, as well. Communications could be clouded or confused; take care to be clear and precise when you reach out to others.

Venus and Jupiter are conjunct in fiery Leo. The two planets are known as the Lesser and Greater Benefics, respectively. When they join forces, they shower all of their subjects with favors and gifts.

Jupiter is also in a harmonious trine with Uranus in fiery Aries. Their alliance bodes well for anyone who's engaged in Jupiterian pursuits like teaching or publication—particularly if they're experimenting with new methods or approaches.

Phases of the Moon

July 1: A highly visible Full Moon in earthy Capricorn sheds light on issues of business, career, and social status—all subjects that are completely opposite the Sun's position in watery Cancer, the sign of home and family life.

July 15: A New Moon in Cancer, its own sign, ushers in a brief period of domestic tranquility. It's a good time to enjoy life in your own domicile, or to invest in home repairs and home improvements.

July 31: A Full Moon in airy Aquarius will bask in the light of the fiery Leo Sun. This is the second Full Moon in a single month—which makes it a rare celestial event known as a Blue Moon.

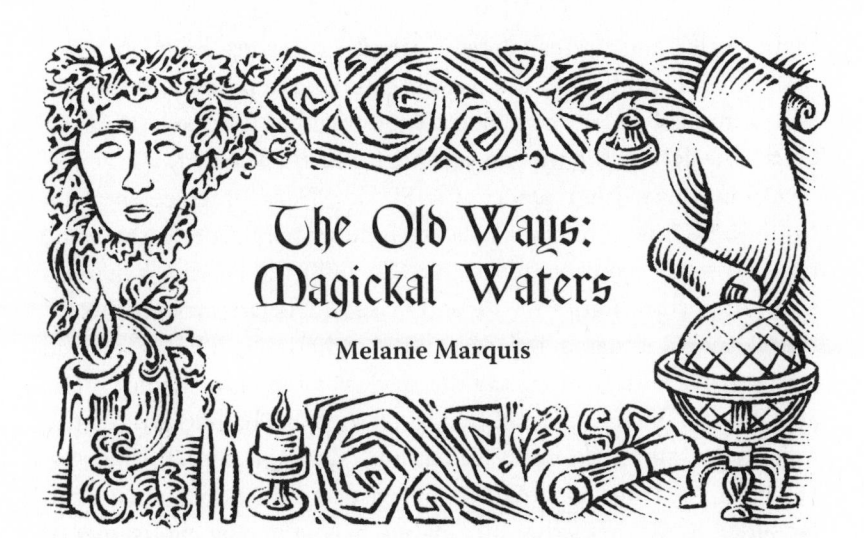

The Old Ways:
Magickal Waters

Melanie Marquis

ALTHOUGH TODAY MANY WESTERN Neopagans think of Midsummer as primarily a fire festival, in older times, many Midsummer celebrations held water and fire in greater equality, two essential aspects whose coming together was symbolic of the holiday's significance as a whole. Midsummer is a time of juxtaposition, when nature illuminates the truth of seemingly disparate aspects coming together for a common purpose. Days will soon begin to shorten, just as the sun reaches the height of its glory. Vegetation is in full bloom, yet it nears the end of its growth cycle, and soon the living crops will fall to either the hands of humans or the tides of nature. We know the coming harvest will bring nourishment and life to the people, just as it means certain death for the crops. These crops rely on both the sun and the rain, so it only makes sense that we honor both the sun (fire) and the rain (water) at the time of Midsummer, when all the plants, all the water, and all the sunshine, are at the pinnacle and height of their power.

In Slavic lands in particular, Midsummer is traditionally associated with both fire *and* water, and rituals are heavily focused on the magickal properties of rivers and streams, as well as on the combining of opposites. A popular Slavic belief holds that on Midsummer night, water and fire can "make friends." Fires are built on river-banks, lovers unite, and the powers of both the moon and the sun pour into field and stream alike, joined together for one last hurrah before the light of the waxing year begins its final decent.

As in many other places, the Slavic Midsummer celebration came to be linked to the Christian holiday held around the same time of year in commemoration of St. John the Baptist, regarded as an important figure in the early rise of Christianity. In Russia, the Ukraine, Lithuania, Belarus, and elsewhere, the holiday is called Ivan Kupala, with "Ivan" being the Slavic version of the name "John," and "Kupala" being a play on the slavic word for "bather," a reference to John the Baptist fondness for bathing (aka baptizing), the masses. However, the true roots of both the word and the holiday may echo far older traditions which pre-date Christianity by thousands of years. Kupala is also the name of an ancient Slavic goddess associated with reproduction, fertility, water, joy, love, herbs, and magick. She brought life and renewal to the earth and the crops through her blessings, and she was traditionally honored around the time of Midsummer.

Water is believed to be endowed with especially magickal properties at the time of Midsummer. In many Slavic lands, taking to the rivers and streams for a group swim was common practice. Since Midsummer was a time when the energies of both the moon and the sun entered and combined in the waters, it was believed that bathing in such charmed water would improve health and increase overall vitality and power. One time-honored Lithuanian tradition is to wash one's face with dew on the morning of Midsummer, in order to increase beauty and preserve youth. Another Lithuanian tradition holds that walking barefoot through the Midsummer morning dew can have a healing effect, preventing the feet from getting chapped. In Russia, a Midsummer brew of water and grass is used to increase one's life force and promote overall good health.

The water of Midsummer not only heals; it can also serve as a powerful medium for divining the future. One divination ritual still widely practiced in Slavic lands on Ivan Kupala concerns love. Wreaths are fashioned from wild herbs and flowers, and are then worn on the head. The wreaths are believed to banish evil spirits and avert the evil eye, and they also act as a symbol of the endless cycles of nature, an emblem of infinity. At sunset, the wreaths are tossed into a river or stream, sometimes set afloat with a burning candle attached at the center. If the wreath floats out far into the river, perhaps even crossing over to the opposite bank, romantic prospects are deemed very good, and love is predicted. If the wreath clings to the edge of the nearest bank or gets stuck and doesn't really go anywhere, prospects for love are not so great, and delays and obstacles for lovers should be expected. If the wreath were to sink, it reveals an untrustworthy lover; if the wreath breaks apart, it signifies another year without a betrothal.

There's also an interesting Slavic method of wax and water divination, practicable anytime, but especially effective on Midsummer. A candle is broken up into pieces, then melted in a metal container. If you want to try this yourself, use a regular cooking pot on the stove or a small cauldron outdoors over an open flame. The molten wax is then carefully poured into a vessel of cold water. The wax forms shapes as it cools, and these symbols are then interpreted according to tradition or intuition. Common symbols and interpretations include the star, signifying good luck; the flower, indicating a new admirer; the flag, predicting an unexpected guest; a man, revealing good friendship and strong alliances; a band or rectangle, indicating a fun trip; and an undulating, or zigzag figure, indicating that wishes will be fulfilled.

Another Slavic Midsummer water divination ritual utilized a bowl of water and two flower blossoms to discern the fate of lovers. The two blossoms, meant to represent the two lovers, were placed on the surface of the water, and their movements were then observed. If the blossoms floated together, the lovers could expect to remain united. If the blossoms drifted apart, so too would the lovers' hearts.

Large bodies of water were also used in Slavic culture for Midsummer divination. One custom was to go out into the middle of a river and make a wish on a pebble. The pebble was then cast into the water, and the number of circles made on the river's surface were carefully observed and counted. If the number of ripples was even, the wish would come true; if odd, the desire would remain unfulfilled.

Midsummer water was believed to have other magickal properties, as well. Ashes were taken from the Midsummer bonfire, then boiled with water. The resulting potion was stored for use throughout the year, to be sprayed on the body whenever the witch had the need to move about quietly without being detected.

If you would like to incorporate more water magick into your Midsummer rituals, try to find natural water sources that are as unpolluted as possible. If such a place doesn't exist in your area, just use your own sink, shower, or bathtub and make do with the water from the tap. You can use your charms to empower the tap water, banishing impurities and charging it with the elemental force of water itself, inviting into it the energies of the oceans, rivers, lakes, seas, the goddess Kupala, etc. For maximum effect, incorporate the elemental force of fire into your Midsummer rituals as well, placing lit candles around the bathtub, holding a torch high as you wade into a river, sitting beside a small campfire as you gaze at the ripples made by a pebble dropped into a small vessel of water, building a fire beside a riverbank—or whatever else you can think of. Trying new things and adding extra details to your traditional sabbat celebrations keeps them vibrant, fulfilling, and effective, and looking to old Slavic traditions is one way to get inspiration for creating your own modern Midsummer magick.

References:

Frazer, Sir James George. *The Golden Bough.* 1922. Reprint, New York: Bartleby.com, 2000.

Kudirka, Juozas. "The Lithuanians: An Ethnic Portrait." "Midsummer Day." Lithuanian Folk Culture Centre, 1996. Accessed October 13, 2013. http://thelithuanians.com/bookthelithuanians /node20.html.

"Russian Culture Days." Accessed October 1, 2013. http:// en.chancefr.ru/?page_id=604.

Slavic Souvenirs Blog. "Ivan Kupala Day." Accessed October 1, 2013. http://blog.slavicsouvenirs.com/ivana-kupala-day.

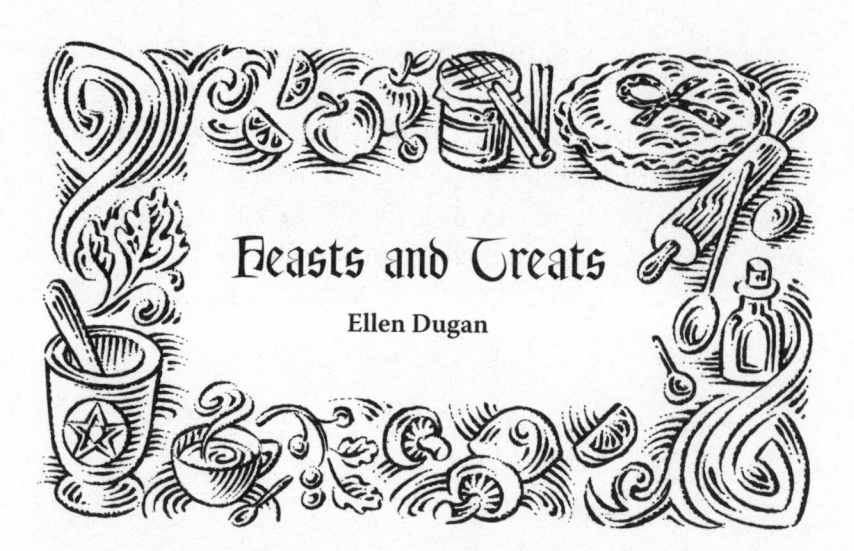

Feasts and Treats

Ellen Dugan

MIDSUMMER HAS ARRIVED, AND the vegetables and herbs are really starting to produce in the gardens! As the price of fresh fruit and vegetables drops at your local market this time of year, make the most of this opportunity. (These four vegetarian friendly recipes certainly do.) This Midsummer, try keeping things light so you can splurge on a decadent dark chocolate fondue for dessert!

Veggie Pizza

This is a classic summer recipe. Here is a tip: arrange the veggies cleverly on top so it looks like a regular pizza.

Prep time: 30 minutes
Cook time: 12–15 minutes to bake crust
Serves: 6–8

2 packages crescent rolls
2 packages fat-free cream cheese
1 cup Greek, nonfat, plain yogurt
1 package (1 ounce) dry Ranch-style dressing mix
Choice of fresh veggies. Cucumber slices, broccoli florets, green
 and red bell peppers, grated carrots, halved cherry tomatoes,
 red onions, or whatever else you like.

Preheat oven to 375 degrees F. Roll out crescent roll dough onto a 9 × 13-inch baking sheet to form the pizza crust. (Gently pat it together so it is all one piece of dough.) Bake the crust for 12 to 15 minutes until golden brown. Let it cool at least 15 minutes without removing it from the baking sheet. In a small mixing bowl combine the cream cheese, plain Greek yogurt, and dry ranch mix. Spread this over the cooled crust. Arrange veggies over the cream cheese mixture and refrigerate for at least one hour. Slice and serve.

Spinach Salad with Walnuts and Cranberries

A light and satisfying salad that you can jazz up by adding fresh sliced strawberries. You can also experiment a bit—I personally prefer this salad without the onions.

Prep time: 20 minutes
Serves: 6–8

1 pound of fresh baby spinach
2 tablespoons diced red onions
½ cup feta cheese crumbles
⅓ cup of chopped walnuts
¼ cup of dried cranberries

Add ingredients to bowl and toss well. Then try this sweet-and-sour dressing recipe. It makes plenty.

1 cup vegetable oil
⅓ cup white vinegar
1 medium onion, grated
¾ cup sugar
1 teaspoon salt
1 teaspoon Worcestershire sauce

Pour ingredients into a jar. Screw on lid tightly and shake the dressing. Serve over salad and refrigerate leftover dressing in the lidded jar.

Dark Chocolate Fondue in a Crockpot

This is a dairy-free, which cuts out a lot of fat as compared to recipes calling for heavy cream. Be warned… this is so good—it's evil!

Prep time: 10 minutes
Melting time: 30 minutes to 1 hour
Serves: 4–10 (depending on how many chocoholics you have!)

12 ounces (1 bag) semisweet chocolate chips (I used Hershey's Special Dark chocolate chips.)
¾ cup almond milk
1 teaspoon vanilla extract
1/8 teaspoon granulated instant coffee
Assorted fruits for dipping (strawberries, bananas, etc.)

Add all ingredients to the crockpot. With crockpot on low, stir occasionally as the chocolate melts. It will take about 30 minutes to 1 hour to melt completely. The fondue will have the consistency of a creamy soup when completely melted. Chop bananas and strawberries into big chunks for dipping. Pretzels, marshmallows, graham crackers, and cubes of angel food cake are wonderful to dip in this fondue as well! Refrigerate any leftovers. You can easily reheat a small portion of leftover fondue in the microwave. Just zap the small portions in 20-second increments.

(Note: I used a mini crockpot that holds 16 ounces for this fondue. Also, long wooden skewers work great for the dipping.)

Heather's Midsummer Magick Lemon Sangria

My coven sister Heather conjured up this sangria recipe. It is amazingly light and refreshing—perfect for Midsummer. You may want to make a double batch as my coven went through this quickly. Also, it's fun to eat the wine-soaked fruit when you finish the sangria!

Prep time: 5 minutes
Chill time: 2 hours
Serves: 4–6

1 bottle of Moscato (or your favorite local semisweet white wine.)
Heather uses a local Missouri wine called *Montelle's Stone House White*

25 ounces white grape juice

¼ cup Limoncello

1–2 shots of whiskey or Southern Comfort

Oranges, limes, and strawberries, sliced

Mix liquids in a large glass pitcher. Stir, and then cover the pitcher with plastic wrap. Refrigerate for at least 2 hours. Add sliced fruit after the drink is well chilled. (Plan on making a double batch!)

Crafty Crafts

Lexa Olick

LITHA REPRESENTS THE LONGEST day of the year. This day will shine brighter than any other. Now is the time to go outside and celebrate the triumph of light. It is a source of energy, life, and success.

Litha is the Summer Solstice. It is a period when light finally overcomes the darkness. It's a time for us to revel in the glory of the sun. It is represented by the element of fire and has the ability to repel evil and bring about prosperity.

The sun deserves more appreciation than it gets. It returns every morning, so it's easy to take it for granted. The sun is a source of light as well as life. It brighten our days while replenishing our energy supply and nourishing our bodies. The sun is a great source of power that we can endlessly tap into.

So for this Litha, make use of solar lighting. We can utilize a wide variety of solar-powered LED lights to not only be more decorative, but also be more energy efficient. It's a gorgeous way to brighten the night while still using the sun's energy.

Litha Solar Orbs

Solar orbs sit by the window to charge all day so they can glow at night. The sun is currently at its strongest, so this is the perfect project to contain that energy. They are made with simple materials. An ordinary glass bowl is quickly transformed into a glowing orb of beauty.

Supplies

1 medium-sized, clear, rounded glass bowl

Frosted-glass spray paint

E6000 adhesive

Solar garden light or solar path light (Look for the most inexpensive ones. The dollar stores start to carry them in the summer.)

Instructions: In order for the bowl to emit an ethereal glow, you first have to coat the inside with spray paint. The frosted-glass spray paint covers glass with an acrylic resin that will scatter the light radiating from inside the bowl. Just one coat of paint will help diffuse the light. It leaves the glass looking milky white during the day, but at night the jar will be ablaze with a warm radiance.

Lay a few sheets of newspaper down in a well-ventilated area. Apply a coat of frosted-glass spray paint inside the bowl, taking care to avoid painting the bottom, which needs to be fully transparent in order for the solar battery to absorb the sun's energy during the day. Otherwise, make sure to cover the bowl in its entirety

Set the bowl aside for about 20 minutes to dry completely. During that time, you can disassemble the solar light.

When you take apart a solar light, you will discover useful materials inside. The top piece unscrews easily, leaving you with the light and battery pack.

The battery pack is what we're looking for. It contains the solar cell, a circuit board, and the LED light. The solar cell is covered by a solar panel that looks like a dark square, but underneath it is the circuit board. The circuit board senses when the sun is shining down on the solar cell and automatically turns off the LED.

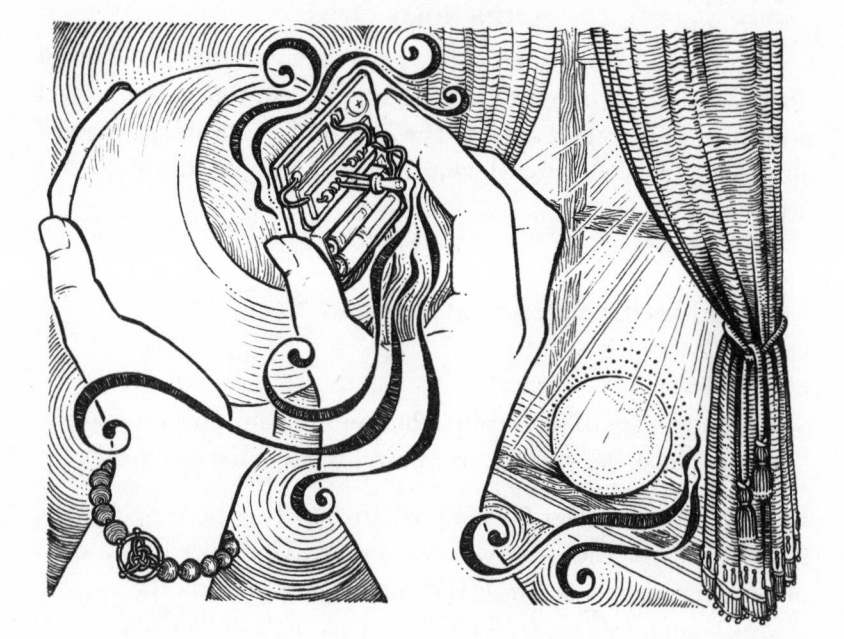

Glue the solar battery pack directly to the bottom of the inside of the glass bowl. Make sure that the solar panel is pressed against the glass because it needs to be in direct sunlight in order to work. Hold it tight to the glass for 1 minute, then let it sit for 24 hours to fully adhere.

This bowl becomes an orb when it is displayed upside down. The bottom of the bowl has the solar pack, so it now becomes the top in order to remain in direct contact with the sun. Place the orb by the window where it can get the most sun, then watch it glow all night!

Time to Complete: About 40 minutes to assemble, but between 24 to 48 hours for the adhesive to completely cure.

Cost: Around $15.00

Fairy Garden Lights

These tiny, little lights add whimsy to your garden. They look like flowers so they blend in during the day, but shine like fireflies once it gets dark.

The solar lights are tucked inside beautiful silk flowers. They are gathered together in a vase to create a magical bouquet of lights. In the morning, you can enjoy the sight of the silk flowers. Then at night, you can watch them transform into a dazzling display of tiny lights! They add a bit of radiance to your nighttime garden.

Supplies

Small solar string lights
E6000 adhesive
Large silk flowers
Decorative vase
Marbles or pebbles

Instructions: For this project, it is best to choose silk flowers with a flat center, such as daisies. A string of solar lights usually have about 16 bulbs, but it depends on the brand. Either way, collect as many flowers as you have bulbs.

Apply a dab of E6000 adhesive onto the side of a solar bulb. Hold it tight against the center of the flower for approximately 1 minute. It will take about 24 hours for the glue to completely dry, but you can continue to attach bulbs to the rest of your flowers in the meantime. As you continue to add more bulbs, push the petals aside so the wire can dangle down onto the stem. Twirl the wire a couple times along the stem so it won't be obtrusive. Apply another dab of E6000 at the bottom of the stem and hold the wiring tightly against it for 1 minute. Once all the bulbs are attached to your flowers, set them aside for 24 hours.

Gather your flowers together and place them in a vase. If you want to weigh your vase down, pour some marbles or pebbles at the bottom. Drape the main wire over the edge of the vase and stake the

battery pack into the ground. Once the lights have charged all day, they will add sparkle to your garden at night.

Time to Complete: Around 30 minutes to assemble, but 24 hours for the glue to fully dry.

Cost: About $25.00

Sustainable Solstice: Into the Woods

Natalie Zaman

TWO TIMES A YEAR, THE sun stands still. Six months ago at the Winter Solstice, the sun was at its lowest altitude in the sky, giving us extra hours of darkness. Reaching its zenith at the Summer Solstice, we experience a longer day. In fact, there are places on the planet where the sun is visible for a full 24 hours. Extended periods of light and heat cause plants to grow and flourish. All is awake and alive. Go out into nature and you will see it everywhere: color and light, and the green—oh, the green.

I enjoy a walk in nature in any season, and each brings its own brand of magic. A summer walk teems with life: in the air, hidden under the leaves... and what are those leaves? In my neck of the woods (bad pun intended), I've found yarrow, milkweed (a favorite of butterflies), and an abundance of dandelions, honeysuckle, and wild blackberries. Every walk in every season reveals new discoveries. There are also plants to avoid, like poison ivy, a few varieties of nightshade, and many mushrooms that look interesting but are best left alone. The trick is to be able to tell one plant from another and to know what to avoid and what's safe to handle.

Part of preserving the Old Ways is learning to use plants for natural remedies and magical work. Many herbs are widely available in shops and online—already identified, cured and dried—but you will be become better acquainted with nature and forge a stronger connection with the plants you work with by finding and collecting them yourself. Take advantage of the long summer days to forage.

Don't be afraid to start very simply. So many plants look alike, and one type can have several different varieties, each with its own unique characteristics. There are plants that should always be handled with caution because some people will have an allergic reaction to certain plants just from touching them. Visit localharvest. org, an online, countrywide, agricultural resource, to find one of the many farms in your neighborhood where you can pick your own fruits, herbs, and vegetables. Beginning this way allows for the potential assistance of local farmers to address your questions and concerns about local vegetation. Websites and books are invaluable, but can't compare with the human touch.

When you feel comfortable, take to the woods, but go out prepared.

Make It Your Own!
You will need:

A natural fiber pouch to collect plants

Scissors

Notebook dedicated to your herbal study (Press the first samples you collect on your own in the notebook to create your own, personal reference. Slip your cuttings in between the blank pages of the notebook, then place a weight on the book to flatten the samples [I put my notebook at the bottom of a pile of heavier books]. When the samples have flattened out, you can glue or tape them to the page and write out any information you have about them, including magical and healing qualities, and where and when you found each one.)

Reference book to ID plants

First-aid kit (Always handy whenever you are out and about in nature!)

When deciding where you will forage, be respectful of the environment and of other peoples' property. Make sure you have permission to cut plants before you take them, even in a public park. Some parks are nature preserves and taking even small specimens could disrupt a delicate ecosystem. Take only what you need, and more importantly, what you can identify. Express gratitude for every plant you cut:

  Name of Plant , *I know you and thank you.*

Consider taking a few seasons to familiarize yourself with your area and the plants that grow there. Watch for changes and patterns of growth and dormant periods as the weather changes and the months go by. Record these changes in your notebook by including samples of the same plant collected under different conditions.

Forage for plants for your magical practices when you've become proficient in identifying them. Clean, preserve, and/or dry your harvest before use. You may come across recipes and formulae that require plants you can't find. Before you go shopping, consider some alternatives: Can you grow any of the ingredients? Would any local plants make suitable substitutes? And you can always be creative and rewrite the spell so that you can use what you have—there's always more than one way to accomplish any task.

Be a locavore (a person who buys locally/closely produced items) in summer and all the seasons!

Litha Ritual: Intertwining Opposites

Dallas Jennifer Cobb

SUMMER SOLSTICE IS A time for the God and Goddess to celebrate their shared energy, to see the power of their passionate union as it grows closer to manifestation. Litha is a time of radiance and absorption, glory and growth, and of the potential for dreams to come true through the power of collaboration—the collaboration of two great powers.

Understanding the energy and meaning of Litha allows us to contemplate power in our own lives. In the darkness, we can contemplate what grows inside of us, and how those dreams, our metaphorical babies, can be fed by the light. At the zenith of the sun we can examine our relationship to power, enlightenment, and passion, and see how it feeds our dreams.

While so many rituals are joyously undertaken in community, on Litha, I like to symbolically explore the relationship between paired, so-called opposites that rely so steadfastly upon one another for their survival: light and dark, waxing and waning, work and leisure, men and women, Lugh and Litha, and in-community and solitary. I spend much of the day alone, undertaking small rituals of emotional, mental, and spiritual observance, and then join in community in the evening to feast and celebrate.

If you are a solitary practitioner, I welcome you to invite a few people to feast with you tonight, and if you are a community-minded person with a strong ritual circle or coven, I welcome you to take time in solitude today to work your private, inner magic.

To understand the intertwining energies, we must look at the commonly held assumptions of what is feminine and what is masculine. Feminine is nurturing, receptive, emotional, related, imperfect, multitasking, unpredictable, nonlinear/cyclical, round, and soft. Alternately, masculine is represented as protective, penetrating, mental, separate, perfect, task focused, predictable, linear, angular, and hard.

We're led to believe that they are polar opposites, two opposing energies. But today, we will celebrate the steps of their sacred dance together, how the God and Goddess come together, intertwine, and collaborate for each of their greatest good. On Litha, we "couple" our internalized male and female energies for fertile and productive results.

While this is written as a "day-long" ritual, it is centered around meals and mealtimes, so that if you are working or busy with other things, you can still be present to the sabbat, and the magic of male and female collaboration.

Rise

On Litha, I like to rise in the darkness and know quiet. I am aware of my containment, my solitude, and my peace. Find out what time the sun will rise in your area, and set your alarm for a good three quarters of an hour before. You'll have time to dress quickly and prepare a warm cup of tea to take with you, outdoors, into the dark.

Savor the darkness, the silence and calm. Walk to a place where you will be able to watch the sun come up. Find a safe spot to sit, and while in the darkness, make quiet lists of what you love about women and femininity. Remember women you love and women who have loved you. Recall their strengths, their power, and their attributes. Know what "being feminine" looks like. Whether you are a man or woman, know your feminine qualities and strengths.

Ask yourself: What do I nurture, love, embrace, and feed?

In the darkness, be with your feminine self, and be at peace.

Stay long enough to see the sun creep up into the sky, the dark turn to light, and feel the cool air warm. Welcome the growing Sun God.

Go home and make a Litha breakfast. Enjoy symbols of the sun's glory, like oranges or eggs with their golden yolks. Add fruits of the Earth's fertility like strawberries or young spinach. Ingest these symbols, and know that feminine and masculine combine together to produce food, life, and sustenance. As you eat, know that you contain both masculine and feminine energy, the impregnated seeds of dreams are within you. With these you can produce your own "babies" (creative ideas, wishes, hopes, desires, and dreams) and grow them to glowing fruition. See yourself as metaphorically pregnant and know that you embody both the earth and the sun, the powers that intertwine to produce life.

Ask yourself: What are my deepest desires? What dreams do I choose to grow?

Stand

When the midday sun has climbed high into the sky, ask the Sun God to walk with you. Go outside to enjoy the splendor of nature. Turn your face to the sun and absorb the radiant light. Use this time to harvest from your own garden, visit a farmers' market or grocery store, and gather the fruits of the season in preparation for tonight's feast.

As you gather foods, see yourself like the Earth Goddess, gathering in the radiance of the Sun God, feeding the life that grows within. Nibble on foods as you shop or harvest, literally feeding yourself. And with each item that you add to your shopping basket, know that you feed your dreams.

Ask yourself: How am I fed and supported to achieve my deepest desires?

Journey

"If I am to utter only one prayer, let it be 'Thank You,'" said German philosopher and mystic Meister Eckhart. Preparing for the evening meal, take time to express your gratitude for the miraculous products of earth and sun. As you wash and chop vegetables, let your thanks flow. Know that these foods are the product of male and female collaboration, the sacred twining of masculine and feminine.

Look within yourself to see the ways in which you harness your masculine energy to provide structure and form for the feminine creativity and content. Know how you use your drive and purpose to create space for receiving and enjoyment.

Ask yourself: What is the fruit of all of my sacred masculine and feminine selves?

Prepare yourself to celebrate in community tonight. Know what you bring to the feast of life, and know what energy and blessings you want to take from the fire. With knowledge of what your metaphorical and literal babies are, know that you take these gifts to the feast in addition to whatever foods you contribute. Your rich life is the result of your inner dance of masculine and feminine, and your great fertility and creativity are nurtured by your energy and light.

Tonight you will nourish seeds sewn, be grateful for friends and family, bless hearth and home, celebrate health and vitality, and accept blessings for the road ahead.

Dance

Walking to the Litha feast, return to the quietness inside you that represents the feminine self. Woman or man, know that you are pregnant with your dreams and great possibility, and that these dreams are fed by light: people, community, joy, laughter, love, and of course, the Sun God.

Prepare yourself to soak in the radiance of community at tonight's feast. Take a candle to add your light to the table, and take food to add your nourishment to the feast, each a representation of the masculine and feminine energy that you possess.

As you walk, ask yourself: What is needed to feed me, and help my dreams to grow?

And when you arrive and as you feast, know that each of us sometimes feels empty, lonely, isolated, and needy, so reach outside yourself tonight to fill these needs, hungers, longings, and desires. Eat, laugh, smile, and play, and let the light shine in. For today, as we understand the sacred dance of God and Goddess, we understand how to use the light to examine our darkness, use satiation to balm our hunger, and use satisfaction to understand our need.

Leap

Whether you place candles on the floor of an apartment (safely), or gather around the roaring bonfire outdoors, ready yourself to take the leap. With both God and Goddess within you, masculine and feminine, know you hold the power for great creation.

Stand within the circle, supported, accepted, and connected. Ask yourself: What actions and nurture will manifest my dreams?

And then, stepping out of the circle, alone again, look into the fire, open yourself to the blessings, and take a leap into the future.

Today we have walked the mini wheel of the year, enacting Shakespeare's "dream within a dream." We start and end in solitude and in between enjoy community; we arrive and leave the day in darkness, and in the midst enjoy the bright, radiant light; we started as a sleepy babe, we sat, we walked, we journeyed, we danced, and finally we leap into the unknown.

The small journey of a day, the journey of the sun and earth in a year, and the journey of a human life, all made possible by the collaboration of mother Goddess and father God.

Go now, as the wheel of the year turns, hold the God and Goddess within, and honor the sacred dance of masculine and feminine within you, and know with these two mighty powers, everything is possible.

Blessed be.

Notes

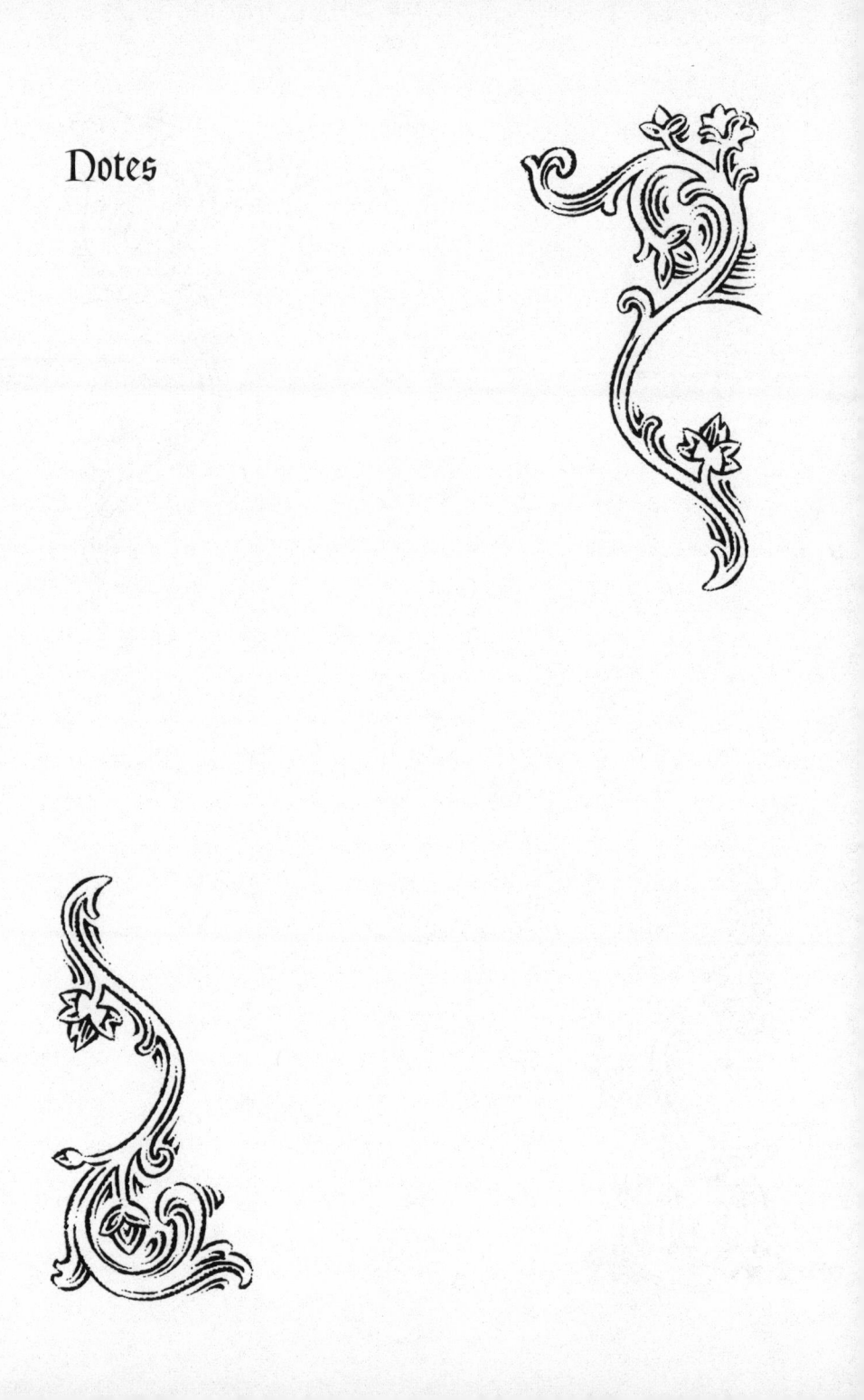

Notes

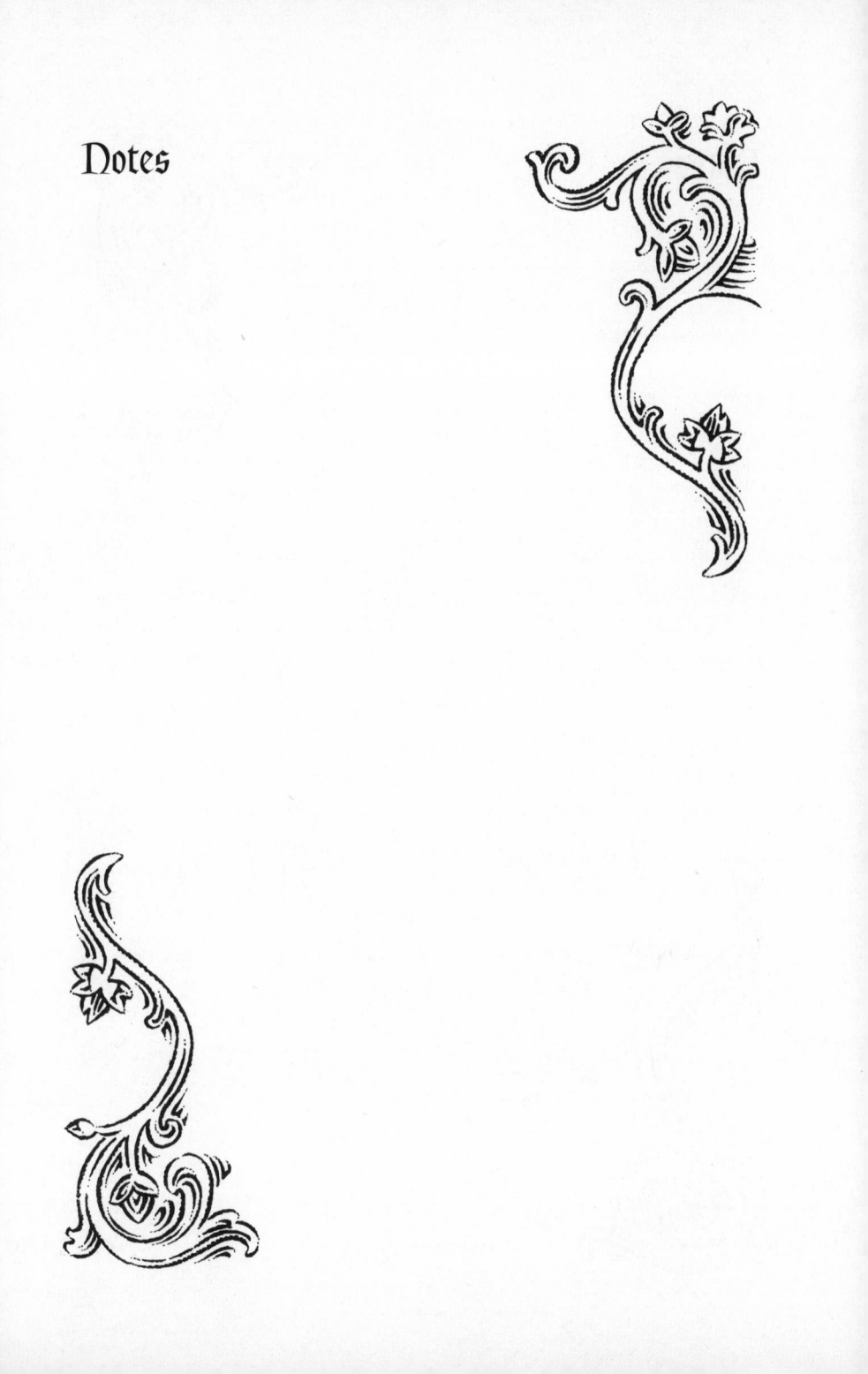

Lammas

Lammas & Lughnasadh

Patricia M. Lafayllve

AUGUST 1 MARKED THE beginning of autumn, and therefore it was time to enter the harvest season. Throughout the medieval period, two popular events occurred on this date. The first, Lammas, was mentioned in the *Anglo-Saxon Chronicle* twice. The first mention of Lammas came during the time northern-area groups broke the peace and warred with the southern people of England. The second time, which happened in 917, the holiday is mentioned specifically: "In this year before Lammas, *Æthelflœd*, the 'Lady of the Mercians,' won the borough called Derby with God's help." In Anglo-Saxon (the same language as Old English) the word was *hlaef-mas*, or "loaf-mass," and seemed to be a celebration of the first fruits of the harvest. At some point on August 1, bread would be made from the first grains of the harvest and then blessed at the local church. One piece of folklore, according to Ronald Hutton's *The Stations of the Sun*, suggests that the bread should then be divided into four parts, each then crumbled into a corner of the barn used as a granary. This would, one presumes, provide for a good harvest, helping fill the granary.

In addition to *hlaef-mas*, Lammas was also referred to as the Gule of August. There are two translations at issue here. First, this may refer to a "Yule" of August. Clearly this hints at the importance of Lammas, meaning there might have been two Yuletides, one in August and one in December. While interesting to speculate on, it is difficult to establish precisely why the beginning of autumn is celebrated on par with the midwinter festivities—Yule and Midsummer are placed at the solstices and would seem to balance once another more effectively. The second translation is simply an Anglicization of a Welsh word, *gwyl*, which simply means "feast." In Welsh, we can see *gwylaust*, which would translate as "the feast of August." Whichever of these is the more correct, it is certain that Lammas remained important in Britain throughout the Middle Ages. August 1 became a day for secular fairs, rent payments, the opening of common lands, and the election of local officials. We see remnants of these practices in annual festivals held in Exeter and Chumleigh in Devon, and in South Queensbury, located near Edinburgh.

Modern pagans often consider Lammas and Lughnasadh to be one and the same. They both occur on August 1, both deal with the first fruits, vegetables, and grains ready to be harvested, and both were centers for fairs. However, the two holidays are not interchangeable. Lughnasadh, also called Lugnasa or Lughnasa, has more to do with the Celtic god, Lugh, than Lammas does. Additionally, while Lammas occurred primarily in Britain, we have records of Lughnasadh practices in Ireland and the Scottish Highlands, and it may have even stretched as far as Gaul.

It is important to remember from the first that the god Lugh was neither a sun nor a harvest god. Lugh was, instead, more related to human skills and professions, as well as with kings and heroes. He was a well-known deity, as evidenced by the many places named for Lugh, including cities in France, Spain, and even Rome. Ronald Hutton suggests that the word "lug" might have been the real source for these names—this would mean that the "Lugoves," followers of the Celtic god of craftsmanship, are not connected with the Irish deity—meaning that there may not have been a wide-ranging pan-Celtic festival at all. Lughnasadh may have been a series of local festivities, but as a whole it does seem, if not pan-Celtic, fairly widespread throughout Ireland and Scotland, including some sections of what was known as Gaul.

We owe a great deal to Máire MacNeill for her work on the festival of Lughnasadh. She studied the remnants of this festival across the British Isles and noted a great many folkloric practices that might otherwise have been lost. MacNeill also suggested that Lammas and Lughnasadh might have been one and the same festival, although this is now discounted by scholars for the reasons already discussed. Here are some of the more interesting practices mentioned by MacNeill in her 1962 work, *The Festival of Lughnasa: A Study of the Survival of the Celtic Festival of the Beginning of Harvest*:

The first cutting of the ripened grains would be taken to a high place and then buried as an offering.

A feast was held that included newly harvested foods and bilberries.

Part of the feast might have come from the meat of a newly sacrificed bull.

Although the specifics are unknown, there may have been a ceremony involving the bull's hide, or a replacement of the old bull with a young one.

A ritual play may have been presented, its theme dealing with a struggle for a goddess or other female spirit culminating in a staged fight.

After the play, the head of the bull might have also been brought to the top of the high place, with an actor playing Lugh exulting in triumph over it.

Another ritual play might have involved the monster Blight (or Famine) trapping Lugh and confining him.

While the sacrificing of animals is not popular as part of Pagan practice in the modern world, many of the other traditions can be as easily followed now as they were then. As one might imagine, these events could take place over days, and MacNeill concludes that Lughnasadh might have been a full three-day festival, August 1–3, involving bonfires as well as the above practices. In a festival such as this, there might well have been an opening rite involving the representative of Lugh arriving to preside over the festival, and another closing ritual bringing the chief god of the area back into place. There seems to be some strong evidence for this practice, found mainly in records from the eighteenth and nineteenth centuries. Up to seventy-eight remains of these sort of offerings have been found at the tops of hills in Ulster and the North Midlands, and also near lakes, rivers, and various holy wells.

On the other hand, there is very little evidence for the use of fires for Lughnasadh in Ireland, nor in Britain. In Ireland the basic tradition was a big, open-air feast. While bonfires were used on other holy days, Lughnasadh seemed to notably lack them. Bonfires can be seen in the Isle of Man, where the holiday was called Laa'l Lhuanys. We see some parallels between Isle of Man practices and those in South Wales, as well. Still, we rarely see bonfires being lit as a part of Lammas nor as a part of Lughnasadh.

Scottish Traditions

Now, in Scotland the celebration of Lughnasadh can be problematic. In Barra during the nineteenth century, the opening day of the harvest (August 15) was considered the Catholic Feast of the Assumption of the Virgin Mary, also called *La-Feill Maire*. This may seem late enough in the month not to matter, except that the accepted calendar changed in 1752. Days shifted at this time, and it is interesting to note that the original La-Feill Maire would have occurred on or about August 1. The key is that this celebration had very little, if anything, to do with the Irish set of rituals.

In Scotland the celebration looked more like this: first, one would rise early in the morning and pick a row of ripened grain. Each member of the family would then take a stalk and walk clockwise, following the sun's direction, around the household fire. A song called "The Paean of Mother Mary" would be sung at this time. Then the embers of the fire would be put in a pot and processed around the house and farmland, everyone singing the Paean again. Here we can see what may be references to pre-Christian practices—the harvesting of grain, the procession of fire across one's property to bless it, and so on—but the focus here is clearly Catholic.

In other parts of Scotland, the Highlanders also held a local custom involving August Eve. Here, they would renew the rituals of protection that has been cast on homes and cattle earlier, in Midsummer. Rowan crosses were placed above doors for protective purposes. Rowan is considered by many pagans to be a protective wood, and spindles, pegs, tool handles, and other objects are often made from it. Rowan seems to have a modern connection to the Celtic Brigid and the Norse Thor, as well as to the Virgin Mary. Out in the barn a ball of cow's hair might be put in the milk pail, or tar daubed on the ears and tails of the farm animals. Blue or red threads may have been tied to their tails and incantations then spoken over udders to ensure a good flow of milk. These practices are far more reminiscent of their pagan roots, even though crosses are set in place over the doors.

⚘

In both Lammas and Lughnasadh, the evidence we have seems to come mostly from early Medieval sources, and their practices seemed to have dominated in the Middle Ages. We see that fire was only a part of the festivals in small, localized areas and was not a standard practice for this celebration. Even throughout the Christianized areas of the broader British Isles, we see the remnants of pre-Christian folkloric practices. While Lammas became more or less secularized as a series of local fairs and elections, Lughnasadh seemed to have retained much of its religious character. Either way, these two festivals have persisted into the modern era. The main modern practice involves the baking of bread and its blessing as well as offering the first harvest grains and vegetables in sacrifice to ensure a better and stronger harvest from August 1 on until the final harvest, near the start of winter.

References

Garmonsway, G.N., trans. *The Anglo-Saxon Chronicle*. London: Everyman's Library, 1984.

Hutton, Ronald. *The Stations of the Sun: A History of the Ritual Year in Britain*. Oxford: Oxford University Press, 1996.

MacNeill, Maire. *The Festival of Lughnasa: A Study of the Survival of the Celtic Festival of the Beginning of Harvest*. Oxford: Oxford University Press, 1962.

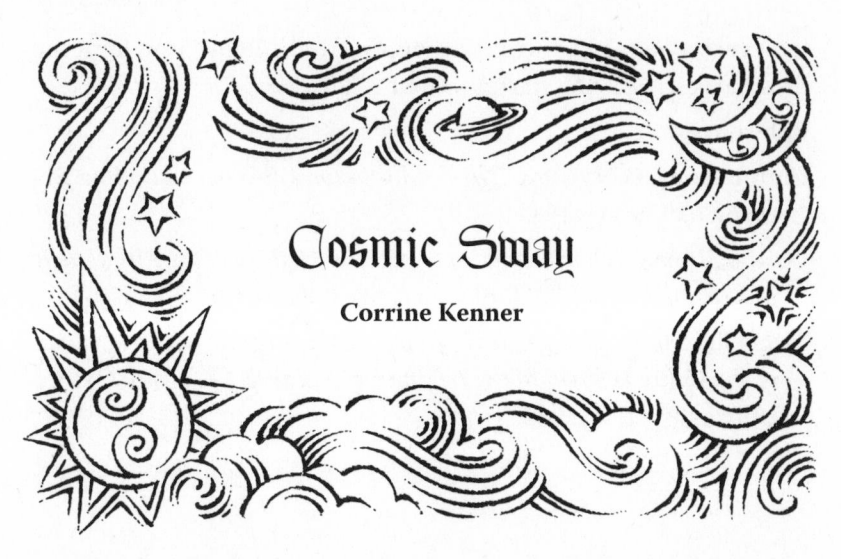

Cosmic Sway

Corrine Kenner

THE CROSS-QUARTER HOLIDAY of Lammas falls during the hottest month of the year, as the Sun makes its way through Leo, the sign it rules. Three planets—Mercury, Jupiter, and Venus—are traveling by his side, which means there are four planets in the fixed fire sign today.

Leo is the sign of fixed fire, and it fuels most regal qualities of all four planets. In their own way, they'll all become more regal, more gregarious, and more dramatic. Jupiter is perfectly happy to don the mantle of the Sun; in ancient myth, Jupiter was the king of the gods, so he's comfortable wearing his brother Apollo's robes.

Mercury, however, tends to be more of a play actor in Leo, drawing attention to himself by aggrandizing his importance and delivering messages that are heavy on style, light on substance. Venus, the planet of love and desire, focuses on her own beauty and sex appeal—especially given the fact that Venus also happens to be one of five planets moving backward through the zodiac today.

In fact, Venus—along with Saturn, Pluto, Neptune, and Uranus—seems to have reversed course. All five are carefully retracing their steps, moving retrograde, almost as though they're magnetically drawn to the irresistible heat and fire of those fiery Leo planets.

Granted, fiery Leo is a sign that's hard to ignore. Just as we can't take our eyes off a flickering campfire, planets in Leo are mesmerizing. We're practically compelled to pay attention to them.

While we typically describe retrograde planets as moving backward through the zodiac, their backtracking motion is simply an optical illusion that occurs when our planet passes them in orbit, like cars traveling side by side on a freeway. Retrograde planets, on the other hand, demand that we focus on internal issues.

Tarot and Astrology

When the Sun, Mercury, Jupiter, and Venus are in Leo, they all assume the guise of the lion tamer in the Strength card. The Sun, as we learned at Midsummer, can handle it. Jupiter, the king of the gods, is also well equipped for a position of command and control.

The clothes don't fit Mercury and Venus quite as well. Mercury corresponds to the Magician card, and the Magician would rather entertain an audience through clever banter than brute force. He's mastered the art of mind over matter, but he'll have to work hard to channel his will into another sentient being. Meanwhile Venus, who's represented by the Empress card, is generally too elegant and refined to lower herself to working with wildlife.

All of the planets in Leo, however, do enjoy their time in the realm—and they become more regal simply by being in close proximity to the Sun. They become more creative, warmhearted, and generous. They also become more dramatic and proud.

Practical Astrology

To align yourself with the planetary energies of this holiday, consider the dramatic contrast between the planets that are moving forward through fiery, outgoing Leo, compared to the five planets in retrograde motion. Their movement through the sky mirrors the way we move through life.

The planets that are retrograde today will inspire us to look back at our own progress, and to reflect on their significance in our lives.

Planetary Positions

The Sun is in fiery Leo. It will move into earthy Virgo on August 23.

The Moon is in airy Aquarius, the humanitarian sign of social groups and progressive causes, futuristic vision, and technological imagination.

Mercury is in fiery Leo, where it can inspire clear thinking and confident self-expression. Mercury will move into earthy Virgo on August 7, and airy Libra on August 26.

Venus is retrograde in fiery Leo, where the planet of love and attraction rewards loyalty with affection.

Mars is in watery Cancer, the sign of home and family life. The planet of action and assertion will move into Leo, a more compatible sign, on August 8.

Jupiter is already in Leo. The expansive planet will move into Virgo on August 11, where it will shift its focus toward clean living. If you eat well, exercise regularly, and maintain a healthy lifestyle, you'll definitely see rewards.

Saturn is still in watery Scorpio, moving retrograde, but it will move into Sagittarius on September 17. Once it's in the sign of philosophy, long-distance travel, and higher education, the ringed planet might loosen its restrictions and limitations—although it will always cling to a systemized pattern of thought and tradition.

The generational outer planets remain in the same signs:

Uranus is retrograde in fiery Aries.

Neptune is retrograde in watery Pisces. On September 1, Neptune will make its closest orbital approach to Earth, and its face will be fully illuminated by the Sun. It's still one of the most distant planets, though, so you won't be able to see it unless you have a powerful telescope.

Pluto is retrograde in earthy Capricorn.

Planets in Aspect

Mercury, in fiery Leo, is in a harmonious trine with Uranus in fiery Aries. The two planets fuel each other's quest for ingenuity and innovation.

Venus, also in Leo, is in an uncomfortable square with Saturn in watery Scorpio. The ringed planet puts arbitrary limits on her socializing.

That's counterbalanced, however, by the fact that Venus is conjunct Jupiter in Leo. When the Greater and Lesser Benefics form a partnership, they shower everyone in their path with blessings and gifts.

Mars, in Cancer, is in a flowing, easygoing trine with Saturn in Scorpio. Neither planet is particularly comfortable in water; Mars is the planet of war, while Saturn is the ringed planet of boundaries and limitations. Both prefer to be solidly grounded on earth, fueled by fire, or strategizing in the heady air. When they're both plunged into the watery depths of emotion, however, they can conduct surveillance missions, so they can understand the needs and desires that drive others.

Mars is also in an uncomfortable square with Uranus in fiery Aries. While both planets share a primal need for freedom and independence, this particular aspect tends to leave them tripping over each other.

Jupiter, in Leo, is square Saturn in Scorpio. The ringed planet could cast long, dark shadows on Jupiter's natural optimism and self-confidence.

Neptune, in Pisces, is in a harmonious sextile with Pluto in Capricorn—which softens Pluto's hard edges, at least for the moment.

Phases of the Moon

August 14: On Lammas, the Moon was full in airy Aquarius. Two weeks later, the Moon will have made its way halfway around the zodiac, where it will join the Sun and become a New Moon in Cancer.

August 29: A Full Moon in watery Pisces will fill the sky, illuminated by the Sun in earthy Virgo. A watery Pisces Moon promises psychic dreams and intuitive flashes of insight.

September 13: A New Moon will be born as the Moon and the Sun conjoin in dutiful, responsible earthy Virgo. Tonight's New Moon will be accompanied by a partial solar eclipse, visible in southern Africa, Madagascar, and Antarctica. A solar eclipse occurs when the Moon passes between the Earth and the Sun; lunar eclipses occur at the full Moon, when the Earth is between the Sun and the Moon. In astrology, eclipses represent sudden and dramatic change. Lunar eclipses tend to be personal, while solar eclipses generally affect widespread groups.

September 28: The Sun in airy Libra will shine on a Full Moon in fiery Aries.

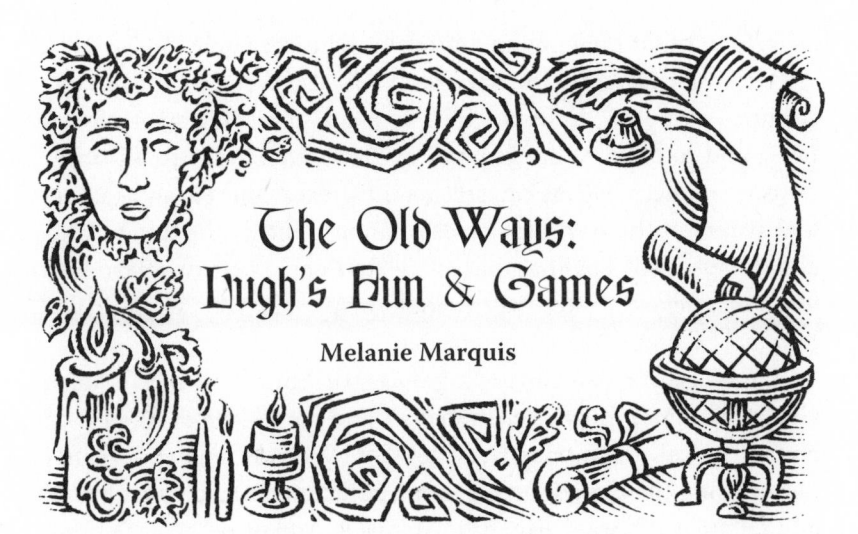

The Old Ways: Lugh's Fun & Games

Melanie Marquis

LUGHNASADH IS ONE OF the least talked about sabbats among western Neopagans who celebrate the wheel of the year. It's sort of an in-between time, not quite fall and yet not really a summer celebration, either, though it's celebrated at the start of the August, halfway between the Summer Solstice and the Autumn Equinox. Lughnasadh marks the first harvest, but for non-farming city folk, it feels a little weird and unnatural to be celebrating a harvest when there is none. We tend to associate harvest time with the heart of fall, and it can get a little confusing trying to differentiate between our Mabon celebrations at the Autumn Equinox, and Lughnasadh, which seems on the surface to be pretty much like Mabon, only it's the first havest rather than the second harvest, and the day doesn't have any special astronomical significance, as Mabon does with the equinox. Take these factors together, and it's easy to see why Lughnasadh is so often overlooked and underdone.

It hasn't always been that way. If we look to the roots of Lughnasadh and examine some of the traditional ways the holiday has been celebrated, we can gain insight that helps us to connect with the energies of the day in a way that feels authentic, even if we don't have crops to harvest or livestock to tend to. In fact, there were many aspects to traditional Lughnasadh rites that were only loosely connected with the idea of the harvest. It was also seen as a time to pay tribute to the past, to honor love, to share good times with loved ones, and to enjoy some fun and excitement. These are all traditions we modern Pagans can still get into, just as our Pagan brothers and sisters of the past did. By examining some of the less talked-about aspects of Lughnasadh, you'll find new ideas to weave into your own personal rites, which could help make your sabbat day a lot more meaningful and memorable.

Lughnasadh, also called Lughnasa, or Lúnasa in the modern Gaelic, was traditionally celebrated around the twelfth of August. In Britain, it's called Lammas, or "loaf mass." When Britain and Ireland began using the Gregorian calendar, adjustments had to be made, and Lughnasadh was pushed to August 1. Today, people celebrate either Old Style Lughnasadh on August 12, or New Style Lughnasadh on August 1. Lughnasadh signals that the growing season is drawing to a close, as the first fruits of the harvest reach maturity. It's a time when themes of fertility and abundance are prevalent, a time when the bounty of the earth and the beauty of its natural cycles are rejoiced in and celebrated. Prevalent symbols of the season include corn, flowers, wells, and mountains.

The origins of Lughnasadh are not exactly certain nor traceable. Little survives in the way of historical record or even oral traditions, and our knowledge of traditional Lughnasadh customs is limited to our ability to discern as much from observing the surviving practices. Lughnasadh most likely has its origins in Ireland, but came to be celebrated widely throughout the Celtic world. Irish legend has it that Lugh (a Celtic hero exalted to the status of deity) started the Lughnasadh tradition by hosting a funeral feast and carnival games in honor of his dead stepmother Tailtiu, who had given her life in order to ready all the fields in Ireland for agriculture, having worked herself to a state of complete exhaustion. Legend has it that Lugh's original funeral feast and carnival games became an annual tradition. This is why many Lughnasadh festivals are called "wake fairs," both as a rememberance of the festival's origins, and also as a symbolic acknowledgment of the fact that summer is nearing its time of "death." As time passed, Lugh's stepmother fell out of the spotlight, and traditions evolved while retaining the more ancient symbolism. Many Lughnasadh festivals came to feature a wake in honor of the corn god, the embodiment of the first harvest. An ear of corn or other fitting symbol was ceremoniously laid to rest in the graveyard, followed by a festival of feasts, games, and dancing. A state of peace and an atmosphere of fun and friendly competition prevailed at Lugh's festival, which was called the Áenach Tailteann. Truces were called, but athletic contests of strength, skill, and fighting prowess were engaged in with full hearts. It was also a time of love, with many romantic partnerships forged for the course of the festival, and longer partnerships also solidified through public handfastings. Gifts were usually exchanged, and varied from gold rings to gold coins split in half, to a knotted red ribbon or even a silver toothpick.

Another interesting tradition associated with the Lughnasadh fairs is the Battle of the Flowers. On the Channel Islands, groups of locals compete to make the best floral arrangements and exhibits, sometimes over forty-five feet long and comprised of more than a hundred thousand blossoms. In modern times, the displays are carried through the town on the backs of flat-bed trucks, parade float style, but the local tradition dates back long before the advent of the automobile. Because of the popularity of the Battle of the Flowers, the Sunday closest to Lughnasadh is sometimes called "Garland Sunday."

If you're looking to add some fun to your Lughnasadh celebration, why not reenact a few of the old ways? You might host your own wake fair in honor of the dying summer, enjoy a temporary Lammas-time hook-up, or even challenge your witchy friends to a battle of the blossoms, seeing who can make the best display of flowers or other foliage. Lughnasadh is a time for fun, whether we find that fun in ancient traditions or in our own modern inventions.

The summer is soon coming to an end, and now is the time to enjoy it while we can.

References:

All Saints Parish. "The Festival of Lughnasa." Accessed October 1, 2013. http://www.allsaintsbrookline.org/celtic/lughnasa.html.

Irish Cultural Society of San Antonio. "Lughnasadh: Celtic Festival of Light." Accessed October 1, 2013. http://www.irishculturalsociety .org/essaysandmisc/lughnasadh.html.

MercianGathering.com. "Lughnasa" by Anna Franklin. Accessed October 1, 2013. http://www.merciangathering.com/lughnasa .htm.

StoryArcheology.com. "Notes on the Festival of Lughnasagh." Accessed October 1, 2013. http://storyarchaeology.com/2012/12/10 /notes-on-the-festival-of-lughnasagh/

Feasts and Treats

Ellen Dugan

AT LUGHNASADH WE CELEBRATE the first harvest. Pork is traditional at this time of year, and I love recipes that beat the heat or that I can cook in a crockpot. You'll love these fun summertime recipes: a healthy guacamole with garden tomatoes, a seasonal peach cobbler, and a peachy fizz drink! Blessed be.

Pulled Pork in a Crockpot

Hands down, this is my favorite summer sandwich. Please note: be sure to let the cooked pork sit for 30 minutes before you shred it up—otherwise it is too hot to handle.

Prep time: 20 minutes
Cook time: 6 hours
Cooling time: 30 minutes
Serves: 6

1 can of beer
8 ounces (1 can) chicken broth
½ cup barbeque sauce (I prefer sweeter sauces, but use your personal favorite)
1 tablespoon dried minced onions

½ teaspoon paprika
½ teaspoon garlic powder
½ teaspoon black pepper
2½ lb. pork shoulder (boneless)

Pour beer, chicken broth, barbeque sauce, dried minced onions, and spices in crockpot and whisk together. Then add pork. Cook on low setting for 6 hours. Reserve a bit of the cooking liquid to keep the shredded pork moist. When the meat is done, remove it from the crockpot, set it on a cutting board, and allow it to cool. Then shred meat and serve on whole-grain buns, with extra sauce on the side.

Healthy Guacamole

Guacamole doesn't have to be loaded with unhealthy and fattening ingredients. In fact, it tastes better when you keep it simple.

Prep time: 10 minutes
Serves: 2–4

2 ripe avocados
1 tomato finely chopped
2 teaspoons dried minced onions
1 lime
Salt and pepper to taste

Cut avocados in half. Remove pit. With a butter knife, make lengthwise and crosswise slices in the avocados halves, so as you scoop them out they fall into the mixing bowl as rough cubes. Chop the tomato and add to the avocado. Add minced onions. Cut the lime in half and squeeze the juice of half of the lime into the bowl. Mash and stir the ingredients gently with a fork. (I like to leave the texture fairly chunky. If you prefer it smooth, then mash it up more.) Add salt and pepper, or more lime juice, to taste. Serve immediately with corn chips.

Peach Cobbler

This is a deceptively simple recipe—but it yields cobbler magick!

Prep time: 20 minutes

Cook time: 25–30 minutes

Serves: 4–6

2 cans sliced canned peaches (Drain the cans of their liquid) Note: You definitely want to use the old-style canned peaches. Don't use fresh or frozen. Trust me on this one.

⅛ teaspoon cinnamon

1 box (15¼ ounces) yellow cake mix—with the dry mix divided in half (Save the rest of the dry mix for another time.)

½ cup (1 stick) cold butter or margarine

Preheat the oven to 350 degrees F. Spray an 8 × 8-inch square pan with nonstick cooking spray. Drain the liquid from both cans of peaches and add the fruit to the bottom of the pan. Sprinkle the cinnamon on top of the peaches.

In a separate bowl add half of the dry yellow cake mix. Using a pastry blender, cut the cold butter into the cake mix. Work until the cake mix and butter resemble rough crumbs. Then sprinkle the crumbly topping evenly on top of the peaches. Bake for 25 to 30 minutes or until the topping is puffed, cake-like, and golden brown. Serve warm with frozen vanilla yogurt or fat-free vanilla Greek yogurt.

Peachy Lemonade Fizz

In keeping with our seasonal peachy theme for Lughnasadh, try this sparkling drink. Please note you could substitute a sweet sparkling wine like Prosecco for the white soda if you wanted to!

Prep time: 20 minutes

Serves: 2

1 cup frozen sliced peaches (or 2 fresh peaches peeled, pitted, and sliced)

½ cup lemonade (per glass)
White soda (Sprite or 7-Up)
Ice cubes
Fresh mint leaf for garnish

Purée peaches and lemonade in blender until smooth. Pour white soda over ice in a rocks glass. Top off with peach lemonade purée. Add a mint leaf for garnish.

Crafty Crafts

Lexa Olick

LAMMAS CELEBRATES THE BEGINNING of the harvest as well as the end of summer. Therefore, you should create decorations that honor the great outdoors and the wonderful gifts of nature. Plants are beginning to wither and seeds are starting to drop, so it's the ideal time to gather those gifts and put them to good use.

Apple Slice Candles

Candles are the one decoration that is appropriate for nearly any occasion. They can be used all year long to enhance your home with their warm light. These candles not only have the fresh, crisp scent of apples, but they are actually made from real apples!

Just one apple can create two beautiful candles. Instead of buying a block of beeswax or a bag of wax pellets, scavenge the pieces of a votive candle. It's the easiest way to purchase candle-making supplies if you are a casual crafter or if you only need to make a few. Votive candles are inexpensive and you won't have to worry about storing leftover wax or wicks.

Because these candles are created from an apple, they are temporary. However, votive candles generally only burn eight to twelve hours, so they make a fitting combination.

Supplies
1 apple
2 unscented votive candles
Knife
Melon baller
Lemon juice
Double boiler

Instructions: Choose an apple of a nice shape and form. I recommend finding the biggest one available so you can create a more impressive candle. Once you have chosen your desired apple, place it on a firm surface and cut it in half lengthwise. These two halves will be the base of your candles.

With a melon baller, carefully scoop out the inside of the apple. As you remove the flesh, create a hollow shell of even thickness. Drizzle lemon juice onto the cut apples to help reduce browning. Place the halves in the refrigerator to chill while you work on preparing your candles.

While color isn't necessarily important, it is best to have candles that complement the skin of your apple. The typical colors are red and green, but cream or white will go well with any apple. Place your votive candle on a firm surface and cut it in half lengthwise while taking care not to harm the wick. You won't be able to cut the candle completely in half because it has a metal wick tab at the bottom. When you reach the wick tab, crack and pull the candle open with your hands and set the wick aside. Continue to slice the candle into smaller pieces so it will be easier to melt. Repeat this step with your second candle.

Fill a large pan with about an inch of water and heat to a simmer. Place a pouring pot inside the pan and fill that pot with your wax pieces. When the wax is fully melted, you are now ready to pour your candles.

Remove your apple halves from the refrigerator. Place the wick tabs you set aside earlier directly in the center of each apple. Care-

fully pour your wax into the hollow areas. Set the apple candles aside until the wax cools completely.

Time to Complete: About 1 hour in order to let the candles fully harden.

Cost: Approximately $5.00

Note: Any unscented candle can instantly be turned into a scented one, or a candle that never had a strong scent can be quickly revitalized. Purchase fragrance oil specifically designed for candle-making. Light the candle and let the wick burn for several minutes. During that time, some of the wax will melt. After a few minutes, blow out the candle. Add a couple drops of fragrance into the melted wax and stir gently with a toothpick. The oil becomes part of the wax when it hardens again. When you light the candle, you will be greeted with a fresher, stronger scent!

Lammas Maize Flower Vase

Dry ingredients add a natural look to an ordinary glass vase. It is filled with the colors of fall, which is appropriate for Lammas since it marks the beginning of autumn. This vase shows off some of the wonderful elements of this season.

Supplies

Clear glass vase (around 7 or 8 inches tall)
Split peas
Corn kernels
Coffee beans
Dried maize flower
Raffia ribbon
Brooch with an autumn-theme design (such as a leaf brooch)

Instructions: The vase looks best when the kernels, peas, and coffee beans are poured as separate layers. Vases vary in sizes, so you will have to eyeball the amount of ingredients you pour into it. I recommend a plain cylinder glass with no texture. When you choose a simple vase, it shows off the texture of the items held within. You don't want any colors or patterns to distract from the natural beauty of the split peas, corn kernels, and coffee beans.

First, place the dried maize flower inside the vase and hold it steady with one hand. Continue to hold it in place as you add the split peas slowly. Once you have poured the desired amount, repeat with the coffee beans and then with the corn kernels. Now that your vase is full, you can let go of the dried maize flower. The dry ingredients lock it in its place and it can now stand proudly on its own.

To decorate the vase, gather 12 strips of raffia ribbon that are about 40 inches long. Wrap them around the vase and tie them in a huge bow at the front, trimming the excess if needed. Embellish the center of the bow by inserting a beautiful autumn brooch at the knot. The pin will easily slip behind the strands of raffia.

Time to Complete: Approximately 20 minutes.
Cost: Around $10.00

Variation: The coffee beans give a nice aroma to this display, but all the dried ingredients can be substituted with birdseed. You can dress up the dried corn maize flower by creating a full and lush bouquet. To do so, add other items to your arrangement, such as wheat or long bird feathers.

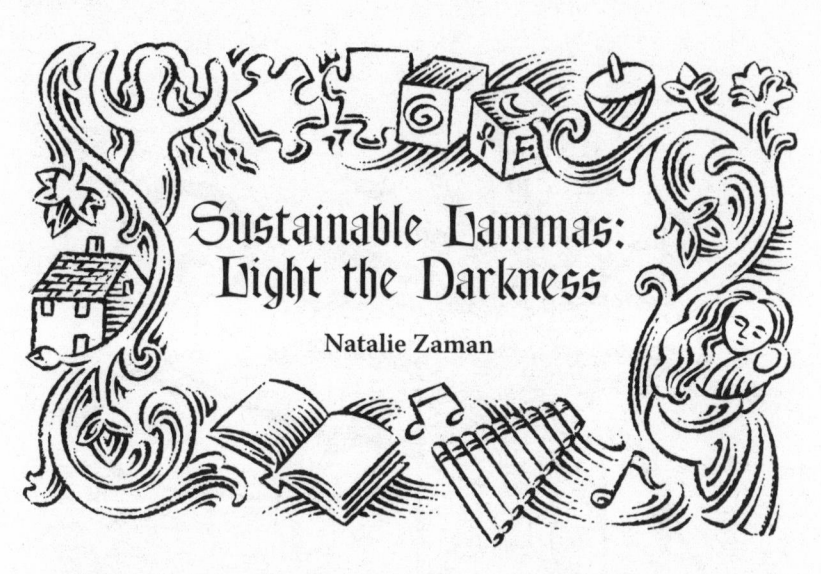

Sustainable Lammas: Light the Darkness

Natalie Zaman

"'Let me light my lamp,' says the star, 'and never debate if it will help to remove the darkness.'"
—Rabindranath Tagore, poet and philosopher

THE LIGHT AND HEAT of the sun is a thread that winds its way through all the sabbats. Ultimately, it determines the fertility of the earth, the form water takes, and the temperature of the air, which together sustain life. Once the Summer Solstice passes, we lose two to three minutes of light each day. By Lammas, daylight is shortened by nearly two hours, and the light continues to wane.

I look forward to summer evenings, the coolness that quells the heat of the day, the velvet twilight that softens the seemingly relentless light, and the rhythmic heartbeat of cricket song. But even in night's darkness, a bit of sunlight survives in a host of marvelous, tiny creatures. Fireflies light up the summer night, not for our benefit, but because they are looking for love.

It starts as soon as the sun goes down, a blink here, and a twinkle there. And as dusk deepens, the wooded curtain of the yard glitters with tiny golden lights. Many is the time I wished I could capture this moment in a bottle—and I did, by making a firefly lantern-habitat.

A lovely representation of the element of fire in a Lammas circle or for use in a summertime ritual in place of a candle, a firefly lantern is easy to craft. Made from a recycled plastic bottle, it is environmentally friendly, as long as the creatures hosted inside are treated with love and respect.

Make It Your Own!
You will need:
An empty plastic water bottle with the label removed (keep the cap)
Nail and hammer
Scissors
Ribbon, yarn, wire, or other type of cord for hanging

Cut the bottle into two pieces—it does not have to be exactly in half. Working first with the screw-capped end, use the hammer and nail to make a hole on one side of the bottle near the neck. Then make another hole on the opposite side. Cut a length of cord and thread each end through each side hole and knot (on the inside of the bottle) to secure. This will create a loop to hang your lantern.

Take the other half of the bottle, and using the hammer and nail again, make 4 to 6 small holes in the closed bottom. These will be air holes for the fireflies; be careful not to make them too large.

Place a few stalks of grass and some drops of honey in the bottom portion of the bottle—firefly comforts—before fitting the open portions into each other. You may have to press in on the plastic to make it fit.

To catch fireflies, use a net rather than your hands if you can (there's less of a chance that they'll get squashed). Carefully put them into your lantern through the screw-cap opening. Take your time and be patient, and don't force any fireflies into the lantern. Ask them to share their time with you:

Little friends, glowing bright,
Will you share your precious light?

Remember to place the screw-cap back on once each firefly is safely inside. An average-sized water bottle should house about six fireflies comfortably.

Include and acknowledge the fireflies in your circle or in your spellwork. Do not keep the them in your lantern for an extended period of time—set them free after an hour or two. A firefly's life span is only about seven to fourteen days, and their dance of light is part of their reproductive cycle, which shouldn't be disrupted for long. To release them, take the lantern to an area where there are shrubs or trees. Place it on the ground and separate the sections. The fireflies will leave on their own. Express your appreciation to the fireflies for sharing their light. Your thanks can be as simple as, *Thanks be to one and all, Merry part, and merry meet again!*

Your firefly lantern can be used throughout the summer. At the end of the season, you can save it to use again next year, recycle the bottle, or use it yet again. Filled with water or ice cubes, the lantern can also be a slow-watering vessel for plants.

Have a de-LIGHT-ful Lammas!

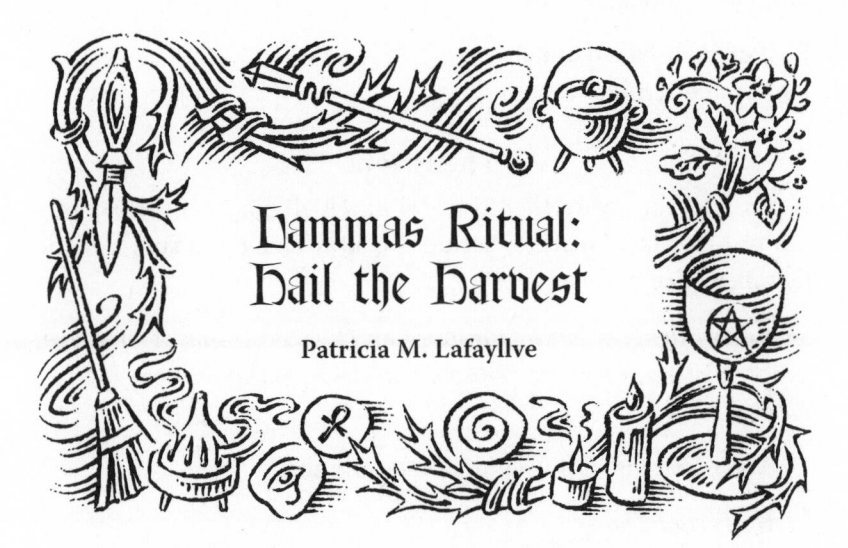

Lammas Ritual: Hail the Harvest

Patricia M. Lafayllve

WHILE LAMMAS AND LUGHNASADH may have different origins, they share a number of similarities. Both occur on August 1, and both involve the first harvest. If you have a garden or access to a farmers' market, a good idea is to get a basketful of whatever fruits, vegetables, and grains are coming into season. You can also do some research to find out which plants are native to your area and find some in your local market. These make excellent offerings, and can also be used to cook the celebratory feast which typically follows rituals of this kind. If possible, find out which grains are ready for harvest in August and make bread from them.

Items Needed

Altar cloth
Altar decorated with seasonal fruits, vegetables, grains, or flowers
Hammer
Offering cup or drinking horn
Offering bowl
Mead, beer, cider, or other offering liquid
Bottle opener (as needed—it is best to open liquids before the ritual, so that they are ready when they are required)

Loaf of fresh-baked bread

Basket of offerings

The Ritual

If possible, the group should travel to a high place, at the top of a hill or other local feature. Set up the altar facing the sun. Lift the hammer. Face the altar.

SAY: *Mighty Mjolnir, Hammer of Thor, Protector of Midgard, make this space holy so that we who have gathered here may be blessed.*

Make the sign of the hammer over the altar.

SAY: *Hail Thor!*

Gathered people SAY: *Hail Thor!*

Place the hammer back on the altar. Raise hands in the air.

SAY: *On this, the first day of autumn, the day of harvest, a holy day, we stand in the presence of our ancestors. Hail to you, those who have prepared the way for us. Hail to you, those who have shared their bread and mead in the halls of the dead. Hail to you, our mothers and fathers, our sisters and brothers, our aunts and uncles, and our grandparents back to the beginning. We ask that you be with us as we share offerings in honor of the harvest season. Hail the ancestors!*

Gathered people SAY: *Hail the ancestors!*

SAY: *On this, the first day of autumn, the day of harvest, a holy day, we stand in the presence of our gods and goddesses. Hail to you, shining ones. Hail to you, our oldest ancestors. Hail to you, who live above us and around us. We ask that you be with us as we share offerings in honor of the harvest season. Hail the gods and goddesses!*

Gathered people SAY: *Hail the gods and goddesses!*

(Note: Specific names of deities can be spoken at this time. This is primarily a Celtic and Anglo-Saxon holiday, so Celtic and Anglo-Saxon deities are highly appropriate. Lugh, particularly, might be a good deity to call on.)

SAY: On this, the first day of autumn, the day of harvest, a holy day, we stand in the presence of the spirits of earth and sky, of water and air, all the spirits who live in this place. Hail to you, those who are seen and unseen! Hail to you, those who walk, or crawl, or swim, or fly. Hail to you who call this place home. We ask that you stand with us as we share offerings in honor of the harvest season. Hail the spirits!

Gathered people SAY: *Hail the spirits!*

Lift cup/drinking horn from the altar. Fill it with liquid. Place your hand over the top and speak a blessing.

SAY: *All you spirits, ancestors, gods and goddesses. We ask that you bless this drink so that the words spoken over it are made holy.*

Pass the cup/drinking horn from one person to the other. Each should speak a blessing for the harvest over the cup, take a sip from it, and pass it to the next person. Add your own blessing when the cup/drinking horn gets passed back to you.

SAY: *We ask that you accept this offering.*

Pour all of liquid into the offering bowl.
Take bread off of the altar.

SAY: *We share this offering with you, gathered ones, for the harvest season has arrived. We will have a moment of silence, while we each consider what the harvest means to us.*

Break bread into four pieces. Then pass the pieces of bread so that everyone can take a piece and eat it. This should be done in silence, but if there is a large group, a chant might be sung after a few moments of silence. Place remaining bread back on the altar. Pick up the basket of vegetables/fruits.

SAY: *Here are the products of the first harvest. We thank you, gathered beings, for this bounty. We thank the sun and the rain. We thank the fertile earth and the farmer's toil. We thank the seeds and the growing plants. We ask that the harvest remain fertile from today's opening of autumn through the final harvest and the beginning of winter's season. Now we make our offering.*

Place the basket of fruits/vegetables in front of the altar, in the center of your gathered company, or in a clear, sunny spot on the hill. Bring the bread to the same place. Finally, bring the offering bowl.

SAY: *We thank you for the harvest and its bounty. We thank you for the bread we eat, the ale we drink, and the work that is to come.*

Pour the liquid onto the bread/basket.

SAY: *This rite is ended. We ask that all who came go in peace, that our ancestors, the gods and goddesses, and those who live on this land be present in our lives in this and in all our affairs. Hail the harvest.*

Gathered people SAY: *Hail the harvest.*

Leave the offering at the top of the hill. If able, you might bury it in its place. A small fire might be lit to burn it, if that is allowed where you are. If you have this rite indoors, and have an outdoor space to leave the offering, do so there. If not, leave the basket, bread, and offering bowl in place on the altar as you feast and spend whatever other time you are going to spend together. After everyone has left, discard the offering.

Notes

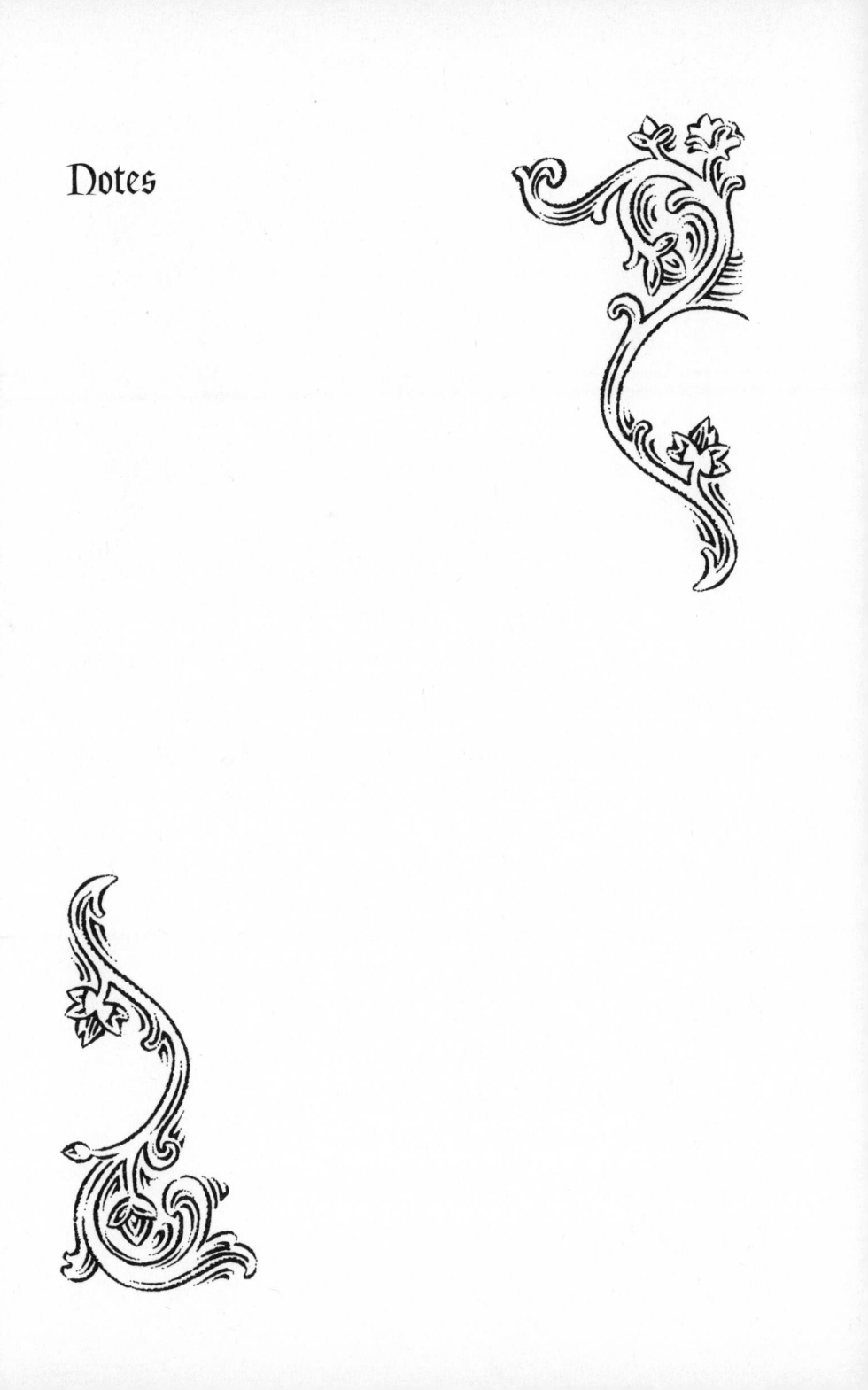

Notes

Mabon

Mabon: The Forgotten Sabbat

Denise Dumars

MANY MODERN WICCANS AND other pagans say that their favorite time of year is autumn, and when asked why, they promptly answer that it is the season of Samhain. Indeed, many pagans are so busy preparing for the Samhain holidays—be they the secular Halloween, the pagan Samhain, the Hispanic Dia del Los Muertos, the Vodou All Saints' Day, or all of the above—that they completely forget that the Autumnal Equinox, called Mabon, is the beginning of the season, the vital balance, tenuous and short though it may be, that ushers in the season the ancestors called simply "winter." What is the Autumnal Equinox? It is the dark sister of the Vernal Equinox—*equinox* meaning "equal night" in Latin.

The Autumnal Equinox—which many modern pagans call Mabon, a name that my good friend, pagan elder Aidan Kelly, coined from a Celtic myth of a hero named Mabon, son of Modron, who figures in Welsh myths and fits in with the modern Wiccan Celtic tradition—is a very directly earth-related holiday, or perhaps more literally, a planetary holiday. It literally refers to the earth's position relative to the sun, in which sunlight is hitting directly on the equator, making day and night virtually equal in the Northern Hemisphere. Depending on the calendar, it can fall (no pun intended!) any time between September 20–24. It is on this night, not on Samhain, that what I like to call The Return of the Darkness is ushered in.

In pagan terms, it marks the second harvest, the first being Lammas, the last being Samhain. This may not mean much to us now here in the Northern Hemisphere when our supermarkets are always full of food, including that which, while not in season, was either forcibly brought forth in greenhouses or flown in from the Southern Hemisphere. American pagans may, in fact, see Thanksgiving in November as the "harvest holiday," in which consuming mass quantities of our indigenous American harvest of turkey, cranberries, potatoes, and pumpkin while watching a ritualized battle known as "football" celebrates the season most effectively, and, living in the modern world, perhaps this does fit the bill.

Let us think to our ancestors, then: Mabon time would have been the time of the fullest harvest, when fruit was hanging heavy on the trees and many crops had to be harvested before they either went to seed or were ruined by the oncoming cold weather. It would, indeed, be a time of thanksgiving, but with slightly ominous overtones: not enough of a harvest meant not enough food for the oncoming winter. Needless to say, our pagan ancestors were very grateful when there was a bountiful harvest, and profusely thanked their gods and goddesses of nature, whether in general or specifically. Gods and goddesses of agriculture and animal husbandry were the deities primarily thanked and honored. So when the equal day/night arrived, it marked a literal turn from the green growing days of spring and summer, just called "summer" by the ancients, to the harvesting and dying-off days of fall and winter, just called "winter" in old Europe.

Many modern pagans mark the day, then, by re-creating a ritual of gratitude for the abundance of the real or symbolic harvest. These rituals can include thanking the gods not only for a bounteous harvest but also for whatever one has harvested symbolically during the year: a year of monetary abundance, an abundance of friends, love, health, etc. These rituals can also include revering the season by using autumn leaves and such fruits as apples and nuts as part of the decorations, as in the cornucopia (see below). Other pagans welcome the holiday as symbolic of stability and harmony: the equality of the day and night mirroring the equality that we either have or hope to have in our own lives. Getting back one's balance can be the goal for the holiday; figuring out what is out of balance in one's life and trying to equal the scales (it is, after all, the time of Libra, the scales) is the idea. So finding balance is important for a lot of pagans at this time.

Yet others can see the darkness oncoming and honor such events in pagan lore such as the descent of Persephone into Hades, while at the same time honoring her mother Demeter, the harvest goddess, whose mourning for her absent daughter brings on the cold and the dark until Persephone returns to her in spring. This myth, which was celebrated in the autumn holidays of Greece, seems relevant to the harvest seasons where my group resides in California because we have a climate quite similar to the Mediterranean countries. We have abundant pomegranates and a growing season that matches that of southern Greece quite closely.

Our bounteous harvest provides appropriate natural symbols: Persephone ate seven pomegranate seeds while in Hades and these enchanted seeds meant that she must return each year to the land of the dead and her husband, Hades, who is more appropriately named Plouton, for Hades is the place where he rules. Calling the Lord of the Dead "Hades" then, is actually considered slang. We get the word "plutocrat," meaning a wealthy and influential person, from his name or its more well-known variation, Pluto. The very best examination of the Persephone myth is recounted along with extremely detailed rites in Jennifer Reif's wonderful book *Mysteries of Demeter.*

Priestess Jennifer Reif does not see the story of Persephone as a "rape." The ancient Greeks in fact had several versions of the story. Here is one version: Persephone, also called Proserpine, was frolicking in the fields with her friends, ready to celebrate the harvest with her mother, Demeter, the Lady of the Harvest and all green growing things. *Demeter*, by the way, simply means "the mother." What happens next is up for debate: some say Hecate was there and, being a trickster goddess, led Persephone to the Underworld, where she met the lonely Lord of the Dead, Plouton. The Greeks were terrified of death, and never portrayed this Lord full-face, so Persephone did not know what he looked like. When she saw him, she realized that he was as handsome as his brother Poseidon, and he was weeping in loneliness. The souls of the dead were bereft as well, as their Lord was too sad to properly welcome them to the Other Side, and he had no Lady beside him to welcome them as hostess, so Persephone was persuaded to stay with him.

Whether this happened or whether handsome Plouton and his black steeds rose out of the ground and so impressed Persephone that she agreed to marry him, or whether, as in later myths, it was an abduction, no one really knows. The next part of the story is more important, however, for the theme of the autumn harvest.

When Demeter finds her daughter gone, she tears her hair and rends her garments in grief. All of the crops that had not yet been harvested began to wither. The weather suddenly became cold. Snow fell in parts of Greece where it had never fallen before. The people were terrified, thinking that as long as Demeter mourned for her lost daughter, the sun would never shine and nothing would grow again and the people and animals would perish.

One version of the tale states that Demeter went on a sort of "harrowing of hell" and stormed into Hades demanding her daughter back. Another says that Hecate brokered a deal. Whatever happened, Persephone had already eaten from the pomegranate of Hades, and was therefore obliged to stay. So a compromise was worked out: Persephone would stay as Lady of Hades for six months of the year, fall and winter, and six months of the year she would return to the living world to stay with her mother, Demeter, who would once again bring spring and summer to the living. A nice metaphor for the seasons and their relationship to life and death, isn't it?

Pomegranates are very much in season in the fall, and in cutting into one, the deep red juice (be careful—it stains!) evokes the elder days of sacrifice. This is an important bit of symbolism not only in the Persephone myth but in many myths of Mabon. In the Teutonic lands, autumn was the time of slaughtering the animals to preserve the meat for winter, and their festival would have centered more on thanking the lord of beasts than on thanking a goddess of agriculture.

Apples, another common autumnal fruit, conveniently display a pentagram in the middle when sliced though their own equators. Here in California the city of Pomona is named for the apple goddess of the harvest in Rome, since it was chosen as the location for the yearly Los Angeles County Fair, which takes place in September and usually has a mannequin dressed as Pomona on display.

Those of us in the autumn of our lives may want to play "September Song" and other songs in which the month symbolizes the change from youth to middle age, for this is the domain of the harvest deities, who are almost always thought of as middle-aged, whether in the person of Demeter, Ceres, the Native American Corn Mother, Yemaya, or many other goddesses seen as motherly and/or in their middle years. The god of animal husbandry, be he Herne or Cernunnos or Cerne, has in his name the origin of the word "kernel," which is applied to the seeds of many types of grain. Osiris, the Egyptian God and leader of the Heliopolitan Cosmogony, is also a god of agriculture when he is depicted with green skin, and as with the Greek god Dionysos he is a sacrificed god, a god who is himself a symbol of the reaping at the harvest, as are Baal and Tammuz in Middle Eastern cultures. The multicultural aspect of the harvest festival cannot be overstated: it is not, as some think, a Celtic rite alone. "Herfest" was its name to the Anglo-Saxons, from which we obviously get the word "harvest," and alternate modern names for the holiday are Harvest Home, Cornucopia, and the Witches' Thanksgiving. The ancient Celtic name for the holiday was not Mabon, but *Alban Elfed*, which means "the light of the water," and symbolically addresses the balance of the Equinox and the oncoming darkness.

The cornucopia, or "horn of plenty," is both the secular and the sacred symbol of fall. Baskets woven in cornucopia shapes are easy to find and, if at all possible, should be stuffed with real leaves, fruits, nuts, etc., to symbolize the bounty of the harvest. They are symbols of prosperity as well, as in ancient times one's prosperity was directly tied to abundance, especially an abundance of crops and livestock!

The literal day and night of the Autumnal Equinox should not be overlooked. Even a small observance, such as marking dawn and/or dusk with a pomegranate or apple placed before an image of Demeter or your favorite harvest deity, is enough. Below is a full ritual for groups that can be adapted for solitary use as well.

After the Autumnal Equinox, each day gets shorter until the Winter Solstice, when the Sun God is reborn.

Cosmic Sway

Corrine Kenner

MABON, THE LAST SABBAT rung on the wheel of the year, symbolizes the cycle of life as it draws to a close. It marks the final harvest and a time of thanksgiving, as the bounty of summer is brought in for the dark days of winter.

We celebrate Mabon on the Autumn Equinox, when the Sun moves into airy Libra. Today, the hours of day and night are equal, balanced evenly on the scales that serve as the emblem of the sign.

On this particular equinox, the days aren't the only thing that are balanced. Mars and Venus are in a unique partnership, too. They're both in airy Gemini, the sign of twins and kindred spirits.

Mars, the red planet named for the ancient god of war, symbolizes energy, action, and aggression. It's a classically masculine symbol—and on this holiday, he just happens to join forces with his feminine counterpart Venus, the goddess of love, beauty, and attraction.

Tarot and Astrology

The partnership between Mars and Venus is easy to visualize in tarot terms—starting with the fact that the airy sign of Gemini corresponds to the Lovers card.

Mars is linked to the Tower card—but that Tower belongs to the Emperor.

Venus corresponds to the Empress card.

All you need to do is pull the Emperor and the Empress cards from your tarot deck, and simply picture the happy royal couple at home in the Lovers card.

Practical Astrology

To align yourself with the planetary energies of Mabon, work with the symbol of the season—a scale. If you happen to be a lawyer or a judge, you might already have a set of scales on your desk. If not, craft a primitive balance from any tools you happen to have on hand, like paper plates, a wooden dowel, and some string.

Proceed to weigh your options. Write your hopes and wishes on pieces of paper, and then measure them against a similar expression of obstacles and fears. Which dreams make up the bulk of your plans for the future? Which fears weigh heaviest on your heart? How can you get them to balance, so you can move forward?

Planetary Positions

The Sun is in airy Libra. It will move into watery Scorpio on October 23.

The Moon is in earthy Capricorn, the sign of business, career, and social status. During this phase, the Moon has difficulty focus on her own home. Instead, she turns her attention to the world of business, finance, and career. It's a pragmatic sign, however, and with any luck, you can use the Moon in Capricorn to balance your home and family responsibilities with the demands of the outside world.

Mercury is retrograde in airy Libra, where it can inspire heartfelt conversations with intimate friends and partners. But be clear in your intentions and your words. Don't let Mercury's backward movement through the sign lead to any miscommunication.

Venus is still in fiery Leo. On October 26, she'll move into a conjunction with Jupiter, the planet of luck and good fortune. She might even bring you luck in love that day. You can see the two planets in early morning sky. Look to the east just before sunrise. Two days later, on October 28, Mars will join them there in a rare, visible, triple conjunction. Venus will move into earthy Virgo on October 8.

Mars is in fiery Leo, fueling a desire for creativity and play. You might be inspired to follow a sudden artistic impulse, or to challenge a friend to a game or good-natured athletic competition. Mars will move into earthy Virgo on September 24.

Jupiter is also in earthy Virgo, where the expansive planet operates a bit more cautiously, and rewards are more closely tied to good behavior.

Saturn is back in fiery Sagittarius after sliding back into watery Scorpio for a few months over the summer. Saturn will now establish itself in the sign of the archer, and it will stay there until December 2017. Saturn in Sagittarius is rigorously methodical in its approach to travel and exploration.

The generational outer planets remain in the same signs:

Uranus is retrograde in fiery Aries. On October 11, Uranus will make its closest orbital approach to Earth. You'll still need a powerful telescope to see it.

Neptune is retrograde in watery Pisces. On September 1, Neptune will make its closest orbital approach to Earth. It's also extremely far away, so you'll need a powerful telescope to see it, too.

Pluto is retrograde in earthy Capricorn.

Planets in Aspect

At the moment the Sun enters airy Libra, the luminary will be in a harmonious sextile with Saturn in fiery Sagittarius. The aspect signifies a period of comfort with authority figures. The sextile also makes it easier to learn from experience. Use this time period to look at your past mistakes in a new light. Don't see them as personal failings; instead think of them as life lessons.

The Moon, in earthy Capricorn, is squaring off against Uranus in fiery Aries. Passions run hot, tempers may flare, and everyone will need to keep their emotions in check.

Uranus is causing trouble with Mercury, too. The messenger planet is blithely moving through airy Libra when he runs into opposition from the planet of rebellion and revolution. While they face off, it's all too easy to jump to conclusions, refuse to compromise, and alienate the people close to you. Thank goodness Mercury moves fast; the aspect won't last more than a day or two.

Mercury is also squaring off against Pluto, in earthy Capricorn. The aspect isn't nearly as damaging to interpersonal relationships. It's still not good: in this case, Pluto tends to wear away at focus and self-discipline. Luckily, however, this too shall pass quickly.

On a more cheerful note, Venus, in fiery Leo, is in a harmonious trine with Uranus in fiery Aries. Here the two planets' energy takes on a pleasant note of optimism and enjoyment.

Mars, in fiery Leo, is squaring off against Saturn in fiery Sagittarius. They're not working together anymore. Instead, they're getting in each other's way, frustrating each other in their individual missions of conquering and control. Here on Earth, it's important to pace yourself, so you don't trip over your goals, too.

Jupiter, in earthy Virgo, is opposite Neptune in watery Pisces. Watch out for a tendency to make promises you can't keep. It's always better to under-promise and over-deliver.

Jupiter is also in a harmonious trine with powerful Pluto in earthy Capricorn, which supercharges a global sense of optimism—especially in financial matters.

Phases of the Moon

September 28: A Full Moon in fiery Aries will shine in the full light of the Sun, which is in airy Libra. A fiery Aries Moon is bold, brave, and independent, and it fuels a desire for fresh starts and new beginnings.

Tonight's Full Moon also features a total lunar eclipse, visible throughout most of North and South America, Europe, Africa, and western Asia. Lunar eclipses occur when the Earth comes between the Sun and the Moon, and the Earth casts a shadow across the face of the Moon.

October 13: A New Moon will be born when the Sun and Moon conjoin in graceful airy Libra, signaling a grace period in close relationships and social interactions.

October 27: A Full Moon in earthy Taurus will be illuminated by the watery Scorpio Sun. Earthy Taurus is ruled by Venus, the goddess of love and attraction, making tonight's Full Moon one of the most romantic of the year. Celebrate with your favorite Taurus comfort food—or make this a date night, and share a gourmet meal and a glass of fine wine.

The Old Ways:
China Moon Festival

Melanie Marquis

THERE'S SOMETHING SPECIAL ABOUT the full moon that occurs every year nearest the Autumn Equinox. Called the "Harvest Moon" by many, it seems to glow a little brighter, and appear a little larger, than most full moons. Maybe it's the hint of autumn chill in the air, or the fact that the darker half of the year is upon us, but something about the autumn full moon brings about a feeling of magick, reminiscence, and wishful thinking. We western Witches aren't the only ones to feel a strong connection to lunar energies around this time of year. In China, autumn is celebrated with the Moon Festival, also called the Mid-Autumn festival. For thousands of years, the Chinese Moon Festival has been a time to get together with friends and family while honoring the moon and welcoming blessings. Second only to the New Year's celebration held in the spring, the Moon Festival has become one of the biggest and most popular national holidays in China. Held on the fifteenth day of the eight month in the Chinese lunar calendar, the Moon Festival falls on variable days, but generally occurs on the full moon around the time of the Autumn Equinox.

The festival is an extension of moon worship practiced in China for thousands of years, dating back at least as early as the Shang

Dynasty over 3,000 years ago. As the moon and the sun are both closely tied to agricultural cycles, it became common custom to offer sacrifices to the sun in the spring, and to make offerings to the moon in the autumn. Over time, these procedures evolved into full-fledged ceremonies, with both the common folks and the Emperor himself making annual sacrifices to the heavenly body and the divine powers therein represented.

In Chinese culture, the moon is often seen as the embodiment of the goddess Chang-O, a deity of good fortune, beauty, and love. Chang-O represents the *yin* aspect of the universe—the female principle, the less aggressive, darker side of the force associated with water, earth, and the moon, while her consort represents the *yang*, the active and positive masculine principle. While Chang-O's myths vary, most involve an account of Chang-O consuming a magickal elixir and then ascending into the heavens to dwell on the moon forevermore. On one night of the year—Mid-Autumn night—Chang-O and her lover reunite, and thus the holiday is often associated with love, romance, and happy reunions. To honor Chang-O and ask for her blessing, offerings of fruit, incense, and pastries are set out on a table under the moonlight. Typically, sacrifices might include watermelon, grapes, apples, plums, and mooncakes, a round pastry with sweet or savory fillings made especially for the Moon Festival.

In modern times, mooncakes are available commercially in packaged boxes, with the fanciest, most luxurious cakes selling for around a $1,000 U.S. dollars a box. Traditionally, however, the mooncakes are made at home, usually by the lady of the house. The flour-based pastries are typically about four inches in diameter, and can be filled with fruit, egg yolks, red bean paste, mung bean paste, lotus paste, meat, or other fillings. Originally, the mooncakes became attached to the Mid-Autumn festival as a way to remember an uprising that happened long ago in which mooncakes with messages hidden inside were passed out to the people, communicating the proposed time of rebellion. Their symbolism has since evolved, and today the mooncakes have come to signify the Mid-Autumn holiday as well as the full moon itself, seen in China as a symbol of completeness and reunion. In addition to leaving a plate of mooncakes out for Chang-O, the pastries are enjoyed by friends and family gathered under the moon to talk about Autumn wishes and to contemplate life's mysteries. As families and friends stand side-by-side gazing at the full moon light and enjoying the taste of sweet fruits and mooncakes, love and good wishes are expressed for those who are close by and far away, as well. A popular Mid-Autumn saying translates as, "Round moon, people reunite!"

Over time, the Moon Festival evolved into a celebration that indeed became a force of unification. As the festival gained greater recognition and developed more structure, it was celebrated by the upper ruling classes and the more common folks alike. The richest merchants and government officials would host lavish parties, bringing people together for music, dancing, and drinking under the full moon light. In the countryside, the farmers would mark the Mid-Autumn celebration more simply, with families placing a few humble offerings under the stars for Chang-O, enjoying the beautiful moon while praying together for a good harvest. Although the festivities and levels of opulence varied, the Moon Festival was something nearly everyone in the region could connect to and enjoy, regardless of one's station in life.

The Moon Festival is a time of unity, but that doesn't mean there's no variation. Different regions and different cultures within China celebrate the day in unique ways. In the Hunan Province, for instance, the Dong people's Moon Festival celebrations include an interesting custom referred to as "stealing moon dishes." It's believed that lunar fairies descend at the time of Mid-Autumn to sprinkle all the fruits and vegetables with a magickal moon dew. Such foodstuffs are referred to as "moon dishes," and eating them is thought to bring joy and good luck, especially in matters of the heart. On Mid-Autumn night, Dong women visit the gardens of their lovers, and pick vegetables (aka the "moon dish") without asking. Depending on which vegetables are picked, the lovers' fortunes can be predicted—large, ripe vegetables are auspicious, with melons in particular signifying a child to come. If fruits or vegetables are found growing in pairs, with two emerging from a single stalk, it's taken as a sign of a long and happy relationship. If a handful of soybeans is picked, it can signify fertility, predicting the couple will soon bear children. Once the vegetables are picked, the "theft" is announced to the lover with a loud cry of, "I've got your vegetables!" followed by an invitation to come to the woman's house for tea or a light snack. In parallel, the Dong men often pick their lover's vegetables on this night, also, cooking and eating them in the open air while thinking of their wishes for love and happiness. Sometimes the men talk loudly about the women, who hide around the area to eavesdrop. If a woman likes what she hears, she might pop out from her hiding spot and ask the man to join her for a more private conversation.

Near China's Changbai mountain, Mid-Autumn is celebrated by building large, conical structures out of pine branches, called moon houses. Friends and family enjoy the moonlight as it filters through the intertwined and overlapping branches.

In parts of south China, many communities practice *shāo tǎ*, or tower burning. Large towers are built from tiles and bricks, then bamboo and wood are placed inside the structure and set ablaze. It's believed that the rising flames will carry to the heavens the people's wishes for a bountiful harvest and good luck in life.

In modern times, regardless of variations, millenia-old traditions are still a mainstay of many Chinese Mid-Autumn celebrations. People still get together with family, friends, and lovers to make offerings to the moon, dance, and feast on mooncakes. Although the mooncakes might be store-bought and the well-wishes often delivered through text message these days, the enduring tradition of moon worship at the heart of the Mid-Autumn festival still prevails. Why not celebrate this year's autumnal shift with a Moon Festival of your own? It's a great excuse to reunite with your loved ones and party under the bright and beautiful autumn moon!

References:

ChinaHighlights.com. "Mid-Autumn Festival." Accessed October 1, 2013. http://www.chinahighlights.com/festivals/mid-autumn -festival.htm.

China.org. "Traditional Chinese Festivals." "Mid-Autumn Festival." Accessed October 1, 2013. http://www.china.org.cn/english /features/Festivals/78311.htm.

Cultural China. "The Customs of Mid-Autumn Festival." Accessed October 1, 2013. http://traditions.cultural-china.com /en/214Traditions9596.html.

Feasts and Treats

Ellen Dugan

AUTUMN EQUINOX. THE SECOND of our harvest festivals. These four fall recipes are all vegetarian friendly and they also include a quick high-protein snack. Three of these do feature the apple. After all, what would this sabbat be without the apple? Apples are in season and they are affordable now, so go grab some from the local farmer's market and don't forget to snag some cider as well! Read on to find a bewitching spin on cider!

Healthier Apple French Toast

I discovered this recently and adapted it to make it healthier and use less sugar. It is wonderful. Try this out on a crisp autumn morning. Or make it for what my family calls "Bruffer." (You know, breakfast foods for supper?)

Prep time: 20 minutes
Cook time: 8 minutes for compote
Serves: 2

For the Compote
Nonstick cooking spray
1 tablespoon margarine

1 apple, cored, peeled and thinly sliced (I like Gala apples for this)
¼ cup maple syrup
¼ teaspoon ground cinnamon

For the French Toast
4 slices whole-wheat bread
1 cup egg beaters
1 teaspoon vanilla extract
Dash of salt
Dash of cinnamon
Nonstick cooking spray

To prepare the compote, heat a nonstick skillet over medium heat. Spray the pan with the cooking spray, then melt one tablespoon margarine in pan. Add apples to pan and sauté for 8 minutes or until fork tender. Stir in maple syrup and ¼ teaspoon of ground cinnamon. Turn down the heat, but keep warm.

To prepare the French toast, whisk the egg beaters, vanilla, salt, and dash of cinnamon in a medium bowl until well blended. Place the bread one slice at a time into the mixture, turn it gently to coat both sides. Heat a large, nonstick skillet. Coat the skillet with cooking spray and then add the coated bread slices. Cook for 2 to 3 minutes on each side or until lightly browned. If you are making a large batch, place finished slices on a heatproof plate in a 250 degree F oven to keep the toast warm. Serve with the warm apple compote. This recipe is easy to double. Enjoy!

High Protein Snack:
Mini Bean and Cheese Quesadilla

Sometimes you just need a midafternoon protein pick-me-up. This is one of my favorites.

Prep time: 10 minutes
Cook time: 2–4 minutes
Serves: 1–4

½ cup canned black beans (drained)
1 tablespoon mild salsa
1 slice low-fat cheddar cheese
1 medium tortilla
Avocado slices (if desired)

Fold ½ cup black beans, 1 tablespoon salsa, and 1 slice cheddar cheese in a small tortilla. (It will be in a half circle shape.) Cook in a dry nonstick pan until cheese is melted and tortilla is lightly browned. Cut into slices with a pizza cutter. Serve immediately with salsa and fresh avocado slices.

Note: Cover and refrigerate the leftover beans for another time. This would also make a fun appetizer for a party or a nifty after-school snack for the kids. Instead of making only one for yourself, just continue to make the quesadillas one at a time (until you run out of beans) and keep them warm in a 250 degree F oven until they are all finished. Then serve.

Apple Oatmeal Crisp

This is a favorite at my house. It's especially good and satisfying on a crisp autumn night.

Prep time: 30 minutes
Cook time: 40–45 minutes
Serves: 8–10

1 cup packed brown sugar
1 cup all-purpose flour
1 cup rolled oats
½ cup butter, melted
3 cups sliced apples, cored and peeled (3–4 medium size apples); I like Gala apples for this recipe
½ cup white sugar
2 teaspoons ground cinnamon

Preheat oven to 350 degrees F and coat an 8 × 8-inch square pan with nonstick cooking spray. In a large bowl combine brown sugar, flour, oats, and melted butter. Mix until crumbly. Place half of this mixture into the bottom of the pan. Pat this out gently so it covers the pan like a thick crust. Spread the apples evenly over the crumb mixture. In a small bowl, mix the white sugar and cinnamon. Then sprinkle this mixture over the top of the apples. Top the crisp with the remaining crumb mixture. Bake in preheated oven for 40 to 45 minutes or until golden brown. Serve warm with frozen vanilla yogurt/vanilla ice cream, or fat-free Greek vanilla yogurt.

Beverage: Hot Caramel Apple Cider for Adults

Here is a spiked apple cider for the grown-ups that tastes like a caramel apple! Quick, go find a crock pot and a few mugs!

Prep time: 20 minutes
Serves: 4–6

4 cups apple cider
1 cup caramel flavored vodka
1 tablespoon brown sugar
2 teaspoons cinnamon

Add ingredients to a crock pot and stir until sugar has melted and cinnamon is well blended. Warm this brew up with the heat on LOW. (Otherwise the alcohol burns off.) Serve garnished with apple slices in mugs or rim rocks glasses with brown sugar, and serve with a cinnamon stick.

Crafty Crafts

Lexa Olick

MABON CELEBRATIONS REVOLVE AROUND the gathering of the crops. Great reverence is paid to the last sheaf of corn that is harvested. It is believed that the spirit of the corn resides in the crops, but is made homeless after the harvest. Many traditions use animal names, such as the "cutting of the hare" or the "cutting of the crow," to describe the harvesting of the last sheaf. Just like the corn spirit, these animals are also left homeless.

As a result, the last sheaf is usually made into corn dollies. Normally, corn dollies are kept to encourage future harvests, but numerous talismans are made to encourage prosperity and good fortune. However, corn husks are also knotted into wreaths or crafted into besoms, so they don't always have to resemble a living figure.

Spirit of the Corn Wreath

Indian corn is a symbol of the harvest. While it is eaten in rare occasions, it has firmly made its place in craft projects and that is perfectly fitting because it comes in a beautiful array of colors. Just one ear has gorgeous shades of burgundy, yellow, red, orange, or brown. There are no two exactly alike, so they become the ideal prop for an autumn celebration.

Indian corn is a symbol for protection and luck, which makes it a great material for wreath making. After all, wreaths are usually displayed on our front doors. It protects our families and becomes a focal point of our homes.

The husks of the corn are peeled back, so when they are arranged into a circular wreath it looks very similar to a lion's mane. The pointy husks also resemble a sunburst once completed. These wreaths are very simple to construct, but have amazing results.

Supplies
Approximately 35 miniature ears of Indian corn
12 inch straw wreath
8 dried sunflowers
11-inch plastic canvas circle
Hot glue
Scissors
Spanish moss
Craft glue

Instructions: The straw wreath is the foundation of your Mabon decoration. You may not be able to see it once the project is complete, but it is the "skeleton" that keeps your wreath together and allows it to be hung. Plastic canvas is sold for needlework décor, but we're going to use it as part of our skeleton for the wreath. You can purchase a plastic canvas circle, but if one is not available locally, you can make your own. Just buy an ordinary sheet of plastic canvas and cut your own circle with a diameter of 11 inches.

Lay the straw wreath down on a flat surface. Apply hot glue on the edge of the plastic canvas circle and secure it to the center of the wreath. This is the skeleton of your wreath, which you will be building upon in the following steps.

Apply hot glue onto one side of an ear of Indian corn and firmly place it on top of the wreath. The corn will overlap the plastic canvas, but it should not cover it completely. Continue until the entire wreath is covered. Take care not to get any loose glue on the corn husks. You need around 35 ears of miniature Indian corn, but since the sizes of the ears vary, you could need more or less. Indian corn is a seasonal item, so be sure to stock up on it when autumn approaches.

When all the Indian corn is securely glued to your wreath, loosen the corn husks around it. Be careful while you fluff out the husks. You want them to blossom around the wreath, but don't handle them so roughly that they break.

Now that you have covered the straw wreath, it is time to cover the plastic canvas. The center of the wreath is made with sunflowers. When you buy sunflowers from a craft store, they are naturally dried, which means they retain their golden color. Their petals are reminiscent of the sun's rays in the very same way that the corn husks are arranged to resemble a sunburst.

The plastic canvas has evenly spaced holes that allow yarn to be woven throughout it, but you can ignore them for this project. Trim the sunflowers off their stem. If the stems are too thick to cut with regular scissors, try garden shears. Apply hot glue onto the underside of the flower head and hold it firmly against the plastic canvas. Work from the outside in. The first row should overlap the tips of the Indian corn. Continue until the entire plastic canvas is hidden.

None of the sunflowers or ears of Indian corn will be perfectly shaped, so you will have a few gaps in your wreath. To cover any sign of the white plastic canvas, hide it with Spanish moss. Add craft glue to a small amount of moss and gently push it between any gaps. Continue to add the moss little by little until all the gaps are filled.

Time to Complete: About 1 hour.

Cost: Around $40.00. Luckily, Mabon is in the fall when Indian corn is readily available. It is a seasonal item, so if you were to make this project at another point in time during the year, you would have to conduct a more rigorous search to buy Indian corn and the prices would be higher. For that reason, I recommend buying them in stores as soon as they become available.

Variation: I mentioned earlier that the sunflowers capture the rays of the sun and that the corn husks of the wreath resemble a sunburst when the project is completed. To fully emphasize that point, mist the wreath with aerosol glitter spray. The spray glitter goes on evenly and dries clear so that the wreath will sparkle and shine. It's also lightweight, so it won't weigh down or damage the fragile husks. I recommend choosing a glittery spray in shades of gold so that it matches the autumn season and the colors of the Indian corn. The added sparkle is a decorative way to capture the energy of the corn spirit!

Sustainable Mabon: From Bulb to Braid

Natalie Zaman

SPRING IS THE SEASON for planting, and fall for harvesting—or is it? Sabbat dates revolve around the planting year, but science also plays its part. The exact position of the sun is calculated to determine the change of season. We've assigned dates and hours to mark the passage of time, but truly, the lines are blurred, and there are exceptions to every rule. The earth is always alive and receptive, and there are plants that grow in the God season. One such is the versatile and very magical garlic.

Garlic is a slow-growing bulb that thrives in cool conditions. It is planted at the waning of the year where it is kept safe in the dormant earth until it is ready to be harvested after spring (in some areas garlic is planted in the spring and harvested in late fall). Even after it's been pulled from the earth, the bulbs take almost a full month to mature.

Like honey, garlic is a wonder substance. As an herbal remedy, there is hardly a malady upon which it won't have a positive effect. Magically, garlic provides protection, and can be used as an aphrodisiac (perhaps because it is known to decrease blood pressure and keep the blood moving).

The sabbat of Mabon celebrates plenty and preparation for the season to come, and the ritualistic planting of garlic is one means of honoring this tradition. Planting year-round helps enhance the fertility of the soil.

Make It Your Own!
You will need:

Garlic cloves (Bulbs that have sprouted stems are good for planting; it avoids waste and like a potato that has sprouted eyes, these can be used to generate new crops.)

Patch of ground or a pot to plant your garlic (Be sure to choose ground that has not been used for garlic or onions before, and in a patch that doesn't retain water; standing water promotes rot.)

Salt

At the equinox, or when you are sure that the weather will be steadily cool, wait for the new moon and then mark out a plot of earth to plant your garlic. A new moon is a good time for beginnings, and so perfect for this work. If it is possible, make your plot round, to honor the wheel of the year.

Sprinkle the salt in a circle around your pot or around the edge of your plot if you are planting the garlic in the ground. The ring of salt will offer protection for your plants, the clockwise movement reinforces the desire for protection and growth.

Make small holes 5 centimeters deep and place a clove in each, point-side up. Plant the cloves about 20 centimeters apart. As you cover them with earth, give them an autumnal blessing.

Rest well and grow,
Under frost under snow.
Widen and swell,
My cupboards to fill.

Keep the plants mulched throughout the winter. In the spring, your garlic will produce flower stalks. Wait until the stalks begin to turn brown before harvesting; when this happens will vary depending on your location and climate. In my area (the East Coast of the USA), it's usually between the Summer Solstice and Lammas.

Once pulled from the earth, the garlic will need three to four weeks to cure. Once you have established a steady garlic crop, you will be planting and curing at about the same time. Lay the harvested garlic bulbs in a cool, dry place where they can mature undisturbed. When the stalks are dried and the outer bulbs are papery, you can trim the stalks and store the bulbs in a cool, dry, and well-aired container, or you can keep the stalks long and braid them.

Making garlic braids at the Autumnal Equinox not only preserves your garlic, but honors the God and Goddess as we transit from one season to the next. We are leaving the Goddess season, and will enter the God's at Samhain. There are many resources available with instructions on how to make a braid. When you are comfortable with the technique, weave your garlic bulbs together with a magical intention. Speak one line for each strand as you work it into a braid:

> *Maiden, Mother, Crone.*
> *Child, Father, Elder.*
> *Seedling, Sproutling, Fruit.*

When a set of three strands is complete, seal them with this sentiment:

> *All are one.*

Repeat the process until your braid is complete. If you have an abundance of garlic, make each braid consist of 8 sets of 3 garlic bulbs—8 for the sabbats and 3 for the faces of the God and Goddess.

Blessings for a good harvest, preparation for winter, and return of the light.

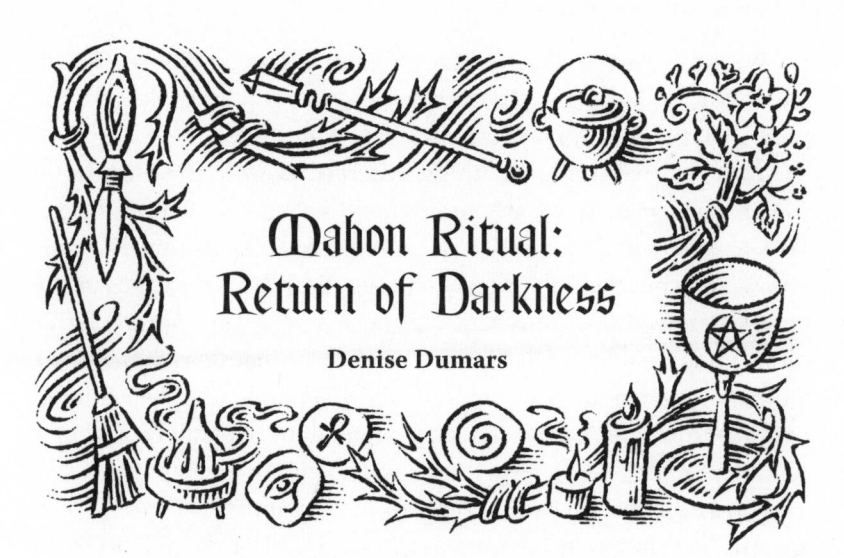

Mabon Ritual: Return of Darkness

Denise Dumars

IN OUR GROUP, THE Iseum of Isis Paedusis in the Fellowship of Isis, "Who's going to bring the blackberry wine?" is often the most important question in planning Mabon! We hold a gratitude ritual to thank the gods and goddesses for the bounty of our lives and to ease into the season of darkness. Since we are based in the Egyptian tradition, we often honor the dying god of autumn with Osiris; we make a "corn dolly" resembling Osiris and plant chia seeds or another fast-growing seed on him to simulate his rebirth, and give participants seeds to take home and grow. As Osiris dies, his wife, the goddess Isis, becomes his mourner and assumes the mantle of widow, a symbolic time in the later years of many women's lives that fits with our symbolism of "the autumn of our years." The Greek god Dionysos is also honored as the dying-and-resurrecting god of the season, and the gods of the harvest and of animal husbandry are also honored, including the Green Man in all his guises: the British Herne, the Gaulish Cernunnos, the Slavic Volos, the Norse Odin, or the Hindu Pashupati can be included or whomever your group wishes to include.

We will often have a meditation on gratitude and balance, will dance for the bounty of the goddess and the god and celebrate the feast with the appropriate harvest foods and drink.

This year we tried something different as well: the blessing of the animals, usually a Catholic rite held around St. Francis of Assisi's feast day of October 4. Since it is close to the Autumnal Equinox, many churches of various denominations hold blessings of the animals around this time. Since as pagans we revere nature, let us bless our animals as well! This is a brief event that doesn't make the animals wait around too long for their blessings, nor their human companions! The Animal Blessing can be done separately or before or after the rite.

Have each person with a companion animal or farm animal (yes, we still have farms in Los Angeles County) bring the animal to an outdoor setting. The Priestesses and/or Priests bless each animal in turn. I will use the example of a pet rat of one of our Adepts:

The pet owner stands before the officiant with the animal. The Priestess or Priest (more than one can participate) waves a wand over the animal.

Bless Sweetie, beloved companion of Lauren, with good health and happiness and joy and long life. All hail Sweetie!

Participants repeat. We do not use a sistrum or other noisy object that might frighten the animals, but a song such as "Bless the Beasts and the Children," can be playing softly. A flick of blessed water from the officiant upon the animal can be done if desired. When all are blessed, this part of the rite is done.

Ritual of Gratitude and Abundance

The main ritual can be performed by a circle or as a solitary ritual.

The altar is decorated with harvest motifs including autumn leaves, apples, pomegranates, grapes, pumpkins, nuts, a cornucopia, etc., as well as any autumn plants native to the area. Choose an appropriate incense for the ritual: pine, rosemary, cypress, benzoin, frankincense, myrrh, cedar, and patchouli singly or in some combination are preferred. An anointing oil in the same combination is sometimes used as well. Our group also has a bowl of yerba buena (spearmint, and the original name for San Francisco!) to place on the ground as it was sacred to the Native Americans here in California.

An image or statue of the goddess Demeter and the god Dionysos are placed in the center of the altar. Place candles at the four corners: East, yellow; South, orange; West, red; and North, brown. The altar should face West. In the west place water with sea salt; incense in the east; earth from the place of the ritual in the north, and a white candle along with the orange one in the south. On the feast table have cornbread or other harvest bread, wine of your choosing—we suggest pomegranate and/or blackberry wine—and apple or grape juice.

We begin by placing extra cauldrons of incense at the entrance to the right, and have the participants walk outside and through the smoke as purification when the rite is about to begin, and/or we anoint the participants with oil drawn in the shape of an ankh on the forehead.

Cast a circle with sword, athame, or wand, moving clockwise to include the entire space, including the altar, participants, feast table, and any other space that might be used (such as a sound system). Light candles and incense.

The officiant of choice begins by explaining the equality of day and night, in balance on the Autumnal Equinox. Then, instead of the traditional calling of the quarters and center, begin with words by authors through the ages, beginning in the West and continuing clockwise, ending in the middle:

O wild west Wind,
Thou breath of Autumn's being
—Percy Shelley

Looking on the happy Autumn-fields,
And thinking of the days that are no more.
—Alfred, Lord Tennyson

O Autumn, laden with fruit, and stained
With the blood of the grape, pass not, but sit
Beneath my shady roof; there thou may'st rest,
And tune thy jolly voice to my fresh pipe,
And all the daughters of the year shall dance!
Sing now the lusty song of fruit and flowers.
—William Blake, "To Autumn"

There is an old tale goes that Herne the Hunter
Sometime a keeper here in Windsor forest,
Doth all the winter-time, at still midnight,
Walk round about an oak, with great ragg'd horns...
—William Shakespeare, *The Merry Wives of Windsor*

Envied by us all
The leaves of maple turn so
Beautiful, then fall
—Shiko

Play "The Green Man" by the band XTC, found here, to call Dionysos: http://www.youtube.com/watch?v=hbhQURN9Szw

Encourage guests to dance and sing along (some practice in advance may be nice, but not required) and follow the rhythm with drums, tambourine, sistrum, etc.

After the dance, pour a glass of wine for Dionysus and place it before his image. Now call Demeter while passing a pomegranate around the circle, or holding one if solitary:

Mother Demeter, queen of the harvest,
We ask you to join us
As we are grateful for your bounty,
And for your sacrifice
In parting with your daughter
For the dark months of the year.
Dearest Demeter, please continue to bless us
With your harvest of pomegranates,

As we gather your tears
To drop to the ground to offer for your daughter.

The pomegranate is now placed on the altar before Demeter. Participants are seated. A meditation on gratitude will begin. It can be read by a participant or pre-recorded:

Take three deep breaths in and out, and with each breath visualize your head connected to the stars, your feet connected to the earth. Feel the earth beneath your feet and the cosmos above. Now visualize the following: Imagine that you are in a deep forest; take a few moments to look around and orient yourself. What does the forest look like? (Pause here for 30 seconds.) Take another deep breath. Now walk through the forest until you reach a clearing in the trees. There is Dionysos, hiding in the forest from those who would sacrifice him. He is holding a glass of wine, sporting a grapevine in his hair, and wearing a Greek robe. What does he look like? Take a moment to visualize him. (Pause for 30 seconds.) Now approach him, bow to him, and speak your gratitude and whatever else you wish to say to him. Then allow him to respond to you. What does he say or do? (Pause for 1 minute.) Thank him and continue through the forest until you walk out of it and find yourself in a field of autumn wheat. Walk through the wheat (pause for 30 seconds). Soon you come upon a woman in Greek mourning dress and veil; this is Demeter. She is holding a pomegranate in one hand and a sheaf of ripe wheat in the other. What does she say or do? Greet her by placing your hand on your heart. What does she look like? Speak your gratitude and whatever else you wish to say to her (pause for at least 1 minute). Move along through the grain until you come to an open field. Take three deep breaths and open your eyes.

❧

After the meditation, pass paper and pen to each participant. Encourage them to jot down any impressions they had during the meditation on what Dionysos and Demeter said or did. Then give them another piece of paper, and ask each to write a petition of gratitude for something good that has come to pass during the year. Each participant may also ask for something he or she wants to come to fruition, but only after offering gratitude. Each places a petition before the deity image of choice.

Now cornbread and wine or juice are passed around. Participants first thank the deities for the harvest, and toast Demeter and Dionysos. They then say to each other:

May you never hunger; may you never thirst.

Ask the participants if anyone has a personal toast, and let each one who wishes to speak do so and continue to toast.

After the "cakes and ale" are consumed and toasts made, seal the deal by making noise with drums, sistra, etc. Ground the ritual energy by placing palms on the floor. Now begin thanking the deities:

Demeter, goddess of grain, we thank you for your many blessings. Go if you must, but stay if you will. Hail and farewell; blessed be!

Dionysos, god of wine, we thank you for your many blessings. Go if you must, but stay if you will. Hail and farewell; blessed be!

Beginning with the South, thank the quarters and center:

Powers of the South, of autumn's flame, we thank you. (Extinguish candle in the south).

Powers of the West, of autumn's tides, we thank you. (Extinguish candle.)

Powers of the North, of autumn's fields, we thank you. (Extinguish candle.)

Powers of the east, of autumn's breezes, we thank you. (Extinguish candle.)

Power of the center, of autumn's spirit, we thank you. (Extinguish white candle.)

Open circle by going widdershins (counterclockwise), then join the circle and have everyone stand and hold hands, saying:

The circle is open, but never broken, merry meet and merry part and merry meet again!

Now the feast begins! Put on more music if desired. Gather and burn the petitions in a heatproof container such as a cauldron outdoors after the ritual is over.

Sources and Recommended Reading:

Dugan, Ellen. *Autumn Equinox: The Enchantment of Mabon.* Llewellyn, 2005.

Halstead, John. "Mabon, Mabon-Not," The Allergic Pagan, www.patheos.com/blog.

Kelly, Aidan A. *Crafting the Art of Magic: Book 1.* Llewellyn, 1991.

Regula, DeTraci. *The Mysteries of Isis: Her Worship and Magick.* Llewellyn, 1995.

Reif, Jennifer. *Mysteries of Demeter: Rebirth of the Pagan Way.* Weiser, 1999.

Wigington, Maggie. "All About Mabon, the Autumn Equinox," *About.com. Paganism/Wicca.* http://paganwiccan.about.com.

Notes

Notes